THE ARCHAICON

A Collection of Unusual, Archaic English

Selected, with an Introduction

by

J. ERNEST BARLOUGH

The Scarecrow Press, Inc.
Metuchen, N.J.   1974

Library of Congress Cataloging in Publication Data

Barlough, J   Ernest, 1953-
    The archaicon; a collection of unusual archaic
English.

    Bibliography: p.
    1. English language--Obsolete words--Dictionaries.
2. English language--Etymology. I. Title.
PE1667.B3   427'.09   73-14926
ISBN 0-8108-0683-5

To

MY PARENTS

and, of course,

to

GARY

TABLE OF CONTENTS

INTRODUCTION

Like a mighty river is a language, full of streaming currents and gushing waters, surging downstream from the bosom of its highland mother on its coursing run to the sea. Water collecting in channels moves downward and outward to connect with other flowing tides to form feeders and tributaries, and over the entire land a vast and intricate network of interrelated streams spreads growing fingers.

But in the back country, in the woodlands and the thousand and one hidden recesses of the earth, where time is measured by slower hands, there are the bayous, the lagoons, and the secret worlds where the white abada and the crafty tod, the screeching kae and frightful paddock dwell, by the murky lair of the hideous Anthropophaginian. Here, in this unknown country, where mysterious creatures rear their heads, is where the explorer sets up his camp --in the land of forgotten words.

Many dictionaries, glossaries and collections, some of which are listed in the bibliography at the end of this book, have been written investigating the archaic and obsolete areas of the English language, but The Archaicon is not concerned with the totality of this vast amount of researched knowledge which would take volumes to record. Rather, it has been conceived as a selective collection of unusual archaic English, of words that are not only no longer widely used but are interestingly different--"wondrous strange," as Shakespeare wrote. Often, however, a simple definition is not sufficient to give one a real feeling for a word, so many complete quotations have been included which show the words in context, and which enable the reader to see them as they were used in their own times, mostly by authors of wide renown. Many times several quotations are given to reveal the extent of the popularity of a particular word.

It is, of course, impossible for a book such as The Archaicon to exist without the assistance of the invaluable dictionaries that have been made earlier by others; indeed, without the Herculean labors involved in such works as John Florio's A Worlde of Words, Nathan Bailey's Universal Etymological Dictionary, Thomas Blount's Glossographia, Henry Cockeram's The English Dictionarie, Francis Grose's Classical Dictionary of the Vulgar Tongue, Samuel Johnson's Dictionary of the English Language, Robert Nares' Glossary, Sir James Murray's New English Dictionary (20 volumes), the Oxford English Dictionary (13 volumes), Hunter & Morris's Universal Dictionary of the English Language (4 volumes), Joseph Wright's English Dialect Dictionary, and many others, The Archaicon, which now invites the reader on a journey of discovery into that hidden land of language, could never have been written.

J. E. B.

Los Angeles, California
April 14th, 1973

THE ARCHAICON

__ABACK:__ An ornamental tablet or compartment, usually
square or rectangular, or any similar architectural design;
a cartouche.   The word comes through the French abaque,
from the Latin abacus, the term for the square stone above
a pillar or column of a building.

> In the centre, or midst ... there was an Aback,
> or Square, wherein this Elogie was written.
> --Ben Jonson: Part of the King's Entertainment
>   in Passing to His Coronation (1603); lines 218-
>   219.

__ABADA:__ Also spelled abda or abath, this was an early name
for the rhinoceros, often used in a foreign sense.   It comes
primarily from the Portuguese abada, the name for the female rhinoceros.   It was in common use by many early
British explorers, such as Hakluyt and others who wrote
for his Voyages.

> In Bengala are found great numbers of Abdas or
> Rhinocerotes, whose horne (growing up from his
> snowt,) is good against poyson, and is much
> accounted of throughout all India.
> --Samuel Purchas: Purchas His Pilgrimage (1613);
>   Book I.

__ABEIGH:__ At a safe distance; aloof; a little aside; a little
ways off.   From the Scottish dialects, the derivation of this
word is obscure; it possibly comes from the Norse beig,
"fear"; but a corruption of the phrase "at bay" as a source
has also been suggested.

> When thou an' I were young and skeigh,
> An' stable-meals at fairs were driegh,
> How thou wad prance, an' snore, an' skriegh
>   An' tak the road!

Town's-bodies ran, and stood abeigh,
                An' ca't thee mad.
--Robert Burns: The Auld Farmer's New-Year
Morning Salutation to His Auld Mare, Maggie
(1787); stanza 8.

ABIGAIL: The popularity of the character of a maid in
Beaumont & Fletcher's play, The Scornful Lady (1616),
named Abigail, probably prompted the use of this word as
a synonym for a lady's waiting-maid or maidservant.   There
is also a passage in I Kings xxv in reference to Abigail,
the wife of David: "And she fell at his feet, and said:
Upon me let this iniquity be, my lord.   Let thy handmaid
speak, I beseech thee, in thy ears, and hear the words of
thy servant." This source has been somewhat discounted
as of late because of the great popularity of Biblical names
during this period, but it cannot be denied that it definitely
was an influence on the later use of this word.   It was
primarily in fashion in the 17th and 18th centuries, and can
be found in Congreve's The Old Bachelor, in Pepys' diary,
in Carlyle, in Smollett's Humphrey Clinker, as well as in
the following:

> The woman was dressed with a quiet neatness that
> seemed to stamp her profession as that of an abi-
> gail--black cloak with long cape, of that peculiar
> silk which seems spun on purpose for ladies'
> maids.
> --Edward George Bulwer-Lytton: The Caxtons
> (1849).

ABRAHAM, ABRAM: These two forms are corruptions of
the word auburn, which was sometimes written as abern or
abron, and taken also to mean "fair" or "handsome." Auburn comes to us through the Old French and Middle English
from the Latin alburnus, derived from albus, "white." The
present meaning was influenced by an association of this
word with the Middle English brun, "brown."

> FIRST CITIZEN: And to make us no better thought
> of, a little help will serve; for once we stood up
> about the corn, he himself stuck not to call us the
> many-headed multitude.
>
> THIRD CITIZEN: We have been call'd so of many;
> not that our heads are some brown, some black,
> some abram, some bald, but that our wits are so

diversely color'd: and truly I think, if all our
wits were to issue out of one skull, they would
fly east, west, north, south; and their consent of
one direct way should be at once to all the points
o'th'compass.
--William Shakespeare: Coriolanus (1608); Act II,
Scene 3.

ABROOK: An older form of the verb brook, which meant
"to tolerate, to endure, to suffer, to put up with." It
comes through the Middle English bruken, "to use, to en-
joy," and the Anglo-Saxon brucan, "to put into practice."

DUKE OF GLOSTER:
Sweet Nell, ill can thy noble mind abrook
The abject people gazing on thy face
With envious looks, still laughing at thy shame,
That erst did follow thy proud chariot-wheels
When thou didst ride in triumph through the streets.
--William Shakespeare: King Henry the Sixth,
Part II (1591); Act II, Scene 4.

ACCOIL: To collect or gather together; to assemble; to
crowd together. From the Old French acoillir, "to gather,
assemble" (modern French accueillir, "to receive, to welcome"), the word has descended through various forms from
the Latin accolligere, "to associate," which was constructed
of ad, "to," and colligere, "to gather." Though used as a
verb here, a noun usage of the word can be found in Robert
Southey's 1814 poem, Roderick, the Last of the Goths.

About the caudron many cookes accoyld,
With hookes and ladles, as need did requyre:
The whyles the viaundes in the vessell boyld,
They did about their businesse sweat, and sorely
toyld.
--Edmund Spenser: The Faerie Queene, Book II
(1590); Canto IX, Stanza 30.

ACCUSE: An old substantive use of the verb, this word
meant "a charge, an accusation; the act of accusing."
Accuse is from the Latin accusare, "to call to account,"
which was constructed of ad, "to," and causa, "a case, a
lawsuit." Our word comes through the Old French acuser,
of the same sense. It can be found in Nathaniel Bacon's
1647 discourse Of Uniformity of the Government of England,
as well as in Shakespeare:

DUKE OF GLOSTER:
Beaufort's red sparkling eyes blab his heart's
    malice,
And Suffolk's cloudy brow his stormy hate;
Sharp Buckingham unburdens with his tongue
The envious load that lies upon his heart;
And dogged York, that reaches at the moon,
Whose overweening arm I have pluckt back,
By false accuse doth level at my life.
--William Shakespeare: King Henry the Sixth,
    Part II (1591); Act III, Scene 1.

ACELDAMA: Pronounced with a hard "c" and accented on
the third syllable, this was the name of the field near Jerusalem which was bought with the blood-money taken and
then relinquished by Judas Iscariot before his suicide. St.
Matthew relates: "And the chief priests took the pieces of
silver, and said, 'It is not lawful to put them into the
treasury, seeing that it is the price of blood.' And after
they had consulted together, they bought with them the potter's
field, as a burial place for strangers. For this reason that
field has been called even to this day, Haceldama, that is,
the Field of Blood." The word is taken from the Aramaic
phrase ōkēl damō, literally meaning "field of blood," and
so in later contexts has come to mean any scene of great
slaughter or bloodshed. It can be found in many places in
literature, including John Cleaveland's poem Content (1658),
Thomas DeQuincey's The Caesars (1859), and in Young:

To see, before each glance of piercing thought,
All cloud, all shadow, blown remote; and leave
No mystery--but that of Love Divine,
Which lifts us on the seraph's flaming wing,
From earth's Aceldama, this field of blood,
Of inward anguish, and of outward ill,
From darkness, and from dust, to such a scene!
--Edward Young: Night Thoughts (1742); Night
    Sixth, lines 99-105.

ACTON: A stuffed jacket or vest, originally made of
quilted cotton, worn immediately beneath the suit of mail;
later, a leather jacket plated with mail. The word comes
through many varied influences: the Old French auqueton
(later hocqueton, hocton) (see the modern French hoqueton,
"padding"); the Spanish alcoton, "cotton, padding material";
the Arabic alqūtun, "cotton." This form was used principally from the twelfth to the sixteenth centuries, but influence

by the French has created other forms such as <u>haqueton</u>, <u>hacqueton</u>, <u>haketon</u>, <u>hacton</u>, some of which are <u>still</u> used in <u>historical</u> study. It can be found readily in older literature, such as in Chaucer's <u>Rime of Sir Thopas</u> (1386), in Caxton's <u>Jason</u>, in Holinshed's <u>Chronicles</u>; Sir Walter Scott was fond of it, and he used it in his <u>Fair Maid of Perth</u> and in the following:

> But Cranstoun's lance, of more avail,
> Pierced through, like silk, the Borderer's mail;
> Through shield and jack and acton passed,
> Deep in his bosom broke at last.
> --Sir Walter Scott: <u>The Lay of the Last Minstrel</u>
>   (1805); Canto III, stanza 6.

ADDEBTED: An old form, principally Scottish, of "indebted," this word comes to us through the Old French <u>endeter</u>, <u>endetter</u>, which descended from the late Latin <u>indebitare</u>. <u>Debere</u>, "to owe," is the basic Latin source, constructed of <u>de</u>, "from," and <u>habere</u>, "to have," the origin of many an English word. Douglas used it in 1513 when he was translating the <u>Aeneid</u>, as did Scott:

> Master George took a crumpled paper from the
> fellow's hand, and said, muttering betwixt his
> teeth: "'Humbly showeth--um--um--his Majesty's
> maist gracious mother--um--um--justly addebted
> and owing the sum of fifteen marks--'"
> --Sir Walter Scott: <u>The Fortunes of Nigel</u> (1822);
>   chapter 4.

ADHORN: A humorous word meaning "to plant horns on" (i.e. to cuckold). Reference is drawn in usage between <u>adhorn</u> and <u>adorn</u>, as seen in the quote. <u>Horn</u> is descended from the Indo-European base <u>ker-</u>, "the upper portion of the body" or "the head," and is related to older words such as the Latin <u>cornu</u> and the Greek <u>keras</u>, both meaning "horn." Chapman seems to have liked this word, and it can be found in <u>All Fools</u> as well as in the following:

> THARSALIO: As who should say, are not we mad
> wenches, that can lead our blind husbands thus by
> the noses? Do you not brag amongst yourselves
> how grossly you abuse their honest credulities?
> how they adore you for Saints: and you believe it?
> while you adhorne their temples, and they believe
> it not?

    --George Chapman: The Widow's Tears (1612);
    Act I, Scene 1.

ADMINICULATE: This is a word still in use today in Scottish law, meaning "to support by corroboratory evidence," "to give credibility to." From the Latin adminiculare, "to prop up, to support."

> In the present case, no person, who had heard the witnesses describe the appearance of the young woman before she left Saddletree's house, and contrasted it with that of her state and condition at her return to her father's, could have any doubt that the fact of delivery had taken place, as set forth in her own declaration, which was, therefore, not a solitary piece of testimony, but adminiculated and supported by the strongest circumstantial proof.
> --Sir Walter Scott: The Heart of Midlothian (1818); chapter 23.

AFFRAP: To encounter; to strike down; to beat to the ground. An old word from the Italian affrappare, "to beat, to knock," and the French frapper, "to strike, to hit."

> They bene ymett, both ready to affrap,
> When suddeinly that warriour gan abace
> His threatned speare, as if some new mishap
> Had him betide, or hidden danger did entrap.
> --Edmund Spenser: The Faerie Queene, Book II (1590); Canto I, stanza 26.

AGLY: An old Scottish adverb, meaning variously "crooked," "off the right track," "amiss," "asquint," "off the straight," etc. It was formed from the verb glee, whose origin is unknown. But this word itself is not quite so obscure, witness the following well-known quotation:

> The best-laid schemes o' mice an' men
>   Gang aft agley.
> --Robert Burns: To A Mouse (1785); stanza 7.

AGRIOT, EGRIOT: A variety of tart, sour cherry; a black cherry. The word came into English from the French agriote (modern French, griotte), same sense.

> Yet some fruits, which grow not to be black, are

of the nature of berries, sweetest such as are
paler; as the coeur-cherry, which inclineth more
to white, is sweeter than the red; but the egriot
is more sour.
--Francis Bacon: Sylva Sylvarum (1626); paragraph 509.

A HALL: This was a cry or exclamation used to clear the
way or to make room in a large place that was full of people crowded together, usually for the purpose of arranging
a dance.   It was also used as a general cry for people to
come together during a festive occasion or celebration, and
to summon servants.   The basic meaning of the word hall
is "to cover," also evident in the word conceal.   Scott used
it in his poem Marmion, and so did Chapman:

ARGUS: A hall, a hall: let no more citizens in
there.
--George Chapman: The Widow's Tears (1612);
Act III, Scene 1.

AHIND, AHINT: This is an old adverb meaning "behind" or
"after."   Hind comes through Middle English, possibly influenced by the Anglo-Saxon word hindan, "from behind." Early
Middle English, along with "behind" had "athind," a fore-
runner of this word.   In more modern works it can be found
in Alexander Ross's Helenore (1768), and in Scott's Waverley.

"And it's for certain the very fairies ... are no
half sae visible in our days.   I canna depone to
having ever seen ane mysell, but I ance heard ane
whistle ahint me in the moss. "
--Sir Walter Scott: *The Black Dwarf (1816); chapter 4.

ALCATOTE: A simpleton, fool, or idiot; dumb-bell.   The
origin of this word is unknown.   Its earliest form is alki-
totle, and has been suggested to be associated with the older
English alce, "subject to fits of epilepsy."   The Latin word
alca, "an auk," has also been suggested, the auk being considered a stupid bird.   Perhaps the second part of the word
is related to toti, meaning "giddy, silly," which would make
the general meaning of the word "silly bird. "

SECCO: Spadone, am I a cuckold or no cuckold?
SPADONE: Why, you know I [am] an ignorant,

unable trifle in such business; an oaf, a simple
alcatote, an innocent.
--John Ford: The Fancies, Chaste and Noble
     (1635); Act IV, scene 1.

ALFORGE, ALFORJA: A wallet or leather saddlebag--hence,
cheek-pouches, especially those of a baboon or some similar
ape. This word comes from the Portuguese alforge and the
Spanish alforja, and the Arabic al-khorj, "store, supply,
provision," which is derived from kharaja, "to proceed."

The apothecary ... was a little old withered man,
with a forehead about an inch high, a nose turned
up at the end, large cheek-bones that helped to
form a pit for his little grey eyes, a great bag of
loose skin hanging down on each side in wrinkles
like the alforjas of a baboon.
--Tobias Smollett: Roderick Random (1748); chap-
     ter 18.

ALLENARLY, ALL-ANERLY: Solely; merely; solitarily; all
alone; only.   Still in limited use in Scottish law, this word
is derived from the adverb "all" and the adverb "anerly,"
meaning singly, alone.

"But we are to hold in remembrance that Scotland,
though it be our native land, and the land of our
fathers, is not like Goshen, in Egypt, on whilk the
sun of the heavens and of the gospel shineth allenarly, and leaveth the rest of the world in utter
darkness."
--Sir Walter Scott: The Heart of Midlothian (1818);
     chapter 39.

ALPHABET: An index in alphabetical order, as can be seen
from the quotation.   And, of course, "alphabet" is from the
first two letters of the Greek alphabet.

Then out and walked alone on foot to the Temple,
it being a fine frost, thinking to have seen a play
all alone; but there, missing of any bills, con-
cluded there was none, and so back home; and
there with my brother reducing the names of all
my books to an alphabet, which kept us till 7 or
8 at night.
--Samuel Pepys' Diary: December 25th, 1666.

AMBAGITORY: Devious; roundabout; indirect. From the
Latin ambages, "a roundabout way." Modern English has
the forms ambage, ambagious, etc.

> But without further tyranny over my readers, or
> display of the extent of my own reading, I shall
> content myself with borrowing a single incident
> from the memorable hunting at Lude, commemor-
> ated in the ingenious Mr. Gunn's essay on the
> Caladonian Harp, and so proceed in my story with
> all the brevity that my natural style of composi-
> tion, partaking of what scholars call the peri-
> phrastic and ambagitory, and the vulgar the cir-
> cumbendibus, will permit me.
> --Sir Walter Scott: Waverley (1814); chapter 24.

> He read long and attentively various tedious and
> embarrassed letters, in which the writers, placing
> before him the glory of God, and the freedom and
> liberties of England, as their supreme ends, could
> not, by all the ambagitory expressions they made
> use of, prevent the shrewd eye of Markham Ever-
> ard from seeing that self-interest and views of
> ambition were the principal moving-springs at the
> bottom of their plots.
> --Sir Walter Scott: Woodstock (1826); chapter 5.

ANATOMY, ATOMY: An old word, popular with the Eliza-
bethans and Jacobeans, for "a skeleton"--hence, a skinny
person, a "scarecrow." From the Greek anatomia, "a dis-
section," constructed from ana, "up," and temnein, "to cut."
Shelley used it in his Epipsychidion (1821), but the word had
great popularity with Shakespeare:

> ANTIPHOLUS OF EPHESUS:
> Along with them
> They brought one Pinch, a hungry lean-faced vil-
>   lain,
> A mere anatomy, a mountebank,
> A threadbare juggler, and a fortune-teller,
> A needy, hollow-eyed, sharp-looking wretch,
> A living-dead man.
> --The Comedy of Errors (ca. 1590); Act V, scene
>   1.

> ROMEO:
> O, tell me, friar, tell me,

In what vile part of this anatomy
Doth my name lodge? tell me, that I may sack
The hateful mansion.
--<u>Romeo and Juliet</u> (ca. 1594); Act III, scene 3.

CONSTANCE:
O, that my tongue were in the thunder's mouth!
Then with a passion would I shake the world;
And rouse from sleep that fell anatomy
Which cannot hear a lady's feeble voice,
Which scorns a modern invocation.
--<u>King John</u> (ca. 1595); Act III, scene 4.

ANDREW: A Highland broadsword, the "andrea ferrara,"
named for its maker. In the first quote the word is used
in this sense; in the second, it means a gentleman's servant or valet. Another example, as with <u>abigail,</u> of the use
of a proper name in specific and varied senses.

PETRUCHIO: Here are no such cold pities.
ANTONIO: By Saint Jaques,
They shall not find me one! Here's old tough
    Andrew,
A special friend of mine, and he but hold,
I'll strike 'em such a hornpipe!
--John Fletcher: <u>The Chances</u> (1627); Act I, Scene
    8.

LADY WISHFORT: What, have you made a passive
bawd of me?--this exceeds all precedent; I am
brought to fine uses, to become a botcher of sec-
ond-hand marriages between Abigails and Andrews!
--William Congreve: <u>The Way of the World</u> (1700);
    Act V, Scene 1.

ANGELIQUE: The angelot, an old type of guitar, popular in
France. From the French <u>angelique,</u> "angelical," the
French name.

Met with Mr. Chetwind and dined with him at Har-
graves, the cornechandler in St. Martins-lane,
where a good dinner. Where he showed me some
good pictures and an instrument he called an
Angelique.
--Samuel Pepys' <u>Diary:</u> June 23rd, 1660.

ANLACE: A short, small, double-bladed wood-knife or

dagger, worn at the waist, broad at the hilt and tapering quickly to the point; obsolete by the 15th century. This word is extremely difficult to trace. The Old Welsh anglas, "sword," is probably the same word, and the basic meaning was probably "awl," from the Germanic base alisna. It is used extensively in very old writings: it appears in a Latinized form, anelacius or anelatius in Matthew Paris in 1259; in Havelock the Dane (1300); Sir Ferumbras (ca. 1380); the Morte d'Arthur in 1440. In more modern writers, it has appeared in Byron's Childe Harold's Pilgrimage (1812) and in Scott:

> His harp in silken scarf was slung,
> And by his side an anlace hung.
> --Sir Walter Scott: Rokeby (1813); Canto V, stanza 15.

Other forms of the word include anelas, analasse, anlasse, etc.

ANTHROPOPHAGINIAN: A cannibal; one who eats human flesh. Used as the singular form of "Anthropophagi" with a resounding effect, the suffix taken in somewhat of a locative sense, as in Carthage, Carthaginian. The word comes from the Latin anthropophagus and the Greek anthropagos, meaning "man-eating, cannibal." Constructed from anthropos, "man," and phagein, "to eat."

> HOST: There's his chamber, his house, his castle, his standing-bed, and truckle-bed; 'tis painted about with the story of the Prodigal, fresh and new. Go knock and call; he'll speak like an Anthropophaginian unto thee: knock, I say.
> --William Shakespeare: The Merry Wives of Windsor (1601); Act IV, Scene 5.

ANTRE: A cave, hollow, lair, or den. Taken from the French word antre, having descended from the Latin antrum and the Greek antron, all having the same meaning. Keats used it in 1818 in Endymion, and so did Meredith in The Egoist (1879).

> OTHELLO: I ran it through, even from my boyish days
> To the very moment that he bade me tell it;
> Wherein I spake of most disastrous chances,
> Of moving accidents by flood and field;

Of hair-breadth scapes i'th'imminent deadly breach;
Of being taken by the insolent foe,
And sold to slavery; of my redemption thence,
And portance in my travel's history:
Wherein of antres vast and deserts idle,
Rough quarries, rocks, and hills whose heads
    touch heaven,
It was my hint to speak.
--William Shakespeare: Othello (1604); Act I,
    Scene 3.

ANYTHINGARIAN: A contemptuous term for a person of no
fixed or decided creed or viewpoint, one indifferent to all
beliefs. "Modern neo-Platonism" (Kingsley). Used earlier
by Swift in his Polite Conversations (1738).

'What did he want wi' proofs o' the being o' God,
an' o' the doctrine o' original sin? He could see
enough o' them ayont the shop-door, ony tide.
They made puir Rabbie Burns an anythingarian,
wi' their blethers, an' he was near gaun the same
gate."
--Charles Kingsley: Alton Locke (1850); chapter
    22.

APPERIL: Risk; peril; danger; jeopardy. Old form of the
noun "peril," descended from the Latin periculum, "danger,"
and experiri, "to attempt."

APEMANTUS:
Let me stay at thine apperil, Timon:
I come to observe; I give thee warning on't.
--William Shakespeare: Timon of Athens (ca.
    1607); Act I, Scene 2.

SERJEANT:
You must to prison, sir,
Unless you can find bail the creditor likes.
SIR MOTH INTEREST: I would fain find it, if
    you'd shew me where.
SIR DIAPHANOUS SILKWORM:
It is a terrible action; more indeed
Than many a man is worth; and is call'd Fright-
    bail.
CAPT. IRONSIDE: Faith, I will bail him at mine
    own apperil.
--Ben Jonson: The Magnetic Lady (1632); Act V,
    Scene 6.

APRICOCK: An apricot.   A word of many and varied his-
tories: French abricot; Portuguese albricoque; Arabic al-
barkŭk; Middle Greek praikokion; from the Latin praecoquus,
"early fruit," constructed from prae, "before," and coquere,
"to cook. "

> GARDENER:
> Go, bind thou up yon dangling apricocks,
> Which, like unruly children, make their sire
> Stoop with oppression of their prodigal weight:
> Give some supportance to the bending twigs.
> --William Shakespeare: King Richard the Second
>   (1595); Act III, Scene 4.

AQUILON: The north or the north-north-east wind.   This
word comes through the Old French aquilon, the Portuguese
aquilao, and the Italian aquilone, from the Latin aquilo,
"north. " In 1374 Chaucer used it; so did Shakespeare:

> AJAX:
> Thou, trumpet, there's my purse.
> Now crack thy lungs, and split thy brazen pipe:
> Blow, villain, till thy sphered bias cheek
> Outswell the colic of puft Aquilon:
> Come, stretch thy chest, and let thy eyes spout
>   blood;
> Thou blow'st for Hector.
> --William Shakespeare: Troilus and Cressida (ca.
>   1600); Act IV, Scene 5.

ARBALEST: An old crossbow, consisting of a steel bow
fitted crosswise to a wood launching shaft, which was fur-
nished with a trigger mechanism for drawing and letting slip
the bowstring, thus discharging ammunition such as stones,
arrows, rocks, etc.   Etymologically, the word comes through
the Anglo-French arb(e)leste, the Old French arbaleste (modern French arbalète), the Provencal arbalesta, albaresta.
The word comes ultimately from the Latin arcuballista,
which was constructed of arcus, "bow," and ballista, "a
military device for hurling missiles. " There is no definite
modern spelling, and the word thus has many different
forms: arblast, arbalist, arbalestre, arbalester, arblaster,
arcubalist, awblaster, etc.   It is a very old word: it was
used in Alisaunder (ca. 1300); in Arthur and Merlin (ca.
1330); Sir Ferumbras (ca. 1380); The Romance of the Rose
(ca. 1400); Caxton's Chronicles of England (1480).   In more
modern works, see Southey's Joan of Arc and Robert

Browning's Sordello (1840).

> "Unbend thy arblast, and come into the moonlight, "
> said the Scot, "or, by St. Andrew, I will pin thee
> to the earth, be what or whom thou wilt! "
> --Sir Walter Scott: The Talisman (1825); chapter
>   12.

ARBER, ERBER: The windpipe or esophagus; the throat;
also, the whole of an animal's entrails. From the French
herbière, with same meaning. Another very ancient word,
that can be found in Sir Tristram (ca. 1320) and Sir Gawain
and the Green Knight (ca. 1340).

> ROBIN HOOD:
> On, my Marian:
> I did but take the assay.
> MARIAN:
> You stop one's mouth,
> And yet you bid one speak--when the arbor's
>   made--
> ROBIN: Pull'd down, and paunch turn'd out.
> MARIAN: He that undoes him,
> Doth cleave the brisket bone, upon the spoon
> Of which a little gristle grows; you call it--
> ROBIN: The raven's bone.
> --Ben Jonson: The Sad Shepherd (1637); Act I,
>   Scene 2.

ARBORET: A little tree or shrub; also, a small grove
planted with many trees and shrubs. The word is a diminutive formation from the Latin word for tree, arbor. See
it in Drayton's Polyolbion, Milton's Paradise Lost, and
Southey's Madoc.

> It was a chosen plott of fertile land,
> Emongst wide waves sett, like a litle nest,
> As if it had by Natures cunning hand
> Bene choycely picked out from all the rest,
> And laid forth for ensample of the best:
> No dainty flowre or herbe, that growes on grownd,
> No arborett with painted blossomes drest,
> And smelling sweete, but there it might be fownd
> To bud out faire, and her sweete smels throwe
>   all arownd.
> --Edmund Spenser: The Faerie Queene, Book II
>   (1590); Canto VI, stanza 12.

ARGENTINE: Of, made of, or containing silver; silvery.
From the French argentin and the Latin argentinus, "of sil-
ver," from argentum, "silver." The word can be found in
Holinshed's Chronicles, and in Wilfred Holme's poem The
Fall and Evil Success of Rebellion (1572).

>   DIANA: Awake, and tell thy dream,
>   PERICLES: Celestial Dian, goddess argentine,
>   I will obey thee.
>   --William Shakespeare: Pericles (ca. 1606); Act
>   V, Scene 1.

ARGENT-VIVE: Quicksilver or mercury. Through the
French argent vif, taken from the Latin of Pliny, argentum
vivum, "living silver."

>   SIR EPICURE MAMMON:
>   Such was Pythagoras' thigh, Pandora's tub,
>   And, all that fable of Medea's charms,
>   The manner of our work; the bulls, our furnace,
>   Still breathing fire; our argent-vive, the dragon:
>   The dragon's teeth, mercury sublimate,
>   That keeps the whiteness, hardness, and the biting.
>   --Ben Jonson: The Alchemist (1610); Act II, Scene
>   1.

ARGIN, ARGINE: A rampart or embankment before a fort,
topped with a fortification. The word comes through the
Italian argine from the Latin argerem, adgerem, from agger,
"mound." A description can be found in Paul Ive's Practice
of Fortification (1589).

>   TAMBURLAINE:
>   It must have privy ditches, countermines,
>   And secret issuings to defend the ditch;
>   It must have high argins and covered ways
>   To keep the bulwark fronts from battery,
>   And parapets to hide the musketeers.
>   --Christopher Marlowe: Tamburlaine The Great,
>   Part II (1587); Act III, Scene 2.

ARISTIPPUS: A 17th-century name for canary wine, originally made in the Canary Islands. It comes from the name
of a Greek philosopher, Aristippus (ca. 435-ca. 360 B.C.),
founder of the Cyrenaic school, which professed the belief
that all human sensations can be reduced to two emotions,
pleasure and pain. Needless to say, the old philosopher

was luxuriant in his lifestyle, and it is from this fact that his name is associated with canary wine. Defoe used the word, as did Middleton:

> SIR BOUNTEOUS PROGRESS:
> O for a bowl of fat canary,
> Rich Aristippus, sparkling sherry!
> Some nectar else from Juno's dairy;
> O these draughts would make us merry!
> --Thomas Middleton: A Mad World, My Masters
>   (1608); Act V, Scene 2.

ASINEGO, ASINICO, ASSINEGO: A little ass or donkey; hence, a fool, dolt, blockhead, dumb-bell. Popular in the 17th and 18th centuries, the word came from the Spanish diminutive form of asno, "ass." See Sir Thomas Herbert's Travels; also employed by Ben Jonson.

> THERSITES: Thou hast no more brain than I have in mine elbows; an assinego may tutor thee: thou scurvy-valiant ass! thou art here but to thrash Trojans; and thou art bought and sold among those of any wit, like a barbarian slave. If thou use to beat me, I will begin at thy heel, and tell what thou art by inches, thou thing of no bowels, thou!
> --William Shakespeare: Troilus and Cressida (ca. 1600); Act II, Scene 1.

ASKANCE: A verbal use of this word, meaning "to look aside" or "to turn away." It comes to us through the Middle English askaunce, but further origins are uncertain.

> Men's faults do seldom to themselves appear;
> Their own transgressions partially they smother:
> This guilt would seem death-worthy in thy brother.
>   O, how are they wrapt in with infamies
>   That from their own misdeeds askance their
>   eyes!
> --William Shakespeare: Lucrece (1594); lines 633-637.

ASTUCIOUS: Astute or crafty; cunning; wily; shrewd; keen; sharp. Through the Old French, this word comes from the Latin word of the same meaning, astutus.

> "I will answer you, my Liege, if you will tell me in sincerity, whether you want war or peace, "

replied Dunois, with a frankness which, while it
arose out of his own native openness and intrepid-
ity of character, made him from time to time a
considerable favourite with Louis, who, like all
astucious persons, was as desirous of looking into
the hearts of others, as of concealing his own.
--Sir Walter Scott: Quentin Durward (1823); chapter 9.

In the same council-room of the conventual palace
of the Dominicans, King Robert was seated with
his brother Albany, whose affected austerity of
virtue, and real art and dissimulation, maintained
so high an influence over the feeble-minded monarch. It was indeed natural, that one who seldom
saw things according to their real forms and out-
lines, should view them according to the light in
which they were presented to him by a bold astucious man, possessing the claim of such near re-
lationship.
--Sir Walter Scott: The Fair Maid of Perth (1828);
chapter 21.

Also see Anna Jameson's Characteristics of Women:
Moral, Poetical, and Historical (1846).

AUMAIL: Enamel. From the noun amel, "enamel," a re-
fashioning of that word. It can be located in Jeremiah Wif-
fen's translation of Tasso's Jerusalem Delivered (1824), as
well as in the following:

Below her ham her weed did somewhat trayne,
And her streight legs most bravely were embayld
In gilden buskins of costly cordwayne,
All bard with golden bendes, which were entayld
With curious antickes, and full fayre aumayld.
--Edmund Spenser: The Faerie Queene, Book II
(1590); Canto III, stanza 27.

AUNT: An old woman or gossip; in other senses, a prosti-
tute, loose woman, concubine. The word comes through
Old French from the Latin amita, aunt. It was popular with
Shakespeare:

PUCK:
And sometimes lurk I in a gossip's bowl,
In very likeness of a roasted crab;

And when she drinks, against her lips I bob,
And on her wither'd dewlap pour the ale.
The wisest aunt, telling the saddest tale,
Sometime for three-foot stool mistaketh me;
Then slip I from her bum, down topples she,
And 'tailor' cries, and falls into a cough;
And then the whole quire hold their hips and loff,
And waxen in their mirth, and neeze, and swear
A merrier hour was never wasted there.
--A Midsummer Night's Dream (1594); Act II,
    Scene 1.

AUTOLYCUS:
The lark, that tirra-lirra chants,
    With hey! with hey! the thrush and the jay,
Are summer songs for me and my aunts,
    While we lie tumbling in the hay.
--The Winter's Tale (1610); Act IV, Scene 2.

Also found in Richard III.

AVENTAIL, AVENTAYLE: The movable mouthpiece of a
helmet, which can be raised or lowered to admit fresh air.
The word comes from the Old French esventail, "air-hole,"
from esventer, "to refresh, to cool." A very old word; it
can be located in Sir Gawain and the Green Knight (ca. 1340)
and in Chaucer's Troylus and Criseyde (1374).

He entered the cell of the ancient priest,
And lifted his barred aventayle
To hail the Monk of Saint Mary's aisle.
--Sir Walter Scott: The Lay of the Last Minstrel
    (1805); Canto II, stanza 3.

Scott also employed the word in his Marmion (1808).

AVENTINE: A strong, secure military position or defensive
fortification; a "strong tower." This word is taken from the
Latin Aventinus, the name of one of the seven hills of Rome,
all of which were strategic positions. It lies south of the
others, between the River Tiber and the Caelian hill, southwest of the Circus Maximus.

AESOPUS: 'Tis given out lately,
The consul Aretinus, Caesar's spy,
Said at his table, ere a month expired,
For being gall'd in our last comedy,

He'd silence us for ever.
PARIS:
I expect
No favour from him; my strong Aventine is,
That great Domitian, whom we oft have cheer'd
In his most sullen moods, will once return,
Who can repair, with ease, the consul's ruins.
--Philip Massinger: The Roman Actor (1626);
    Act I, Scene 1.

AWNY: Bristly; bearded; stubbly. This is an adjective
from the noun awn: "the bristly, fibrous 'beard' of the
grain-sheath of barley, oats, and other grasses." This
word is apparently from the Old Norse word ögn, "chaff,"
akin to the Old High German agana, the Middle High German agene, agne, ane (modern German ahne). The basic
meaning is "sharp, pointed."

    Let husky wheat the haughs adorn,
    An' aits set up their awnie horn.
    --Robert Burns: Scotch Drink (1786); stanza 3.

AZURN: Azure. A variation on the noun, similar to heath-
ern, leathern, southern, etc. Through the Middle English
and the Old French, this word is derived from the Arabic
lāzaward and the Persian lāzhuward, "lapis lazuli," a reference to that stone's sky-blue color.

    By the rushy-fringéd bank,
    Where grows the willow and the osier dank,
        My sliding chariot stays,
    Thick set with agate, and the azurn sheen
        Of turkis blue, and emerald green,
        That in the channel strays.
    --John Milton: Comus (1634); lines 890-895.

-B-

BABION: An ape, especially the baboon; also spelled bavian.
The word later came to be a derisive term directed toward
persons. It came from the French babion and the Old
French babuin, and is related to many similar words in other languages, such as the Dutch baviaan and the German
pavian. It was most popular in the 17th century: Drayton
employed it, as did Philip Massinger in The Parliament of
Love (1624).

AMORPHUS: I am neither your Minotaur, nor your Centaur, nor your satyr, nor your hyaena, nor your babion, but your mere traveller, believe me.
--Ben Jonson: Cynthia's Revels (1600); Act I, Scene 1.

BABLIAMINY: This is a humorous use of the common word babble. Babble is probably an echoic word, but can be traced back to certain older words as influences, such as the Latin balbutire, "to stammer" and the Sanskrit balbuthah, "one who stammers."

DAMPIT: Out, you babliaminy, you unfeathered, cremitoried quean, you cullisance of scabiosity!
AUDREY: Good words, Master Dampit, to speak before a maid and a virgin!
--Thomas Middleton: A Trick to Catch the Old One (1608); Act IV, Scene 5.

BACHARACH: A type of wine that was considered one of the finest in Europe, named after a village on the Rhine where it originated. The word exists in a wide variety of spellings, such as bachrag, baccharach, backrag, bachrach, back-rack, back-rac, etc. Usages can be found in Fletcher and Massinger's The Beggar's Bush (1620) and in Scott's The Abbot (1820); it was also employed by Longfellow.

Restored the fainting high and mighty
With brandy, wine, and aqua-vitae;
And made 'em stoutly overcome
With Bacrack, Hoccamore, and Mum.
--Samuel Butler: Hudibras, Part Third (1678); Canto III, lines 297-300.

BACHELOR: A spinster, maid, or unmarried woman. This word is from the Old French bacheler, the Provencal bacalar, the Italian baccalare, coming from the Latin baccalaris, of uncertain origin. In medieval Latin this word signified "a young knight, not old enough, or having too few vassals, to display his own banner, and who therefore followed the banner of another." The original sense is most probably from the baccalaria, a land-division in the Middle Ages, the type and size of which varied considerably. The word is probably connected with the early Latin vacca, "cow," in which sense it could mean "pastureland" or "grazing-land." Whatever the precise origin, the principal sense of the word

is that of a "tenant farmer," a person working on the estate
of a lord, baron, etc. Apparently it was used without distinction of sex until relatively recent times.

> POLISH: Your lady-aunt has choice in the house
>   for you:
> We do not trust your uncle: he would keep you
> A batchelor still, by keeping of your portion;
> And keep you not alone without a husband,
> But in a sickness; ay, and the green sickness,
> The maiden's malady; which is a sickness:
> A kind of a disease, I can assure you.
> --Ben Jonson: The Magnetic Lady (1632); Act II,
>   Scene 1.

BACCARE, BACKARE: An exclamation or cry meaning:
"Go back! Get away! Keep back!" The origin is doubtful;
perhaps it is a mincing of "back there!" or some type of
playful construction of "back-er" meaning "farther back."
Because it is pronounced as having three syllables, it has
also been suggested that this is an attempt at Latinizing
English (Nares). Uses can be found in Nicholas Udall's
Ralph Roister-Doister (1553), Lyly's Mydas (1592), and in
the following:

> GREMIO:
> Saving your tale, Petruchio, I pray,
> Let us, that are poor petitioners, speak too:
> Baccare! you are marvellous forward.
> --William Shakespeare: The Taming of the Shrew
>   (ca. 1595); Act II, Scene 1.

BADINER: To talk about trifling things; to speak much, but
say little; to banter; or, also, to tell a joke or jest. From
the French badiner, "to play or frolic," from badin, "silly,
foolish."

> BERINTHIA: But now what shall I do with myself?
> I don't know how in the world to pass my time;
> would Loveless were here to badiner a little.
> Well, he's a charming fellow: I don't wonder his
> wife's so fond of him.
> --Sir John Vanbrugh: The Relapse (1696); Act IV,
>   Scene 3.

BALD-COOT: The common name for the coot, a water-bird
named for its white featherless frontal plate. Hence, this

word has come to be used in reference to a person without hair, a "marble-head" or "baldilocks." It can also mean simply an old man. A modern use occurs in Charles Kingsley's The Saint's Tragedy (1848), Act III.

> ZANTHIA:
> I am as full of pleasure in the touch
> As e'er a white-fac'd puppet of 'em all,
> Juicy, and firm; unfledge 'em of their tires,
> Their wires, their partlets, pins, and perriwigs,
> And they appear like bald-coots in the nest.
> --John Fletcher: The Knight of Malta (1616?);
>   Act I, Scene 1.

BALD-RIB: Similar to the preceding word, the actual meaning is of the cut of pork between the spare-rib and the rump, so called "because the bones thereof are made bald and bare of flesh" (Minsheu). Hence, in a humorous sense, the word means a thin, bony, skinny person. Thomas D'Urfey used it in Laugh and Be Fat, or Pills to Purge Melancholy in 1674, as did Middleton:

> OLIVER: Thou mushroom, thou shot'st up in a night, by lying with thy mistress!
> SIMON: Faith, thou art such a spiny baldrib, all the mistresses in the town will never get thee up.
> --Thomas Middleton: The Mayor of Queenborough (1661); Act III, scene 3.

BALLARD: A type of musical instrument, well-described in the following quotation. The etymology of the word is uncertain.

> Their ballards are a foot above ground, hollow under, with some seventeen keys on the top, on which the player strikes sitting on the ground, with two sticks a foot long, with balls fast'ned on the end: the sound may be heard an English mile. This instrument is one of their most ingenious artifices. To every one of these keys belongs a small iron a foot long, as big as a quill, upon which hangs two gourds under the hollow like bottles, which cause the sound.
> --Larger Observations of Master Richard Jobson touching the River Gambia (1620-1621) in Purchase His Pilgrimes (1625).

BALLOW: Smooth; even; gaunt? Both etymology and meaning of this word are uncertain.

> A horse of greater speed, nor yet a righter hound,
> Not any where 'twixt Kent and Caledon is found.
> Nor yet the level south can show a smoother race,
> Whereas the ballow nag outstrips the winds in
>   chase.
> --Michael Drayton: Polyolbion (1612); Song III.

BANTLING: A word for an infant or small child, probably taken from a corruption of the German word bankling, "bastard," and, indeed, bantling originally was a synonym for bastard. It is derived from bank, "bench," thus drawing a distinction between a child begotten on a bench and one begotten in a bed. "If it has any etymology," says Dr. Johnson, "it is perhaps corrupted from the old word bairn, bairnling, a little child." It can be found throughout the literature of the 16th, 17th, 18th, and 19th centuries: see Francis Quarles's Emblems (1635); Samuel Coleridge's Table Talk; Tennyson's Boadicea. Washington Irving used it in his Knickerbocker's History of New York--and here is an early use:

> BATTE:
> That pretty Cupid, little god of love,
> Whose imped wings with speckled plumes are dight,
> Who woundeth men below, and gods above,
> Roving at random with his feather'd flight:
>   Whilst lovely Venus stands to give the aim,
>   Smiling to see her wanton bantling's game.
> --Michael Drayton: Eclogue VII (1593); stanza 17.

BASINET: A very old word for the small rounded steel headpiece worn by warriors in medieval times, sometimes having a sharp, pointed visor, and often richly adorned with jewelry. It came from the Old French bacinet, and the Latin basinetum, a diminutive form of the word for basin, which the helmet resembles. Many different spellings exist: basnet, basynet, bassenet, bascinet, etc. It can be found in many writings: in Sir Ferumbras (ca. 1380); Morte Arthur (ca. 1440); John Gwillim's Display of Heraldry (1611); Scott's Lord of the Isles and Lytton's novel, The Last of the Barons (1843).

> 'Hark! hark! my lord, an English drum!
> And see ascending squadrons come

Between Tweed's river and the hill,
Foot, horse, and cannon! Hap what hap,
My basnet to a prentice cap,
    Lord Surrey's o'er the Till!
--Sir Walter Scott: Marmion (1808); Canto VI,
    stanza 21.

BASTA: An old exclamation meaning "Stop! Enough! No
more! Cut it out!" taken directly from the Italian and Spanish basta, "enough." Besides in Shakespeare, the word is
in Brome's The Court Beggar and Scott's Ivanhoe.

TRANIO: For who shall bear your part,
And be in Padua here Vincentio's son;
Keep house, and ply his book; welcome his friends;
Visit his countrymen, and banquet them?
LUCENTIO: Basta; content thee; for I have it full.
--William Shakespeare: The Taming of the Shrew
    (ca. 1595); Act I, Scene 1.

"The man of God bears my sign-manual too; but
the duke made us friends again, and it cost me
more sack than I could carry, and all the Rhenish
to boot, to pledge the seer in the way of love and
reconciliation. But, caracco! 't is a vile old
canting slave for all that, whom I will one day
beat out of his devil's livery into all the colours
of the rainbow. Basta! Said I well, old Trap-
bois? Where is thy daughter, man? What says
she to my suit?"
--Sir Walter Scott: The Fortunes of Nigel (1822);
    chapter 23.

BASTARD: A type of sweet Spanish wine, resembling mus-
catel, often applied to different types of similar wines.
Originally "bastard wine," the name was used in connection
with the way in which it was made.

PRINCE HENRY: I give thee this pennyworth of
sugar, clapt even now into my hand by an under-
skinker, one that never spake other English in his
life than "Eight shillings and sixpence," and "You
are welcome," with this shrill addition, "Anon,
anon, sir! Score a pint of bastard in the Half-
moon," or so.
--William Shakespeare: King Henry The Fourth,
    Part I (1597); Act II, Scene 4.

...the worthy potentate, having first sligh
vited Lord Glenvarloch to partake of the li
which he was to pay for, and after having
served that, excepting three poached eggs,
of bastard, and a cup of clary, he was fasti
from everything but sin, set himself seriousl
reinforce the radical moisture.
--Sir Walter Scott: The Fortunes of Nigel (1t
    chapter 23.

BASTINADO: A sound, punishing beating administered wit
a hard stick or club, usually on the bottoms of the feet.
The word comes from the Spanish bastonada, from baston,
"a stick or staff. " An extremely popular word found in
many writers, including Holinshed, Robert Greene in his
Art of Cony-Catching, Samuel Butler in Hudibras, Washington Irving, and in many others.

BASTARD: Here's a large mouth, indeed,
That spits forth death and mountains, rocks and
    seas;
Talks as familiarly of roaring lions
As maids of thirteen do of puppy-dogs!
What cannoneer begot this lusty blood?
He speaks plain cannon, --fire and smoke and
    bounce;
He gives the bastinado with his tongue:
Our ears are cudgell'd; not a word of his
But buffets better than a fist of France:
Zounds, I was never so bethumpt with words
Since I first call'd my brother's father dad.
--William Shakespeare: King John (ca. 1595); Act
    II, Scene 1.

'Dost thou parley, slave? " answered one of the
maskers; "and must I show thee that thou art a
captive, by giving thee incontinently the bastinado? "
--Sir Walter Scott: The Fair Maid of Perth (1828);
    chapter 16.

BAUDRONS, BAUDRANS: A Scottish familiar name for the
cat, like Tom. The origin is obscure; several words can be
considered as possibilities: the Irish beadrac, "playful, " the
Scotch-Gaelic beadrach, "a playful girl, " and beadradh, "a
caress. "

Auld Hornie did the Leigh Kirk watch,

> Just like a winkin baudrons:
> And ay he catch'd the tither wretch,
>   To fry them in his caudrons.
> --Robert Burns: The Ordination (1787); stanza 10.

Also see Samuel Colvil's poem The Whigg's Supplication, or the Scots Hudibras (1657).

BAUSON, BAWSON: A name for the badger. It comes from the adjective bausond which describes the quality of having white spots on a dark background in animals, or having a bright white spot on the head, as the badger does. The Middle English form was bausen, from the Old French bausen, bauzan. Later, the word came to be a derisive term for a fat person, in allusion to the fatness of the badger prior to winter. It can also mean an ugly person or a numbskull. In chapter 28 of The Heart of Midlothian, Sir Walter Scott employs the variation bauson-faced. Since it is a very old word, it has many varied spellings, including bawsym, bauzen, bawzen, bausene, baunsey, etc.

> MOTTO:
> The shepherd wore a sheep-gray cloak,
> Which was of the finest lock,
>   That could be cut with sheer.
> His mittons were of bauzons' skin,
> His cockers were of cordiwin,
>   His hood of miniveer.
> --Michael Drayton: Eclogue IV (1593); stanza 31.

For a more recent example, consult W. H. Ainsworth's The Constable of the Tower (1861).

BAVAROY: An old type of cloak, the name taken from the French bavarois, "Bavarian," indicating connection either with the location itself as an origin or as a style. An eighteenth-century word: Ebenezer Picken used it in his poetry, as did Gay:

> Let the loop'd Bavaroy the fop embrace,
> Or his deep cloak bespatter'd o'er with lace:
> That garment best the winter's rage defends,
> Whose shapeless form in ample plaits depends;
> By various names in various counties known,
> Yet held in all the true Surtout alone;
> Be thine of kersey firm, though small the cost,
> Then brave unwet the rain, unchill'd the frost.
> --John Gay: Trivia (1716); Book I, lines 54-60.

BAWCOCK: An old colloquialism expressing endearment: "Good boy, fine fellow, good lad," popular in the 16th and 17th centuries. Taken directly from the French phrase beau coq, "fine cock."

> FLUELLEN: Got's plood!--Up to the preaches, you rascals! will you not up to the preaches?
> PISTOL: Be merciful, great duke, to men of mold! Abate thy rage, abate thy manly rage! Abate thy rage, great duke!
> Good bawcock, bate thy rage! use lenity, sweet chuck!
> --William Shakespeare: King Henry The Fifth (1599); Act III, Scene 2.

> KING HENRY: What are you?
> PISTOL: As good a gentleman as the emperor.
> KING HENRY: Then you are a better than the king.
> PISTOL: The king's a bawcock, and a heart of gold,
> A lad of life, an imp of fame;
> Of parents good, of fist most valiant:
> I kiss his dirty shoe, and from heart-string
> I love the lovely bully.
> --William Shakespeare: King Henry The Fifth (1599); Act IV, Scene 1.

For a more recent use, see W. H. Ainsworth's The Constable of the Tower (1861).

BAXTER: A baker (sometimes, a female baker). From the Old English baecestre, from bacan, "to bake, to cook." The word is of feminine origin, though rather early lost its feminine association. From the 10th to the 15th centuries it was used for both sexes; it is still in use in some dialects in Scotland, even though in the 16th century a new feminine form, backstress, appeared.

> A near relation of the author's used to tell of having been stopped by the rioters, and escorted home in the manner described. On reaching her own home, one of her attendants, in appearance a baxter, i.e. a baker's lad, handed her out of her chair, and took leave with a bow, which, in the lady's opinion, argued breeding that could hardly be learned beside the oven.

--Sir Walter Scott: The Heart of Midlothian (1818);
chapter 6.

BEAUPERS, BEWPERS: A type of linen fabric formerly
used in the manufacture of flags, ensigns, pennants, etc.
The origin is totally in doubt; some association has been
suggested with the French town of Beaupreau, which is a
center of the linen and woollen industries.

Up betimes and to my office, where we sat all the
morning, and a great rant I did give to Mr. Davis,
of Deptford, and others about their usage of Mi-
chell, in his Bewpers, which he serves in for
flaggs, which did trouble me, but yet it was in
defence of what was truth.
--Samuel Pepys' Diary: March 14th, 1663.

BEAVER, BEVER: The movable mouthpiece of a medieval
war helmet, when worn with the visor attached.   This word
comes from the Old French word for bib, which was derived
from bave, "saliva." Edmund Spenser used it in his Faerie
Queene, Book II, as did Horace Walpole in 1765 in his Castle of Otranto.

HAMLET: Then saw you not his face?
HORATIO: O, yes, my lord; he wore his beaver
up.
--William Shakespeare: Hamlet (1600); Act I,
Scene 2.

BECCO: A cuckold.   From the Italian becco, meaning "he-
goat," another reference (as in adhorn) to the old verb horn,
meaning "to cuckold." Massinger used it in The Bondman
(1623), as did Marston:

MALEVOLE: Do not weep, kind cuckold, take
comfort, man, thy betters have been beccoes:
Agamemnon, emperor of all the merry Greeks,
that tickeled all the true Trojans, was a cornuto
... Hercules, whose back bore up heaven, and
got forty wenches with child in one night.
PIETRO: Nay, 'twas fifty.
--John Marston: The Malcontent (1604); Act IV,
Scene 5.

BEDSTAFF: Used principally in the 17th and 18th centuries,
this was a staff or stick attached to the sides of a bed,

used to hold the bedclothes to keep them from slipping off while changing the sheets. Thus the object came to become a ready weapon at bedside, and was the source of much humor.

> LONGVIL: Well! Pray Mr. Tinder-box, go about it quickly.
> SIR SAMUEL HEARTY: Gad I'll do't instantly, in the twinkling of a bed-staff.
> --Thomas Shadwell: The Virtuoso (1676); Act I, Scene 1.

Also used by Ben Jonson in Every Man In His Humour and in Brome's City Wit.

BEGLERBEG: A title for the governor of a province of the Ottoman empire, just below the grand vizier. The word comes from the Turkish beglerbeg, "bey of beys." Begler is the plural of beg or bey, which is Turkish for "prince, governor." Thus, beglerbeg means "prince of princes," "king of kings," etc. The beglerbeglik was the province over which the beglerbeg ruled. The word can be found in Richard Carew's Survey of Cornwall (1602) as well as in Sir John Cam Hobhouse's Journey through Albania and other Provinces of Turkey, with Lord Byron (1812).

> GAZET: I have a pretty stock,
> And would not have my good parts undiscovered;
> What places of credit are there?
> CARAZIE: There's your beglerbeg.
> GAZET: By no means that; it comes too near the beggar,
> And most prove so, that come there.
> --Philip Massinger: The Renegado (1624); Act III, Scene 4.

BEJESUIT: To make a Jesuit of one; to subject to the teachings of the Jesuits, or to teach one the Jesuit beliefs. Used by Edmund Hickeringill and Thomas Carlyle, as well as by Milton:

> In the mean while if any one would write, and bring his helpful hand to the slow-moving Reformation which we labour under, if truth have spok'n to him before others, or but seem'd at least to speak, who hath so bejesuited us that we should trouble that man with asking licence to do so

worthy a deed?
--John Milton: <u>Areopagitica</u> (1644); paragraph 25.

BELAMY: An old form of address, popular from the 14th
to the 18th centuries, meaning "Good friend." The word is
directly from the French <u>bel ami</u>, "fair friend." Seen in
the <u>Towneley Mystery Plays</u>, and in the following:

> There mournfull cypresse grew in greatest store,
> And trees of bitter gall, and heben sad,
> Dead sleeping poppy, and black hellebore,
> Cold coloquintida, and tetra mad,
> Mortall samnitis, and cicuta bad,
> With which th' unjust Athenians made to dy
> Wise Socrates, who thereof quaffing glad,
> Pourd out his life and last philosophy
> To the fayre Critias, his dearest belamy.
> --Edmund Spenser: <u>The Faerie Queene</u>, Book II
>   (1590); Canto VII, stanza 52.

BELEPER: To cause to become leprous; to afflict with lep-
rosy. Derived from the Greek <u>lepos</u>, "a scale," which is
from <u>lepein</u>, "to peel." Thus the general meaning of lep-
rosy is "scaly."

> CASSILANE:
> You have a law, lords, that without remorse
> Dooms such as are beleper'd with the curse
> Of foul ingratitude unto death.
> PORPHICIO: We have.
> CASSILANE: Then do me justice.
> --John Fletcher: <u>The Laws of Candy</u> (1619?); Act
>   V, Scene 1.

BELLIBONE: A fair maid; young girl, sweet maiden. "A
woman excelling both in beauty and goodness" (Johnson).
The etymology is uncertain; perhaps it is from the French
<u>belle et bonne</u>, "fair and good." cf. bonnibel.

> PERIGOT: The while my flocke did feede thereby
> ... I saw the bouncing Bellibone ... tripping over
> the dale alone ... well decked in a frocke of
> gray ... And in a kirtle of greene saye ... A
> chapelet on her head she wore ... of sweete vio-
> lets therein was store ... My sheepe did leave
> theyr wonted foode ... And gazd on her, as they
> were wood ...

--Edmund Spenser: The Shepheardes Calender:
August (1579); lines 59-75.

BELLY-CHEER: To banquet in a lavish or luxurious manner; to feast in splendor; to "cheer" the "belly."

> Let them assemble in Consistory with their Elders
> and Deacons, according to ancient Ecclesiastical
> rule, to the preserving of Church-discipline, each
> in his several-charge, and not a pack of clergy-
> men by themselves to belly-cheare in their pre-
> sumptuous Sion, or to promote designs, abuse and
> gull the simple Laity, and stir up tumult, as the
> prelates did, for the maintenance of their pride
> and avarice.
> --John Milton: The Tenure of Kings and Magis-
> trates (1650); paragraph 21.

BELLY-TIMBER: Food, supplies, provisions; "Materials to
support the belly" (Johnson). Originally a serious word,
but since Butler a jocular expression for a meal. Seen in
Smollett and Scott, as well as Butler:

> And tho' knights-errant, as some think,
> Of old did neither eat nor drink,
> Because when through deserts vast,
> And regions desolate, they pass'd,
> Where belly-timber, above ground,
> Or under, was not to be found,
> Unless they grazed, there's not one word
> Of their provision on record;
> Which made some confidently write,
> They had no stomachs but to fight.
> --Samuel Butler: Hudibras, Part First (1663);
> Canto I, lines 327-336.

BELSWAGGER, BELLY-SWAGGER: A swaggering gallant; a
whoremaster; a pimp. This word may perhaps have come
from its "belly-swagger" form, "one who swags or sways
his belly."

> PLEASANCE: Be satisfi'd, thy shears shall never
> enter into my cloth. But, look to thy self, thou
> impudent belswagger: I'll be reveng'd; I will.
> --John Dryden: The Kind Keeper (1678); Act IV,
> Scene 1.

BENCH-HOLE: A latrine; a toilet; an outhouse; privy. The origin of the word is rather obvious.

> MARK ANTONY: Thou bleed'st apace.
> SCARUS: I had a wound here that was like a T,
> But now 'tis made an H.
> MARK ANTONY: They do retire.
> SCARUS: We'll beat 'em into bench-holes: I have yet
> Room for six scotches more.
> --William Shakespeare: Antony and Cleopatra
>   (1607); Act IV, Scene 7.

BENCH-WHISTLER: A derisive term for one who sits "idly whistling on a bench." Hence, a slothful, lazy good-for-nothing; a bum.

> GOSTANZO: I could have written as good prose
>   and verse
> As the most beggarly poet of 'em all,
> Either acrostic, Exordion,
> Epithalamions, Satires, Epigrams,
> Sonnets in Dozens, or your Quatorzains
> In any rhyme, Masculine, Feminine,
> Or Sdruciolla [dactyls] or couplets, Blank Verse.
> Y'are but bench-whistlers now-a-days to them
> That were in our times.
> --George Chapman: All Fools (1599); Act II,
>   Scene 1.

BEPISS: To wet with urine, to urinate upon. The origin of piss is unknown, but it is thought to have had an echoic beginning. Used by Bridges in his travesty on Homer, and much earlier by William Caxton.

> JUSTICE:
> You must not threaten her; 'tis against law; Go on.
> OLD BANKS: So, sir, ever since, having a dun
> cow tied up in my back-side, let me go thither,
> or but cast mine eye at her, and if I should be
> hanged I cannot choose, though it be ten times in
> an hour, but run to the cow, and taking up her
> tail, kiss--saving your worship's reverence--my
> cow behind, that the whole town of Edmonton has
> been ready to bepiss themselves laughing me to
> scorn.
> --Thomas Dekker (with John Ford & William Rowley):
>   The Witch of Edmonton (1623); Act IV, Scene 1.

BESWADDLE: To wrap up in swaddling clothes. From the
Anglo-Saxon swathian, "to swathe, to wrap up," from the
Indo-European base sqeudh-, "to conceal, to hide."

> Hence flow alone the sacred gifts of kings,
> Staves, truncheons, feathers, mitres, stars, and
>   strings.
> Hence cradles, see! with lisping statesmen
>   spawn,
> And infant limbs beswaddled in the lawn.
> --Paul Whitehead: Epistle To Doctor Thomson
>   (1755).

BETSO: A small Venetian coin, made of brass, worth about
a half a cent. From the Italian bezzo.

> MOCINIGO: And what must I give you?
> BRAVO: At a word, thirty livres: I'll not bate
> you a betso.
> MOCINIGO: I'll give you twenty.
> BRAVO: You bid like a chapman. Well, 'tis a
> hard time; in hope of your custom hereafter, I'll
> take your money.
> --Shackerley Marmion: The Antiquary (1636); Act
> III, Scene 1.

BETWIT, BETWITT: To reproach; upbraid; find fault with;
rebuke; censure. Emphatic formation of "twit," from the
Anglo-Saxon aetwitan, constructed of aet "at" and witan "to
accuse." Basic sense: accuse, "point a finger at."

> Then to the Dolphin to Sir W. Batten and Pen and
> other company; among others, Mr. Delabar--where
> strange how these men, who at other times are
> all wise men, do now in their drink betwitt and
> reproach one another with their former conditions
> and their actions as to public concernments, till I
> was shamed to see it.
> --Samuel Pepys' Diary: April 2nd, 1661.

> "The snipe need not the woodcock betwit."
> --Old proverb.

BEVER: Beverage; a potation; liquor; drink; a time for
drinking. From the Old French beivre, "to drink," derived
from the Latin bibere, also "to drink."

I send you the roll that you sent for ... as for
herring, I have bought an horseload ... I can get
no eel yet; as for bever, there is promised me
some, but I might not get it yet.
--The Paston Letters: Margaret Paston to John
Paston, March 22nd, 1451(?).

BEZAN: The meaning of this word is relatively uncertain.
It comes from the Dutch bezaan, "mizzen sail," and probably
refers to some type of small sailing craft.

Up by break of day at 5 o'clock, and down by
water to Woolwich: in my way saw the yacht lately built by our virtuosoes (my Lord Brunkard and
others, with the help of Commissioner Pett also)
set out from Greenwich with the little Dutch bezan,
to try for mastery; and before they got to Woolwich the Dutch beat them half-a-mile (and I hear
this afternoon, that, in coming home, it got above
three miles); which all our people are glad of.
--Samuel Pepys' Diary: September 5th, 1662.

BIDDY: A chicken, fowl, or hen; a louse; a duckling, goose,
or swan.   Usually, a call used by children to their fowl.
The origin is unknown, but the Gaelic word for "very small,"
bîdeach, has been suggested.

SIR TOBY BELCH: Why, how now, my bawcock!
how dost thou, chuck?
MALVOLIO: Sir!
SIR TOBY BELCH: Ay, Biddy, come with me.
What, man! 'tis not for gravity to play at cherry-
pit with Satan: hang him, foul collier!
--William Shakespeare: Twelfth Night (1601); Act
III, Scene 4.

BIDSTAND: A highwayman, so named because he bids you
stand and hand over the goods.

SOGLIARDO: Why, I tell you, sir, he has been
the only bidstand that ever kept New-market,
Salisbury-plain, Hockley i' the Hole, Gads-Hill;
all the high places of any request: he has had his
mares and his geldings, he, ha' been worth forty,
threescore, a hundred pound a horse, would ha'
sprung you over hedge, and ditch, like your greyhound, he has done five hundred robberies in his

time, more or less, I assure you.
--Ben Jonson: Every Man Out Of His Humour
(1599); Act IV, Scene 5.

A more modern use is seen in Sala's Captain Dangerous (1863).

BILBO: A sword, rapier, or cutlass of the finest quality, apparently named after the city of Bilbao in Spain where it was made. "Bilbow blades," says Drayton, "blades accounted of the best temper." The swords of Bilbao "are famous over all Europe" (Moll, 1701). Later, the word came to have a specialized meaning in referring to the sword of a braggart or bully. Principally used in the 16th, 17th, and 18th centuries. Drayton used it in his seventeenth Ode, and Scott used it in Woodstock.

SIR JOHN FALSTAFF: But mark the sequel, Master Brook: I suffer'd the pangs of three several deaths; first, an intolerable fright, to be detected with a jealous rotten bellwether; next, to be compass'd, like a good bilbo, in the circumference of a peck, hilt to point, heel to head; and then, to be stopt in, like a strong distillation, with stinking clothes that fretted in their own grease.
--William Shakespeare: The Merry Wives of Windsor (1601); Act III, Scene 5.

BILK: A statement either (a) destitute of truth; or (b) that says nothing. The origin is unknown, though the word was first used in the 17th century as a technical term in the game of cribbage, a synonym for balk.

SQUIRE TUB: He will have the last word, though he talk bilk for't.
CANON HUGH: Bilk! what's that?
SQUIRE TUB: Why, nothing: a word signifying Nothing; and borrowed here to express nothing.
--Ben Jonson: A Tale of a Tub (1633); Act I, Scene 1.

BIRD'S-NIE, BIRD'S-NYE: An old term of endearment roughly equivalent to "sweetheart," derived from a slurring of "myn eye" to "my nye," associated with the familiar term bird. Principally used in the 17th century.

> LODOVICO:
> O my sweet birds-nie! what a wench have I
> Of thee! Crede quod habes, et habes still.
> And I had thought it possible to have been
> Cuckolded, I had been cuckolded.
> --Robert Davenport: The City Nightcap (1624);
>   Act II.

BLACK-POT: A large beer-mug, sometimes called a black-jack, because it was coated with tar. Later usage adapted the meaning to a drunkard or toper. Employed by Robert Greene in his Friar Bacon and Friar Bungay (1590) and by Thomas Heywood in Love's Maistresse (1636).

> When they had entered this apartment, Tummas as
> a matter of course offered, and as a matter of
> course Mr. Stubbs accepted, a "summat" to eat
> and drink, being the respectable relics of a gam-
> mon of bacon, and a whole whiskin, or black pot
> of sufficient double ale.
> --Sir Walter Scott: The Heart of Midlothian (1818);
>   chapter 32.

BLIND MAN'S HOLIDAY: A jocular expression for twilight, that time just before the candles are lit, when it has be-come too dark for further work, and all must rest or "take a holiday." Evening twilight; the end of the working-day.

> The twilight, or rather the hour between the time
> when one can no longer see to read and the lighting
> of the candle, is commonly called blindman's holi-
> day.
> --Samuel Pegge, the Elder: Anonymiana, Or Ten
>   Centuries of Observations (1809); III, paragraph
>   18.

BLOODY-BONES, BLOODY-BONE: A name associated with the ghost of a murdered man who haunts the scene of his murder; used in conjunction with "Rawhead," often by nurses in tales to terrify children.

> GETA: Run for a surgeon, or I faint!
> FIRST GUARD: Bear up, man;
> 'Tis but a scratch.
> GETA: Scoring a man o'er the coxcomb [head]
> Is but a scratch with you: [pox] o' your occupation,
> Your scurvy scuffling trade! I was told before,
> My face was bad enough; but now I look

Like Bloody-Bone and Raw-Head, to fright children;
I am for no use else.
SECOND GUARD: Thou shalt fright men.
--John Fletcher: The Prophetess (1622); Act IV,
   Scene 4.

BLOWZE: A fat, flush-faced woman, with a red, ruddy
complexion; a coarse, untidy woman; a wild, unruly young
girl; a prostitute. "A woman whose hair is dishevelled,
and hanging about her face" (Grose). The origin of the
word is unknown, but it has been used extensively. See
Heywood's Edward IV (1600); Robert Burton's Anatomy of
Melancholy (1621); Richard Braithwait's Whimzies (1631);
John Ford's The Lady's Trial (1639); Robert Herrick's Hesperides (1648); Thomas D'urfey's Pills to Purge Melancholy
(1719), and the following:

   NURSE:
   A joyless, dismal, black, and sorrowful issue:
   Here is the babe, as loathsome as a toad
   Amongst the fairest breeders of our clime:
   The empress sends it thee, thy stamp, thy seal,
   And bids thee christen it with thy dagger's point.
   AARON:
   'Zounds, ye whore! is black so base a hue?--
   Sweet blowze, you are a beateous blossom, sure.
   --William Shakespeare: Titus Andronicus (ca.
      1593); Act IV, Scene 2.

BODKIN: A short, pointed dagger; a stiletto. The history
of this word is obscure; the earliest form in English is
boydekin. It is possible that the word resulted from a corruption of the Welsh word bidogyn, "little dagger," or the
Irish form, bideog. A very old word: see Chaucer's The
Reeve's Tale in The Canterbury Tales; Lydgate's The Fall
of Princes from Bochas (1430); Earl Rivers's Dictes; Sidney's
Arcadia (1580), and this famous quote from Hamlet:

   HAMLET:
   For who would bear the whips and scorns of time,
   The oppressor's wrong, the proud man's contumely,
   The pangs of despised love, the law's delay,
   The insolence of office, and the spurns
   That patient merit of the unworthy takes,
   When he himself might his quietus make
   With a bare bodkin?
   --William Shakespeare: Hamlet (1600); Act III,
      Scene 1.

BOGGARD, BOGHOUSE: A toilet, latrine, privy. The word
comes from the old verb bog, meaning "to defile with excrement." A "low word."

> BRAINS: May you live to be arrested of the pox,
> and die in a dungeon! may inns o' court gentlemen,
> at next trimming, shave your ears and noses off,
> and then duck you in their own boggards!
> --James Shirley: The Witty Fair One (1628); Act
>   IV, Scene 6.

Also, see Nathaniel Ward's The Simple Cobler of
Agavvam in America, Willing to help mend his Native Country, lamentably tattered, both in the upper-Leather and sole,
with all the honest stitches he can take, &c.   (1647).

BOMBARD: A leather bottle or jug, covered with tar; a
black-pot or black-jack. The name is probably from association with some resemblance of the jug to the bombard, an
early type of cannon. From the Latin word bombarda, a
"catapult," probably from bombus, "a humming or whizzing
sound." Later, as in the case of blackpot and borachio, it
came to mean a drunkard. Used by Thomas Heywood in
1635, and by Shakespeare:

> PRINCE HENRY: Why dost thou converse with that
> trunk of humours, that bolting-hutch of beastliness,
> that swoll'n parcel of dropsies, that huge bombard
> of sack, that stuft cloakbag of guts, that roasted
> Manningtree ox with the pudding in his belly, that
> reverend vice, that gray iniquity, that father ruf-
> fian, that vanity in years?
> --William Shakespeare: King Henry The Fourth,
>   Part I (1597); Act II, Scene 4.

BONA-ROBA: A whore; prostitute, especially a showy one.
"A handsome but wanton girl." Principally in use from the
16th through the 19th centuries, the word came from the
Italian buona roba, literally "good dress." Florio: "A
good, wholesome, plumcheeked wench." Used extensively:
seen in John Dryden's The Kind Keeper (1680), and in
Shakespeare and Scott:

> SHALLOW: There was I, and little John Doit of
> Staffordshire, and black George Barnes, and Fran-
> cis Pickbone, and Will Squele a Cotsall man,--you
> had not four such swinge-bucklers in all the inns

o' court again: and, I may say to you, we knew
where the bona-robas were, and had the best of
them all at commandment.
  --William Shakespeare: King Henry The Fourth,
     Part II (1598); Act III, Scene 2.

'Have with you, my lord; you cannot have a better
guide to the infernal regions than myself.   I prom-
ise you there are bona-robas to be found there--
good wine too, ay, and good fellows to drink it
with, though somewhat suffering under the frowns
of Fortune. "
  --Sir Walter Scott: The Fortunes of Nigel (1822);
     chapter 16.

BONNY-WALLIES: Toys; gewgaws; showy trifles.   Of extremely obscure origin; generally in the Scottish dialects.

"At ony rate the warst barn e'er man lay in wad
be a pleasanter abode than Glenallan House, wi' a'
the pictures and black velvet, and silvery bonny-
wawlies belonging to it. "
  --Sir Walter Scott: The Antiquary (1816); chapter
     29.

BOODY: To be sullen; to sulk; mope; pout.   Apparently from
the French bouder, "to be sullen, to pout. "

"Come, " said she, --"don't boody with me; don't
be angry because I speak out some home truths. "
  --Anthony Trollope: Barchester Towers (1857);
     Volume I, chapter 27.

BORACHIO: In Spain, a large bottle, usually of leather, for
holding wine and liquors.   Hence, as in black-pot, a drunkard, a "wine-bag. "   The word comes from the Spanish bor-
racha, and the Italian boraccia, both same sense.   Writers
who used it include Greene and Middleton, along with Jonson:

MEERCRAFT: 'Tis a toy, a trifle!
FABIAN FITZDOTTREL: Trifle! twelve thousand
pound for dogs' skins?
MEERCRAFT: Yes.
But, by my way of dressing, you must know, sir,
And med'cining the leather to a height
Of improved ware, like your borachio
Of Spain, sir, I can fetch nine thousand for't.

--Ben Jonson: The Devil Is an Ass (1616); Act II,
Scene 1.

BOREE, BORY: A kind of old French dance, the bourrée,
originally associated with Auvergne.

> Dick could neatly dance a jig,
>   But Tom was best at borees;
> Tom would pray for ev'ry Whig,
>   And Dick curse all the Tories.
> --Jonathan Swift: Tom Mullinex and Dick (1745);
>   stanza 4.

Also see Act IV, Scene 1 of Etherege's Man of Mode (1676).

BORREL, BOREL: A word popular in the 16th and 17th centuries, originally meaning "pertaining to the laity," and then
evolving into "rude, rough, unmannered, crude." It is possibly derived from bural or "coarse clothing." Used by
George Gascoigne in his poetry, and by William Morris in
The Earthly Paradise (1870).

> "I question much if Catharine ever has such a
> moment to glance on earth and its inhabitants, as
> might lead her to listen to a coarse, ignorant,
> borrel man like me."
> --Sir Walter Scott: The Fair Maid of Perth (1828);
>   chapter 5.

BOSS: A thick, clumpy seat resembling a bundle of straw;
a hassock. Also, "a milkmaid's cushion for the head."
The history of this word and its origin are uncertain, but
linkage with the Dutch has been suggested. It can be located in William Westmacott's A Scripture Herbal (1695) and
in Samuel Carter Hall's book on Ireland (1841).

> Their mangers were placed circular in the middle
> of the room, and divided into several partitions,
> round which they sat on their haunches upon bosses
> of straw.
> --Jonathan Swift: Gulliver's Travels (1726); Part
>   IV, chapter 2.

BOTARGO: An old type of before-meal relish, made from the
eggs of various fish, such as the albacore, mullet, or tuna.
Bailey describes it as "a sausage made of eggs and of the
blood of a sea mullet." The original source is from a

combination of the Coptic indefinite article <u>ou</u> and the Greek
word for "pickle," <u>tarichion</u>.   The English <u>word</u> is a direct
adoption of the Italian <u>botargo</u>.   Found in George Sandys's
<u>Travels</u> (1615); in Jonathan Swift and in Hobhouse, and in the
<u>following</u>:

> So home, Sir William and I; and it being very hot
> weather, I took my flagilette and played upon the
> leads in the garden, where Sir W. Penn came out
> in his shirt into his leads and there we stayed
> talking and singing and drinking of great draughts
> of Clarret and eating botargo and bread and butter
> till 12 at night, it being moonshine.   And so to
> bed--very near fuddled.
> --Samuel Pepys' <u>Diary</u>:   June 5th, 1661.

<u>BOTTOM</u>:   To wind, as a skein.   Dr. Johnson says: "To
wind upon something; to twist thread round something." The
word came from the noun <u>bottom</u>, meaning "something upon
which to wind thread." Drayton employed it in <u>Polyolbion</u>,
as did Shakespeare:

> THURIO:
> Therefore, as you unwind her love from him,
> Lest it should ravel and be good to none,
> You must provide to bottom it on me.
> --William Shakespeare: <u>The Two Gentlemen of</u>
>   <u>Verona</u> (ca. 1598); Act III, Scene 2.

<u>BOURD</u>:   A very old word, used since the 14th century,
meaning "a joke; a jeer; fun; a mockery; merriment."
Through the Middle English <u>bourde</u> and the Old French
<u>bourde</u>, this word is derived from the Provencal <u>borda</u>, "a
deception," a word that is untraceable further.   Used extensively: see <u>Sir Gawain and the Green Knight</u> (1340); Lydgate's <u>Troy</u> (1430); the <u>Knight de la Tour</u> (1450); Thomas
Cranmer's <u>Catechismus</u> (1548); William Fulbecke's <u>Confer-</u>
<u>ence of Civil Law</u> (1602); and Scott's <u>Antiquary</u>, chapter 4.

> BATTE: Gramercy, Borril, for thy company,
> For all thy jests, and all thy merry bourds,
> Upon thy judgment much I shall rely,
> Because I find such wisdom in thy words:
>   Would I might watch, whenever thou dost ward,
>   So much thy love and friendship I regard.
> --Michael Drayton: <u>Eclogue VII</u> (1593); stanza 28.

BOUROCK, BOURACH: A Scottish word for a small hut or
cottage; a mound of stones; a confused jumble; a cluster; also, the home of a shepherd.   The origin is uncertain, but it
perhaps is derived from the old word bour, "bower." Used
by the poet Robert Tannahill, and by Scott:

> "What is that you say, Edie?" said Oldbuck, hop-
> ing, perhaps that his ears had betrayed their duty
> --"what were you speaking about?"
>   "About this bit bourock, your honor," answered
> the undaunted Edie; "I mind the bigging o't."
> --Sir Walter Scott: The Antiquary (1816); chapter
>   4.

BOUSE, BOWSE: An alcoholic drink or liquor; perhaps the
original sense was of the glass out of which the liquor was
drunk.   Also, a fit of drunkenness; a drinking bout.   It is
related to the verb bouse, meaning "to drink to drunkenness,"
to which booze is also connected.   The exact origin is doubtful, and relation with the Dutch buise, "a drinking jug," has
been suggested.   The word was very popular, and can be
found in many writers: Thomas Harman in Caveat for Vagabonds (1567); Robert Herrick in Hesperides (1648); in Robert
Burns's The Twa Dogs and Scotch Drink; William Tennant's
poem Anster Fair (1812); and Capt. Sherard Osborn's Que-
dah; or Stray Leaves from a Journal in Malayan Waters
(1857).

> WELLBORN: No bouse? nor no tobacco?
> TAPWELL: Not a suck, sir;
> Nor the remainder of a single can
> Left by a drunken porter, all night pall'd too.
> --Philip Massinger: A New Way to Pay Old Debts
>   (ca. 1626); Act I, Scene 1.

BOUTADE, BOUTADO: A sudden outbreak; a caprice or
whim; a fancy.   From the Old French bouter, "to put, to
thrust."

> Mean time, his affairs at home went upside down;
> and his two brothers had a wretched time; where
> his first boutade was, to kick both their wives one
> morning out of doors, and his own too, and in
> their stead, gave orders to pick up the first three
> strollers could be met with in the streets.
> --Jonathan Swift: A Tale of a Tub (1704); section
>   IV.

BRABBLE: A clamorous, noisy quarrel or brawl; a petty skirmish. The origin is unknown; perhaps the word is connected with the Dutch brabbelen, "to stammer, " or perhaps it is of echoic origin--probably a combination of the two. Also found in Holinshed's Chronicles; in Heylin's Microcosmus (1622); Shakespeare's Henry V; and, more recently, in Robert Browning.

> FIRST OFFICER: Orsino, this is that Antonio
> That took the Phoenix and her fraught from Candy;
> And this is he that did the Tiger board,
> When your young nephew Titus lost his leg:
> Here in the streets, desperate of shame and state,
> In private brabble did we apprehend him.
> --William Shakespeare: Twelfth Night (1601); Act
>   V, Scene 1.

BRAGGET: New ale spiced with sugar; originally it was made from honey and ale fermented together. Grose describes it as "Mead and ale sweetened with honey. " The word comes from the Welsh bragawd and the Irish bracát; from the Old Celtic bracata, referring to a drink made from grain or malt. Chaucer used it in his Canterbury Tales; so did Thomas Cogan in 1586 in his Haven of Health made for the Comfort of Students; and it can be seen in Gresley's Forest of Arden (1841).

> PEDRO: Out upon her!
> How she turn'd down the bragget!
> JAQUES: Ay, that sunk her.
> PEDRO: That drink was well put to her: what a
>   somersalt,
> When the chair fell, she fetch'd, with her heels
>   upward!
> --John Fletcher: The Woman's Prize (ca. 1612);
>   Act III, Scene 2.

BRAIN: To understand; to conceive within the brain.

> POSTHUMUS LEONATUS: (waking)
> 'Tis still a dream; or else such stuff as madmen
> Tongue, and brain not: either both, or nothing:
> Or senseless speaking, or a speaking such
> As sense cannot untie.
> --William Shakespeare: Cymbeline (1610); Act V,
>   Scene 4.

BRANDENBURGH: An old type of morning gown, with long sleeves, the name coming from the name of a city in Prussia, famous for the manufacture of woollen goods. cf. the French brandebourg.

> DORIMANT: Y' have a very fine brandenburgh on, Sir Fopling.
> --Sir George Etherege: The Man of Mode (1676); Act IV, Scene 2.

BRANDY-PAWNEE: Brandy-and-water. The second element is taken from the Hindu word for "water," pani. "An East-Indian camp-word" (N. E. D.).

> He had passed ten years in Bengal. --Constant dinners, tiffins, pale ale and claret, the prodigious labour of cutcherry, and the refreshment of brandy-pawnee which he was forced to take there, had their effect upon Waterloo Sedley.
> --William Makepeace Thackeray: Vanity Fair (1848); chapter 57.

BREAD AND SALT: An old oath; "to take bread and salt" = to swear.

> MATHED: Pox on 'em, and there be no faith in men, if a man shall not believe oaths: he took bread and salt, by this light, that he would never open his lips.
> --Thomas Dekker (with Thomas Middleton): The Honest Whore, Part I (1604); Act V, Scene 2.

BREED-BATE: Literally, one who "breeds bate," or who causes strife or mischief. "One that breeds quarrels; an incendiary" (Johnson).

> MISTRESS QUICKLY: An honest, willing, kind fellow, as ever servant shall come in house withal; and, I warrant you, no tell-tale nor no breed-bate: his worst fault is, that he is given to prayer; he is something peevish that way.
> --William Shakespeare: The Merry Wives of Windsor (1601); Act I, Scene 4.

BRENDICE: A cup in which health is drunk; a "bumper." From the Italian brindesi, "a drinking a health or toast." cf. the French brinde, "toast, health."

HARMAN: I was in some small hope, this ship
had been of our own country, and brought back my
son. For much about this season I expect him,
good morrow, gentlemen, I go to fill a brendice
to my noble captain's health, pray tell him so; the
youth of our Amboyna I'll send before to welcome
him.
--John Dryden: Amboyna (1672); Act I, Scene 1.

BROCK: A badger. Usually associated with the adjective
"stinking. " Hence, a dirty fellow; a stinker; one given to
"dirty" pranks; a "skunk. " Also the proverb, "To stink
like a brock. " The Old English form is broc; in Irish, the
same; Welsh and Cornish, broch; derived from the Old Celtic
broccos, and probably originating in the Greek word phor-
kos, meaning "white" or "beige. " Found in Skelton, Shakespeare, Jonson, Ramsay, and in the following:

> But then to see how ye're negleckit
> How huff'd, an' cuff'd, an' disrespeckit!
> Lord, man, our gentry care as little
> For delvers, ditchers, an' sic cattle;
> They gang as saucy by poor folk,
> As I wad by a stinking brock.
> --Robert Burns: The Twa Dogs (1786); lines 91-
> 96.

> 'I keep the crown o' the causey when I gae to the
> borough, and rub shouthers wi' a bailie wi' as
> little concern as an he were a brock. "
> --Sir Walter Scott: The Antiquary (1816); chapter
> 21.

BRONSTROPS: A seventeenth-century word popularized by
Middleton, meaning a prostitute or pimp. The original word
is bawdstrott, which was corrupted to bawstrop, which under-
went further evolution into this word. Bawd is from the Old
High German bald, meaning "bold, " and comes into English
through Old French. Webster made reference to Middleton's
use of the word in his Cure for a Cuckold (1661), act IV.

> USHER: What is my sister, centaur?
> COLONEL'S FRIEND: I say thy sister is a bron-
> strops.
> USHER: A bronstrops?
> CHOUGH: Tutor, tutor, ere you go any further,
> tell me the English of that; what is a bronstrops,

pray?
COLONEL'S FRIEND: A bronstrops is in English
a hippocrene.
CHOUGH: A hippocrene; note it, Trim: I love to
understand the English as I go. (Writes).
TRIMTRAM: What's the English of hippocrene?
CHOUGH: Why, bronstrops.
--Thomas Middleton & William Rowley: A Fair
    Quarrel (1617); Act IV, Scene 1.

BUBBLE-AND-SQUEAK: A dish of cold meat, usually beef,
fried with cabbage and/or potatoes, the name deriving from
the sound made during cooking.

I must not introduce even a spare rib here,
    "Bubble and squeak" would spoil my liquid lay.
--Lord Byron: Don Juan (1824); Canto XV, stanza
    71.

BUCKLE-BEGGAR: An 18th-19th centuries word, principally
Scottish, referring to a priest or minister who performed
irregular marriage ceremonies, or who married people in
secret; also known as a "hedge-priest" or "couple-beggar"
or "Gretna Green parson," referring to the small Scottish
border village where eloping English couples fled to be married. The word comes from an allusion to the verb buckle,
representing a joining in wedlock. Buckle comes from the
Latin buccula, the strap of a helmet which passed beneath
the chin in securing; it was a diminutive form of bucca,
"cheek." Hence, the English buckle, and the verb formed
from it.

A hedge-parson, or buckle-beggar, as that order
of priesthood has been irreverently termed, sat on
the duke's left, and was easily distinguished by his
torn band, flapped hat, and the remnants of a rusty
cassock.
--Sir Walter Scott: The Fortunes of Nigel (1822);
    chapter 17.

BUDGER: One who budges; one who moves or stirs. The
verb "budge" comes through the French bouger, "to move,"
the Late Latin bullicare, "to boil," and ultimately from the
Latin bulla, "a bubble, a knob." The general sense is "to
move slightly."

CAIUS MARCIUS:
Let the first budger die the other's slave,
And the gods doom him after!
--William Shakespeare: Coriolanus (1608); Act I,
    Scene 8.

BUFFIN: "A coarse cloth in use for the gowns of the middle classes in the time of Elizabeth" (Fairholt). Of extremely obscure origin.

> (Enter Lady Frugal, Anne, and Mary, in coarse
> habits, weeping.)
> MILLISCENT: What witch hath transform'd you?
> STARGAZE: Is this the glorious shape your cheat-
>   ing brother
> Promised you should appear in?
> MILLISCENT: My young ladies
> In buffin gowns, and green aprons! tear them off;
> Rather show all than be seen thus.
> --Philip Massinger: The City Madam (1632); Act
>   IV, Scene 4.

BULCH, BULCHIN: A bull-calf; the words are used (a) as
terms of endearment:

> MOTHER SAWYER: O, my best love!
> I am on fire, even in the midst of ice,
> Raking my blood up, till my shrunk knees feel
> Thy curled head leaning on them: come, then, my
>   darling;
> If in the air thou hover'st, fall upon me
> In some dark cloud; and as I oft have seen
> Dragons and serpents in the elements,
> Appear thou now so to me. Art thou i'th'sea?
> Muster-up all the monsters from the deep,
> And be the ugliest of them: so that my bulch
> Show but his swarth cheek to me, let earth cleave
> And break from hell, I care not!
> --Thomas Dekker (with John Ford & William Row-
>   ley): The Witch of Edmonton (1623); Act V,
>   Scene 1.

> CAPTAIN ALBO: Let's go now, sweet face; I am
> acquainted with one of the pantomimics; the bul-
> chins will use the Irish captain with respect, and
> you two shall be boxed amongst the better sort.
> --Thomas Middleton & William Rowley: A Fair
>   Quarrel (1617); Act IV, Scene 4.

SPADONE: A plain case; roguery, brokage and
roguery, or call me bulchin.
--John Ford: The Fancies, Chaste and Noble
(1635); Act III, Scene 3.

(b) as a term of reproach or contempt:

YOUNG B.: How is't, Bulchins? Would you had
been with us.
--James Shirley: The Gamester (1633); Act IV,
Scene 1.

The word is a variation of bulkin, with the same
meaning, and is apparently nothing more than "bull" +
"-kin," though Dutch influence has been suggested. Bull is
from the German bulle and the Anglo-Saxon bula.

BULLY-ROCK, BULLY-ROOK: An old term of endearment,
popular in the 16th, 17th, and 18th centuries, meaning generally "good boy," or "fine lad." A later sense is that of
a thug, or hired bully. The origin is obscure; possibly
there was some association between bully as a term of endearment, and rook, meaning "to cheat or swindle." Used
by Thomas Carlyle, as well as by Shakespeare:

HOST: What says my bully-rook? speak scholarly
and wisely.
--William Shakespeare: The Merry Wives of Windsor (1601); Act I, Scene 3.

BUM: A very old word, coming through Middle English, for
the buttocks, or, as Dr. Johnson said so eloquently, "The
part on which we sit." The origin is unknown, though there
are connections with foreign words signifying bottom. Used
by Crowley in 1550; by Alexander Read in his treatise on
chirurgery in 1638, and by Burns in The Jolly Beggars
(1785). In Butler's Hudibras, it is a shortened form of
bumbailiff.

PUCK: The wisest aunt, telling the saddest tale,
Sometime for three-foot stool mistaketh me;
Then slip I from her bum, down topples she,
And 'tailor' cries, and falls into a cough.
--Wm. Shakespeare: A Midsummer Night's Dream
(1594); Act II, Scene 1.

"The big part of her body is her bum."
--Old saying.

BUMBAILIFF, BUMBAILIE: A contemptuous form of "bailiff." "A bailiff of the meanest kind; one that is employed
in arrests" (Johnson). The word comes from "bum" meaning "the posteriors," a formation expressing the idea that
the bailiff was always at the debtor's back, always close
"behind." "Bailiff" is traced back to the Latin word bajulus,
"porter."

> SIR TOBY BELCH: Go, Sir Andrew; scout me for
> him at the corner of the orchard, like a bum-
> baily: so soon as ever thou seest him, draw; and,
> as thou draw'st, swear horrible; for it comes to
> pass oft, that a terrible oath, with a swaggering
> accent sharply twang'd off, gives manhood more
> approbation then ever proof itself would have
> earn'd him. Away!
> --William Shakespeare: Twelfth Night (1601); Act
>   III, Scene 4.

BUM-BLADE, BUMB-BLADE: Some type of large sword.
The name is possibly used in the same sense as "bumbailiff," but this time in reference to a sword, possibly one
that would always "pink" its man, causing him to flee.

> PAGE: I'll not stand idle. Draw! My little rapier
> Against your bumb blades! I'll one by one dis-
>   patch you,
> Then house this instrument of death and horror.
> --Philip Massinger: The City Madam (1632); Act
>   I, Scene 2.

BUMBO, BUMBOO, BOMBO: An alcoholic beverage described by Smollett as "composed of rum, sugar, water,
and nutmeg." Grose says it is made of "brandy, water,
and sugar," and sometimes gin was used. The word comes
from the Italian bombo, "drink." In the Sailor's Word-book
(1867) it is described as "weak cold punch."

> Then he asked if I had ever received the sacra-
> ment, or taken the oaths; to which question I re-
> plying in the negative, he held up his hands, as-
> sured me he could do me no service, wished I
> might not be in a state of reprobation, and re-
> turned to his messmates, who were making merry
> in the ward-room, round a table well stored with
> bumbo and wine.
> --Tobias Smollett: Roderick Random (1748); chap-
>   ter 34.

BUNG, BOUNG: A thieves' word for a pickpocket or a purse, "that which is pickpocketed." The origin is unknown, but there is a resemblance to the Old English word for purse, pung. Used by Dekker in The Roaring Girl.

> DOLL TEARSHEET: Away, you cut-purse rascal! you filthy bung, away!
> --William Shakespeare: King Henry The Fourth, Part II (1598); Act II, Scene 4.

BUTTER-BOX: Literally, a "box for butter," but used as a popular term of contempt for a Dutchman, because of the notion that the Dutch were great eaters of butter. Other forms exist, such as butter-bag, butter-mouth, etc. It can be found in Thomas Dekker's The Shoemaker's Holiday (1600) and in Henry Stubbe's justification of the Dutch War (1672).

> GRIMALDI:
> Were't not for shame now,
> I could turn honest, and forswear my trade:
> Which, next to being truss'd up at the mainyard
> By some low country butterbox, I hate
> As deadly as I do fasting, or long grace
> When meat cools on the table.
> --Philip Massinger: The Renegado (1624); Act II, Scene 5.

BUTTERED ALE: A drink made of sugar, cinnamon, butter, and beer, and brewed with hops.

> So meeting in my way W. Swan, I took him to a house thereabout and gave him a morning draught of buttered ale--he telling me still much of his fanatiques stories, as if he were a great zealot, when I know him to be a very rogue.
> --Samuel Pepys' Diary: December 5th, 1662.

BUZZ, BUZZ-WIG: An old type of extremely large and bushy perriwig; also, the person who wears such a wig; a "bigwig." The origin is probably a shortening of busby, another large wig worn in the 18th century. Found in Mary Russell Mitford's Our Village (1826), and in Thomas De-Quincey.

> The reverend gentleman was equipped in a buzz wig, upon the top of which was an equilateral cocked hat.

--Sir Walter Scott: <u>The Antiquary</u> (1816); chapter
17.

BUZZARD: A worthless, good-for-nothing, foolish person; a
dunce; a gullible, ignorant fellow; also, a coward. The
word comes from the notion of the buzzard as an inferior
type of hawk; hence, the sense of worthlessness, useless-
ness. From the Old French <u>busart</u> and the Provencal of the
same form; the origin is the <u>Latin</u> word for hawk, <u>buteo</u>.
Found in Langland's <u>Piers Plowman</u> (1377) and in <u>Roger</u> Ascham; and, more recently, in <u>Washington Irving</u>.

'Ha! you guess who I mean, Frank?"
'Not I, indeed," answered Tunstall. "Scotch
Janet, I suppose, the laundress."
'Off with Janet in her own bucking-basket!--no,
no, no! You blind buzzard, do you not know I
mean pretty Mrs. Marget?"
--Sir Walter Scott: <u>The Fortunes of Nigel</u> (1822);
chapter 2.

"An old wise man's shadow is better than a young
buzzard's sword."
--Old proverb.

BUZZGLOAK: A thieves' word for a pickpocket, similar to
<u>bung</u>. The first element is from the verb <u>buzz</u>, meaning
"to pick a pocket, to filch," and the second, <u>gloak</u>, means
"man" or "fellow." Both elements are of unknown origin.
Used by George Sala in <u>Twice Round the Clock</u> (1859), and
in the following:

'He who surreptitiously accumulates <u>bustle</u> money
is, in fact, nothing better than a <u>buzz gloak</u>!"
--Edward George Bulwer-Lytton: <u>Paul Clifford</u>
(1830); chapter 6.

BYRLAKIN: An old contraction of an even older oath, "By
our Ladykin." Many forms appear: <u>berlady</u>, <u>birlady</u>, <u>bela-
kin</u>, etc. Used by Skelton and Fletcher; and by Shakespeare
in <u>Romeo and Juliet</u> and the following:

BOTTOM: There are things in this comedy of
<u>Pyramus and Thisby</u> that will never please. First,
Pyramus must draw a sword to kill himself; which
the ladies cannot abide. How answer you that?
SNOUT: By'rlakin, a parlous fear.

> STARVELING: I believe we must leave the killing
> out, when all is done.
> --William Shakespeare: A Midsummer Night's
>   Dream (1594); Act III, Scene 1.

-C-

CACAFUEGO, CACAFUGO, CACAFOGO: A bragging, blustering bully; a windbag. This word comes from the Spanish
and Portuguese cagar, "to discharge excrement," and the
Spanish fuego, "fire," derived from the Latin word for
hearth, focus. Thus, literally "shit-fire." In 1577, Sir
Francis Drake captured a Spanish galleon called the Cacafuego, and association with this event has been suggested as
having influenced the use of the word. Also, Bailey, in
1731, says that the cacafuego was the name of a Spanish
type of fly that discharged a bright light from its body at
night.

> HOST: Haunted, my house is haunted with goblins
> ... I will nail up my doors, and wall up my girl
> like an anchoress; or she will be ravisht before
> our faces, by rascals and cacafugo's.
> --John Webster (possibly with Philip Massinger &
>   William Rowley): The Fair Maid of the Inn
>   (1625); Act III, Scene 1.

CADOUK: An unexpected occurrence, good or bad; a wind-
fall. Also, forfeited assets. From the French caduc, "falling, crumbling," with the notion of something "falling" to
someone. Generally used in the Scottish dialects.

> "Wherefore, finding that Fortune had changed sides,
> that the borrowings and lendings went on as before
> out of our pay, while the caduacs and casualties
> were all cut off, I e'en gave up my commission
> and took service with Wallenstein in Walter Butler's
> Irish regiment. "
> --Sir Walter Scott: A Legend of Montrose (1819);
>   chapter 2.

CAKE-HOUSE: A bakery; a place where cakes and pastries
are prepared and/or sold. Found also in Samuel Pepys and
in Vicesimus Knox (1777).

> "There is no young gentleman of these parts, who

might be in rank or fortune a match for Miss
Julia, that I think at all likely to play such a
character. But on the other side of the lake,
nearly opposite to Mervyn Hall, is a d---d cake-
house, the resort of walking gentlemen of all de-
scriptions, poets, players, painters, musicians,
who come to rave, and recite, and madden, about
this picturesque land of ours ... But were Julia
my daughter, it is one of those sort of fellows
that I should fear on her account. "
  --Sir Walter Scott: Guy Mannering (1815); chapter
  16.

CALIVER: A type of light musket or hand-gun, originally of
one certain caliber, first appearing in the 16th century; except for the pistol it was the most lightweight type of fire-
arm. The word caliver is apparently the very same word
as caliber, merely corrupted. Caliber itself comes through
the French calibre, the Italian calibro, and the Spanish
calibre, but its exact origin is unknown. It has been suggested that it comes from the Arabic qālib, "A mold for
casting metal, " or qalaba, "to twist, to turn, " again in reference to the bore. Calipers also comes from caliber. It
can be found in many writers: In Shakespeare's Henry IV;
in Holinshed's Scottish Chronicles (1587); in Robert Barret's
Theorike and Pracktike of Moderne Warres, Discoursed in
Dialogue Wise (1598); in Fulbecke (1602); and in Hume's history of England (1761).

"You ride well provided, sir, " said the host, looking at the weapons as he placed on the table the
mulled sack which the traveller had ordered.
  "Yes, mine host; I have found the use on't in
dangerous times, and I do not, like your modern
grandees, turn off my followers the instant they
are useless. "
  "Ay, sir?" said Giles Gosling; "then you are
from the Low Countries, the land of pike and caliver?"
  --Sir Walter Scott: Kenilworth (1821); chapter 1.

CALLET, CALOT, KALLAT: A rude, rough, untidy woman;
a nagging wife; a prostitute; a beggar's mistress; any lewd
woman. The etymology is uncertain; there is a possibility
of connection with the French caillette, "fool, " a word which
is a diminutive of caille, "quail" (the quail being considered
a foolish bird). Also, the French calotte, a small kind of

bonnet or cap, and the Irish <u>caille</u>, "girl," have been considered, the latter more recently, but the exact history of the word is most obscure. Found in Thomas More; in Holland's <u>Livy</u> (1600); in John Still's <u>Gammer Gurton's Needle</u> (1575); in Robert Burns. Shakespeare used it in <u>The Winter's Tale</u>, <u>King Henry VI, Part III</u>, and in the following:

> EMILIA:
> He call'd her whore: a beggar in his drink
> Could not have laid such terms upon his callet.
> --William Shakespeare: <u>Othello</u> (1604); Act IV,
>   Scene 2.

<u>CALLYMOOCHER</u>: Some type of term of ridicule or contempt, meaning perhaps "an idler, a lazy good-for-nothing"; but both exact meaning and origin are unknown.

> SIMON: Look you, neighbours, before you be too hasty, let Oliver the fustian-weaver stand as fair as I do, and the devil do him good on't.
> OLIVER: I do, thou upstart callymoocher, I do.
> --Thomas Middleton: <u>The Mayor of Queenborough</u>
>   (1661); Act III, Scene 3.

<u>CANDLE-WASTER</u>: He or that which wastes candles by study or work late into the night; one who sits up late, like a student. Also, scornfully applied to an unthrifty or unwise person, a drunkard, or a poor student. Used principally in the 17th century. Dr. Johnson says: "That which consumes candles; a spendthrift." The word can be seen in Edward Blount's <u>The Hospitall of Incurable Fooles</u> (1600).

> LEONATO:
> If such a one will smile, and stroke his beard,
> Bid sorrow wag, cry 'hem' when he should groan,
> Patch grief with proverbs, make misfortune drunk
> With candle-wasters,--bring him yet to me,
> And I of him will gather patience.
> --William Shakespeare: <u>Much Ado About Nothing</u>
>   (1599); Act V, Scene 1.

> HEDON: Heart, was there ever so prosperous an invention thus unluckily perverted, and spoil'd by a whoreson book-worm, a candle-waster?
> --Ben Jonson: <u>Cynthia's Revels</u> (1600); Act III,
>   Scene 2.

CAPERHAY: To dance to the tune of a country dance. The etymology is uncertain, but the word was probably formed from the verb caper, "to leap in a frolicsome manner," and the noun hay, a kind of old country dance, in some ways resembling a square-dance. Dr. Johnson tells us: "To dance the hay: to dance in a ring; probably from dancing round a hay cock."

> PRINCE JOHN:
> Mad Gloster mute, all mirth turn'd to despair?
> Why, now you see what 'tis to cross a king,
> Deal against princes of the royal blood,
> You'll snarl and rail, but now your tongue is bed-
> rid,
> Come, caperhay, set all at six and seven;
> What, musest thou with thought of hell or heaven?
> --Look About You (Anonymous) (ca. 1600); scene
> 13.

CAPPIE: A Scottish word signifying a type of small drinking mug; also, a type of beer, "cap-ale." The word is a diminutive rendering of cap, "a wooden dish or bowl, often with two ears or handles, formerly used as a drinking vessel." (N.E.D.). Cap is a later form of cop, which is derived from the Old English copp, "cup, mug," or the Old Norse koppr, "small jug used in dairies."

> 'I will make them repent meddling with your good
> name."
> "My gude name! What the sorrow is the mat-
> ter wi' my name, Mr. Bindloose?" said the irri-
> table client. 'I think ye hae been at the wee
> cappie this morning, for as early as it is."
> --Sir Walter Scott: St. Ronan's Well (1823); chap-
> ter 14.

CAPUCCIO, CAPUCHE: The long and pointed hood of a cloak or cape, especially the one worn by the Capuchin monks; also spelled capoch. Capuccio was acquired directly from the Italian, and capuche comes through the French from the Italian; the essential meaning is as in the Italian cappa, "cape, cloak." Cap and cape are related words. It can be found in John Cleaveland's The Rustick Rampant (1658) and in George Payne Rainsford James's Forest Days (1843). Here is an older use:

> Next after him went Doubt, who was yclad [dressed]

In a discolour'd cote of straunge disguyse,
That at his backe a brode capuccio had,
And sleeves dependaunt Albanese-wyse.
--Edmund Spenser: The Faerie Queene, Book III
(1590); Canto XII, stanza 10.

CARCANET: Originally carcan, an ornamental or jewelled
collar or necklace, sometimes of gold, or any similar orna-
ment for the head. Also, the iron collar used in prisons
for confining prisoners. The word is from the French
carcan, "collar of gold" and the Breton kerchen, "breast;
circle of the neck. " Possibly related to the Latin circus,
"ring or circle. " The word was used frequently: in Stanyhurst's translation; in Holland's Pliny (1600); in Jeremy Taylor's The Great Exemplar of Sanctity and Holy Life (1649);
in Shakespeare's The Comedy of Errors; Massinger's The
City Madam; in Robert Herrick's Hesperides (1648); in Marston's Antonio and Mellida (1630); in Tennyson; in Sala's
Captain Dangerous (1863); and in Scott:

His high-crowned gray hat lay on the floor, covered with dust, but encircled by a carcanet of
large balas rubies.
--Sir Walter Scott: The Fortunes of Nigel (1822);
chapter 5.

CARK: To load or burden with sorrow or care; to worry,
to trouble; to cause to be anxious. Dr. Johnson says: "To
be careful; to be solicitous; to be anxious. It is now very
little used, and always in an ill sense. " Also, to complain.
The word comes from many forms: the Middle English
carken, karken; the Old Northern French carkier, karkier,
carquier, garkier, "to load, to burden"; derived from the
late Latin carricare, "to load. " Carriage and charge are
related words.

Thee nor carketh care nor slander;
Nothing but the small cold worm
Fretteth thine enshrouded form.
--Alfred, Lord Tennyson: A Dirge (1830); stanza
2.

CARLOT: A fellow; a peasant; common man; a rough fellow, a boor. Earlier, a bondman or villein. The word
comes from the Old Norse karl, "freeman. " Other influences include the Middle High German karl, the Old High
German charlo, the Old English ceorl, the Middle Dutch

kērel, and the Frisian tzerl.   Karl also appears in the form
of a proper name, as the Old English Carl and the French
and English Charles.

> PHEBE: Know'st thou the youth that spoke to me
> erewhile?
> SILVIUS:
> Not very well, but I have met him oft;
> And he hath bought the cottage and the bounds
> That the old carlot once was master of.
> --William Shakespeare: As You Like It (1600);
>   Act III, Scene 5.

CARRIWITCHET, CARWITCHET: A pun; a petty play on
words.   Also, a riddle or quibble.   The origin is unknown,
but the word obtained a moderate usage: See Jonson's
Bartholomew Fair, Act V (1614); Dryden's The Wild Gallant,
Act I (1662).   Also appearing in the works of Arbuthnot and
John Taylor, the Water-Poet.

> 'He of them who declares himself recreant, should,
> d--n him, be restricted to muddy ale, and the
> patronage of the Waterman's Company.   I promise
> you, that many a pretty fellow has been mortally
> wounded with a quibble or a carwitchet at the Mer-
> maid, and sent from thence, in a pitiable estate,
> to Wit's hospital in the Vintry, where they languish
> to this day amongst fools and aldermen. "
> --Sir Walter Scott: The Fortunes of Nigel (1822);
>   chapter 13.

CARSE: A stretch of low, flat, fertile land near a river,
especially in Scotland, referring to the wet, marshy character they possess.   The origin of the word is uncertain, but
perhaps it is merely a pluralized form of carr, meaning "a
marshy bog-land. " Found also in Barbour's Bruce (1375).

> Here am I on my way to Inverness. I have ram-
> bled over the rich, fertile carses of Falkirk and
> Stirling, and am delighted with their appearance:
> richly waving crops of wheat, barley, &c. , but no
> harvest at all yet.
> --Robert Burns to Gavin Hamilton: August 28th,
>   1787.

CAT'S-MEAT: Cat food, usually horsemeat, sold by street
vendors.   Later, the word came to be a slang word for the

lungs. Used by Nashe, Massinger, Edward Howard, and by
Dickens:

> "Thomas Burton is purveyor of cat's meat to the
> Lord Mayor and Sheriffs, and several members of
> the Common Council (the announcement of this
> gentleman's name was received with breathless in-
> terest.)"
> --Charles Dickens: The Pickwick Papers (1837);
>   chapter 33.

CATSO: A low, rough person; a scoundrel; a beggar; a very
rogue. Used principally in the 17th century, the word originated in the Italian cazzo, the male organ; and used as an
exclamation by women, meaning variously "What! I don't
believe it! God forbid!" Both Urquhart and Motteux made
use of the word in their translations of Rabelais.

> CARLO: These be our nimble-spirited catsos, that
> have their evasions at pleasure, will run over a
> bog like your wild Irish; no sooner started, but
> they'll leap from one thing to another, like a
> squirrel, heigh!
> --Ben Jonson: Every Man Out of His Humour
>   (1599); Act II, Scene 1.

CAXON: A type of perriwig, now obsolete. The origin is
unknown; possibly the wig was named after a person, perhaps a wigmaker.

> But, hark you, Latter! as you mean
> To be a bishop, or a dean,
> And must, of course, look grave, and big,
> I'd have you get a better wig:
> You know full well when, cheek by jole,
> We waited on his grace at Knowl;
> Though that trim artist, barber Jackson,
> Spent a whole hour about your caxon,
> With irons hot, and fingers plastic,
> To make it look ecclesiastic;
> With all his pains, and combs, and care,
> He scarce cou'd curl a single hair.
> --James Cawthorn: A Letter to a Clergyman
>   (1756); lines 33-44.

CELLARESS: A woman, usually a nun, who had charge of
the provisions in a cellar. Formed from "cellarer," usually

the monk who had charge of the cellar of a monastery.
From the Middle English celerer, and adopted from the Anglo-French celerer, and the Old French celerier, which was
formed from celier, "cellar. "

> The abbess's Norman pride of birth, and the real
> interest which she took in her niece's advance-
> ment, overcame all scruples; and the venerable
> mother might be seen in unwonted bustle, now giv-
> ing orders to the gardener for decking the apart-
> ment with flowers, now to her cellaress, her pre-
> centrix, and the lay-sisters of the kitchen, for
> preparing a splendid banquet.
> --Sir Walter Scott: The Betrothed (1825); chapter
>   17.

CHAMBER-LYE: Urine, especially when used for cleansing.
It was bottled until it fermented, and was once used much
for washing clothes and dressing wheat, after having been
kept in a large vat for a considerable length of time and
mixed with lime. Also, it was used as a drink for horses,
"to make them look well in their skins. " The word can be
found in Barnaby Googe's translation of Heresbachius (1577);
in Robert Sharrock's history on Vegetables (1660); in Edward
Jarman Lance's The Cottage Farmer (1842), and in Shake-
peare:

> SECOND CARRIER: I think this be the most vil-
> lainous house in all London road for fleas: I am
> stung like a tench.
> FIRST CARRIER: Like a tench! by the mass,
> there is ne'er a king christen could be better bit
> than I have been since the first cock.
> SECOND CARRIER: Why, they will allow us ne'er
> a jordan, and then we leak in the chimney; and
> your chamber-lie breeds fleas like a loach.
> --William Shakespeare: King Henry The Fourth,
>   Part I (1597); Act II, Scene 1.

CHARNECO, CHARNACO, CHARNICO: A type of sweet wine,
popular in the 16th and 17th centuries, probably named from
the village of Charneca near Lisbon, where it was famous;
but it has also been suggested to come from the Spanish
charneca, a turpentine-tree. Later, it came to mean any
type of strong liquor, as Ash said in 1775: "Any strong
liquor which is like to bring drunken fellows to the stocks. "
Found in Beaumont & Fletcher, in Thomas Heywood, and in
the following:

> FIRST NEIGHBOUR: Here, neighbour Horner, I
> drink to you in a cup of sack: and fear not,
> neighbour, you shall do well enough.
> SECOND NEIGHBOUR: And here, neighbour, here's
> a cup of charneco.
> --William Shakespeare: King Henry The Sixth,
> Part II (1591); Act II, Scene 3.

CHEWET: A small blackbird; a crow with red legs and
shiny black feathers, with a loud voice.   Hence, in a figurative use, a screeching talker, one who interrupts.   From
the French chouette, same meaning.

> EARL OF WORCESTER: Hear me, my liege:
> For mine own part, I could be well content
> To entertain the lag-end of my life
> With quiet hours; for, I do protest,
> I have not sought the day of this dislike.
> KING HENRY: You have not sought it! how comes
> it, then?
> SIR JOHN FALSTAFF: Rebellion lay in his way,
> and he found it.
> PRINCE HENRY: Peace, chewet, peace!
> --William Shakespeare: King Henry The Fourth,
> Part I (1597); Act V, Scene 1.

CHINKS: Pieces of coin money, the word being echoic in
origin, and the verb, meaning "to cause a clinking sound, as
of coins being knocked together" exists.   It can be found in
Thomas Tusser's 500 Points of Good Husbandry (1573); Holinshed's work on Ireland (1577); in Jonathan Swift and Thomas
Hood; and in many old sayings, such as: "So we get the
chink we will bear the stink" (i. e. "money in any form is
welcome"); "No chink, no drink, " etc.

> ROMEO: What is her mother?
> NURSE: Marry, bachelor,
> Her mother is the lady of the house,
> And a good lady, and a wise and virtuous:
> I nursed her daughter, that you talkt withal;
> I tell you, he that can lay hold of her
> Shall have the chinks.
> --William Shakespeare: Romeo and Juliet (ca.
> 1594); Act I, Scene 5.

CHITTY-FACE(D): A term of reproach or contempt; in the
17th century the prevailing meaning was "thin-faced, pinch-

faced, gaunt-faced, " and in the 18th and 19th centuries, it
was "baby-faced. " In the 17th century, Cotgrave said: "a
wretched fellow, one out of whose nose hunger drops. " The
origin is possibly seen in the French chicheface, "thin-face. "
Perhaps in English the word has been influenced by chit or
chitty, meaning "freckled. " There is also a connection with
chichevache, the name of a legendary monster that fed only
on patient wives, and thus, from the scarcity of the food,
was always thin and hungry-looking. Middleton used the
word in 1622, and it can also be found in William Godwin's
Things As They Are, or the Adventures of Caleb Williams
(1794).

> SPUNGIUS: As I am a pagan from my cod-piece
> downward, that white-faced monkey frights me too.
> I stole but a dirty pudding, last day, out of an
> alms-basket, to give my dog when he was hungry,
> and the peaking chitty-face page hit me in the
> teeth with it.
> --Philip Massinger & Thomas Dekker: The Vir-
>   gin-Martyr (ca. 1622); Act II, Scene 1.

> MRS. FRAIL: My account, pray what's the mat-
> ter?
> BEN: Why, father came and found me squabling
> with yon chitty-fac'd thing, as he would have me
> marry, --so he ask'd what was the matter.
> --William Congreve: Love For Love (1695); Act
>   IV, Scene 13.

CHUCK: An old expression of endearment, applied to wives,
husbands, children, and associates. The origin is unknown,
but it is possibly a corruption of chick or chicken. Found
in 1628 in John Earle's Microcosmographie; in 1770 in Samuel Foote's The Lame Lover; in Emily Bronte's Wuthering
Heights, chapter 34 (1845); in Kingsley's Hereward the Wake,
chapter 19 (1866). Shakespeare employed it in Twelfth Night,
and in the following:

> ARMADO: Sweet Lord Longaville, rein thy tongue.
> LONGAVILLE: I must rather give it the rein, for
> it runs against Hector.
> DUMAINE: Ay, and Hector's a greyhound.
> ARMADO: The sweet war-man is dead and rotten;
> sweet chucks, beat not the bones of the buried:
> when he breathed, he was a man.
> --William Shakespeare: Love's Labour's Lost (ca.
>   1595); Act V, Scene 2.

PISTOL:
Be merciful, great duke, to men of mould!
Abate thy rage, abate thy manly rage!
Abate thy rage, great duke!
Good bawcock, bate thy rage! use lenity, sweet
  chuck!
--William Shakespeare: King Henry The Fifth
  (1599); Act III, Scene 2.

CHURCH-BUCKET: The bucket kept in the corner of the
parish church for use in case of fire.

KING: What they will do with this poor prince,
the gods know, and I fear.
DION: Why, sir, they'll flay him, and make
church-buckets of's skin, to quench rebellion; then
clap a rivet in's sconce, and hang him up for a
sign.
--Francis Beaumont & John Fletcher: Philaster
  (1611); Act V, Scene 3.

CIRCUS: A finger-ring or a geometrical ring or circle.
From the Latin circus and the Greek kirkos, "circle."

"Sooner shall grass in Hyde Park Circus grow,
And Wits take lodgings in the sound of Bow;
Sooner let earth, air, sea, to chaos fall,
Men, monkeys, lapdogs, parrots, perish all!"
--Alexander Pope: The Rape of the Lock (1714);
  Canto IV, lines 117-120.

CLACHAN: In Scottish dialects usually, a word signifying a
"small village or hamlet of the Highlands, containing a
church." The word also can mean a "village ale-house."
The origin of the word is seen in the Gaelic word clach,
"stone."

"I am ashamed to look no man in the face," said
Robin Oig, something moved; "and, moreover, I
will look you in the face this blessed day, if you
will bide at the clachan down yonder."
--Sir Walter Scott: The Two Drovers (1827).

CLAP-DISH: A wooden dish with a cover that shut with a
loud clapping sound, used by lepers, beggars, and vagrants,
to give a warning of their approach, and to receive alms.

LEONORA: Of all men
I ever saw yet, in my settled judgment,
'Spite of thy barber, tailor, and perfumer,
And thine adulterate and borrow'd helps,
Thou art the ugliest creature; and when trimm'd up
To the height, as thou imagin'st, in mine eyes,
A leper with a clap-dish, (to give notice
He is infectious,) in respect of thee,
Appears a young Adonis.
    --Philip Massinger: The Parliament of Love (1624);
        Act II, Scene 2.

CLAPPERCLAW: To claw or scratch with the open hand or
with the nails; to beat, to maul; to scratch in a fight; hence,
to abuse, scold, revile; "To tongue-beat; to scold" (Johnson). The etymology is vague and uncertain.

    HOST: He will clapper-claw thee tightly, bully.
    DOCTOR CAIUS: Clapper-de-claw! vat is dat?
    HOST: That is, he will make thee amends.
    DOCTOR CAIUS: By gar, me do look he shall
    clapper-de-claw me; for, by gar, me vill have it.
    --William Shakespeare: The Merry Wives of Wind-
        sor (1601); Act II, Scene 3.

CLAUDICATION: The act of limping or halting. Adapted
from the Latin claudicare, "to be lame."

    "Honoured sir, I have lately contracted a very
    honest and undissembled claudication in my left
    foot, which will be a double affliction to me, if
    according to your Tatler of this day, it must pass
    upon the world for a piece of singularity and af-
    fectation. I must, therefore, humbly beg leave to
    limp along the streets after my own way, or I
    shall be inevitably ruined in coach-hire. As soon
    as I am tolerably recovered, I promise to walk
    as upright as a ghost in a tragedy, being not of a
    stature to spare an inch of height that I can any
    way pretend to."
    --Richard Steele in The Tatler, No. 80 (1709);
        paragraph 7.

CLENCHPOOP, CLINCHPOOP: A term of reproach or contempt for a person considered low or uncultured; a lout.
The etymology is obscure, but perhaps connected with someone who "clenches" the "poops" of ships, or someone who

"clinches" the bolts in shipbuilding.

> SIMPLICITY: A goodly gentleman ostler! I think
> none of all you will believe him.
> FRAUD: What a clenchpoop drudge is this! I can
> forbear him no more.
> --Robert Wilson, the Elder: The Three Ladies of
>   London (1584); Act II.

CLYSTER-PIPE: A syringe; used contemptuously as an appellation for a medical man.   Through the French clystère
and the Latin clyster, the word originates in the Greek word
kluster, same sense, derived from the verb kluzein, "to
rinse out, wash," "to cleanse."

> DOCTOR: Take again your bed, sir,
> Sleep is a sovereign physic.
> ANTONINUS: Take an ass's head, sir:
> Confusion on your fooleries, your charms!--
> Thou stinking clyster-pipe, where's the god of
>   rest,
> Thy pills and base apothecary drugs
> Threaten'd to bring unto me? Out, you impostors!
> Quacksalving, cheating mountebanks! your skill
> Is to make sound men sick, and sick men kill.
> --Philip Massinger & Thomas Dekker: The Vir-
>   gin-Martyr (ca. 1622); Act IV, Scene 1.

COCK-AND-PIE: A mild oath or asseveration, principally
in use from the 16th to the 19th centuries.   The original
form is "God-and-pye," the pye referring to the set of rules
used before the Reformation in England, to select the cor-
rect church service for the day.   Uses of the word are
numerous: see Robert Crowley's Epigrams (1550); Arthur
Dent's A Plaine Man's Pathway to Heaven (1622); Sir Walter
Scott's Kenilworth (1821); William M. Thackeray's The Newcomes (1854), and the following:

> PAGE: Come, gentle Master Slender, come; we
> stay for you.
> SLENDER: I'll eat nothing, I thank you, sir.
> PAGE: By cock and pie, you shall not choose,
> sir: come, come.
> SLENDER: Nay, pray you, lead the way.
> --William Shakespeare: The Merry Wives of Wind-
>   sor (1601); Act I, Scene 1.

COCKLOCHE: An old expression of reproach for a silly
fool. Used principally in the 17th century, the word comes
from the French coqueluche, "a hood" or "a darling," perhaps originally coming from the Latin word for hood,
cucullus. See Sala's Captain Dangerous (1863) and the following:

> TREEDLE: Gentlemen, I have an ambition to be
> your eternal slave.
> FOWLER: 'Tis granted.
> TUTOR: And I to be your everlasting servant.
> AIMWELL: 'Tis granted.
> CLARE: A couple of cockloches.
> --James Shirley: The Witty Fair One (1628); Act
> II, Scene 2.

COCK-SHUT TIME: An old term for night or the evening
twilight, "When a man cannot discern a dog from a wolf"
(Florio). The origin is probably in the word cockshoot,
which was an opening in a glade or a wood, through which
woodcocks at twilight would "shoot" out and be able to be
caught by hunters in nets. But perhaps it also refers to
the time when poultry are "shut up" for the night in their
houses. For uses, see Henry Kingsley's Mademoiselle
Mathilde, and the following:

> KING RICHARD: Saw'st thou the melancholy lord
> Northumberland?
> SIR RICHARD RATCLIFF: Thomas the Earl of
> Surrey, and himself,
> Much about cock-shut time, from troop to troop
> Went through the army, cheering up the soldiers.
> --William Shakespeare: King Richard The Third
> (1593); Act V, Scene 3.

Also used by Middleton and by Ben Jonson.

COFFEE-WIT: A person who frequented English coffee
houses in the late seventeenth and early eighteenth centuries.
The quotation following provides a good description:

> LYDIA: Now, what is the coffee-wit?
> DAPPERWIT: He is a lying, censorious, gossip-
> ing, quibbling wretch, and sets people together by
> the ears over that sober drink, coffee: he is a
> wit, as he is a commentator, upon the Gazette;
> and he rails at the pirates of Algier, the Grand

Signior of Constantinople, and the Christian Grand
Signior.
--William Wycherley: Love In a Wood (1671); Act
    II, Scene 1.

COLT: A verb formed from the noun, referring to the
friskiness of the young animal: Hence, to frolic; to cheat;
to fool.   The noun is of very obscure origin, though it may
be related to such words as the Dutch kuld "family" and the
Danish koltring, "big man. " Uses can be found in North's
Plutarch (1580); in Beaumont & Fletcher and in Fletcher
alone; and by Shakespeare, in Cymbeline (1611) and in the
following:

> SIR JOHN FALSTAFF: 'Sblood, I'll not bear mine
> own flesh so far a-foot again for all the coin in
> thy father's exchequer.   What a plague mean ye to
> colt me thus?
> PRINCE HENRY: Thou liest; thou art not colted,
> thou art uncolted.
> SIR JOHN FALSTAFF: I prithee, good Prince
> Hal, help me to my horse, good king's son.
> --William Shakespeare: King Henry The Fourth,
>   Part I (1597); Act II, Scene 2.

COMMIS: A clerk or deputy of a foreign country; from the
French commis, and the Latin committere, "to set together,
to employ. "

> That gentleman had never held any rank, nor ever
> been in the army before ... yet this clerk in of-
> fice, this commis, contrary to all military estab-
> lishments, was now a lieutenant-colonel.
> --The Annual Register for the Year 1780: History
>   of Europe, page 129.

COMMODIOSITY: Fitness; advantage; convenience.   From the
Latin commodiosus, "suitable"; from commodious.

> LENTULO: Thou blind gentleman! unless it be
> for my commodiosity, I'll teach thee to be blind,
> and go so bravely.
> --Anonymous: Rare Triumphs of Love and Fortune
>   (1582); Act III.

COMMOIGNE: A fellow-monk, a brother-monk, a fellow-
friar. Adopted from the Old French commoine, constructed

of com an intensive and moine, "monk. "

> Right worthy and worshipful Sir, I recommend me
> to you, and thank you for the good, true, and
> diligent labour you have had for the matter be-
> tween the Prior of Bromholme and his commoigne
> apostata, Johne Wortes, that nameth himself Pas-
> ton, and affirmeth him untruly to be my cousin.
> --The Paston Letters: From William Paston, No-
> vember 5th, 1425.

COMPOTATOR: A person who drinks in the company of
another; a fellow-drinker; a partner in a binge.   The word
is from the Old French compotateur, from the Latin verb
meaning "to drink. " Used by Archibald Campbell in 1767
in his Lexephoras, and by Hawthorne:

> My letters of introduction have been of the utmost
> service, enabling me to make the acquaintance of
> several distinguished characters who, until now,
> have seemed as remote from the sphere of my
> personal intercourse as the wits of Queen Anne's
> time or Ben Jonson's compotators at the Mermaid.
> --Nathaniel Hawthorne: P's Correspondence in
> Mosses From an Old Manse (1846).

COMROGUE: Originally a serious, and then a humorous,
term for an associate or friend; a "fellow-rogue. " Rogue
is of uncertain origin, though perhaps it is connected in
some way with the Latin rogare, "to ask. " Massinger used
it in The City Madam, and so did Thomas Heywood; it is
found in Richard Head's Canting Academy, or the Devil's
Cabinet opened (1673); in Jonathan Swift and Thomas Bridges;
and in Jonson:

> GROOM: By what name so ever you call it, here
> will be a Masque, and shall be a Masque, when
> you and the rest of your comrogues shall sit dis-
> guis'd in the stocks.
> --Ben Jonson: The Masque of Augurs (1622); lines
> 54-57.

CONDIDDLE: To steal; to purloin; to make away with. Used
principally in the 18th and 19th centuries, condiddle is from
the old verb diddle, meaning "to swindle. "

> "Twig the old connoisseur, " said the squire to the

knight, "He is condiddling the drawing."
--Sir Walter Scott: St. Ronan's Well (1823); chap-
    ter 4.

CONDOG: To agree or to "concur." Popular in the 16th and
17th centuries, this word was probably invented by some wit
who was supposedly imitating "concur" by replacing the
syllable cur with the "synonym" dog. Heywood used it in
the Royal King (1637), and it was used earlier by Lyly:

> ALCUMIST: So is it; and often doth it happen that
> the just proportion of the fire and all things con-
> cur.
> RAFFE: Concur? condog! I will away.
> --John Lyly: Galathea (ca. 1584); Act III, Scene
>   3.

CONKY: A popular nickname, principally in the last century, given to a person with a large nose; thus, "nosey."
The origin is uncertain, but perhaps there is a connection
with the French word conque, "shell."

> "It was a robbery, miss, that hardly anybody could
> have been down upon," said Blathers. "This here
> Conkey Chickweed--"
> "Conkey means Nosey, ma'am," interposed Duff.
> "Of course the lady knows that, don't she?" de-
> manded Mr. Blathers. "Always interrupting, you
> are, partner!"
> --Charles Dickens: Oliver Twist (1839); chapter
>   31.

CONQUASSATION: A rough and severe shaking; a violent
agitation or tumbling. From the Latin conquassatio, derived
from quassare, "to shake." In 1767 it was used by Andrew
Campbell in his Lexephoras, and here is an earlier use:

> RALPH: Be in readiness, for he's coming this
> way, alone too; stand to't like gentlemen and yeo-
> men: so soon as he is in sight, I'll go fetch my
> master.
> SWEETBALL: I have had a conquassation in my
> cerebrum ever since the disaster, and now it takes
> me again; if it turn to a megrim, I shall hardly
> abide the sight of him.
> --Thomas Middleton: Anything For a Quiet Life
>   (ca. 1617); Act III, Scene 2.

CONY-CATCH: To swindle, to cheat, to fool, to take in. Popular from the 16th to the 18th centuries, first used extensively by Robert Greene (for the etymology, see the following word). In 1660 it was used in Hickeringhill's Jamaica, and was prevalent in many writers, including Shakespeare:

> GREMIO: Take heed, Signior Baptista, lest you be cony-catch in this business: I dare swear this is the right Vincentio.
> --Wm. Shakespeare: The Taming of the Shrew (ca. 1595); Act V, Scene 1.

CONY-CATCHER: One who catches rabbits; or, a swindler, one who catches "conies," an old word for one who is easily duped. The term was made famous in 1591 by Robert Greene in his pamphlet on thievery. 'To catch a cony is, in the old cant of thieves, to cheat" (Johnson). "Cony" was originally the name for the rabbit, the latter being originally the name for a young rabbit. From the Old French conil, the Spanish conejo; from the Latin word for "rabbit" or "burrow," cuniculus.

> "Merry, thou hast me on the hip there, thou old miserly cony-catcher!"
> --Sir Walter Scott: The Fortunes of Nigel (1822); chapter 23.

COOLING-CARD: In a card-game, the winning card. From the verb "cool," referring to the fact that the card "cools the anxiety" of the other players (i.e. they know they have lost).

> MARGARET: Wilt thou accept of ransom--yea or no?
> EARL OF SUFFOLK (aside): Fond man, remember that thou hast a wife;
> Then how can Margaret be thy paramour?
> MARGARET: I were best to leave him, for he will not hear.
> EARL OF SUFFOLK (aside): There all is marr'd; there lies a cooling-card.
> --William Shakespeare: King Henry The Sixth, Part I (ca. 1591); Act V, Scene 3.

COPEMAN, COPESMAN: A merchant, trader, or vendor; a dealer; later, a fence who dealt with river thieves. Copesman is the original form, from cope, meaning "a bargain."

The later form may also have been influenced by the Dutch word koopman. The formation is similar to many other words, such as herdsman, tradesman, craftsman, etc. It can be found in William Painter's The Palace of Pleasure (1566); in Claudius Hollyband and in John Colquhoun; and in Ben Jonson:

> VOLPONE:
> Assure thee, Celia, he that would sell thee,
> Only for hope of gain, and that uncertain,
> He would have sold his part of Paradise
> For ready money, had he met a cope-man.
> --Ben Jonson: Volpone (1606); Act III, Scene 5.

CORDWAIN: Spanish cordovan leather, originally made at Cordova, of tanned and dressed goat-skins, and later of horsehide. The leather was widely used in the manufacture of shoes, especially for the wealthy and the nobility, from about the 12th to around the 16th centuries. The word comes through the Middle English corduane, the Old French cordoan, the Italian cordovano, the Old Spanish cordovan, "of Cordova or Cordoba," ultimately from the Latin name of that town, Corduba. It was used by Chaucer, Spenser, and Drayton; Scott brought it back in the following:

> The person I mean was a buxom dame of about thirty, her fingers loaded with many a silver ring, and three or four of gold; her ankles liberally displayed from under her numerous blue, white, and scarlet short petticoats, and attired in hose of the finest and whitest lamb's-wool, which arose from shoes of Spanish cordwain, fastened with silver buckles.
> --Sir Walter Scott: Redgauntlet (1824); letter 12.

CORNER-CREEPER: Literally, one who "creeps around corners," hence a furtive, stealthy, wary individual; one who is up to no good and is proceeding cautiously so as not to be discovered; often called a "spider-catcher." Also, then, a thief or robber. Principally used in the 16th and 17th centuries, the word also meant, as illustrated in the quotation, Roman Catholics who "creeped around corners" in attempts to sneak up on people of other religions in order to convert them. John Hacket employed the word in 1670 in his Life of Archbishop Williams.

> The controversy with Rome was at that moment keen. Agents of conversion to the Romish Church,

corner-creepers as they were called, penetrated
everywhere. Two young brothers of Falkland himself were won over by them.
--Matthew Arnold: Falkland (1879); paragraph 12.

COSTARD: A variety of large apple; thus, humorously, the
head. The origin is unknown, but connection with the
French coste, "rib," thus meaning a ribbed apple as the
costard is, has been suggested.

> MERRYGREEK (strikes Roister): I knock your
> costard, if ye offer to strike me.
> ROISTER: Strikest thou indeed, and I offer but in
> jest?
> MERRYGREEK: Yea, and rap ye again, except ye
> can sit in rest.
> --Nicholas Udall: Ralph Roister Doister (ca. 1550);
>   Act III, Scene 5.

Also employed by Shakespeare in King Lear and King
Richard III, and by Scott in Rob Roy.

COUPLE-BEGGAR See buckle-beggar.

COUTEAU-DE-CHASSE: A large knife (a couteau) used as a
weapon; a large hunting-knife. From the Old French coutel,
"knife" (Latin cultellus) and the French chasse, "hunting,
pursuit." Used by William Shenstone; by Richardson in
Clarissa Harlowe (1748); and by Smollett in Roderick Random
(1748).

> Amid this scene of confusion, a gentleman, plainly
> dressed in a riding-habit, with a black cockade in
> his hat, but without any arms except a couteau-de-
> chasse, walked into the apartment without cere-
> mony.
> --Sir Walter Scott: Redgauntlet (1824); chapter 23.

COZIER, COSIER: A cobbler or shoemaker. Adapted from
the Old French cousere, "tailor," from coudre, "to sew."
Used by Robert Armin, the author of A Nest of Ninnies, and
by Shakespeare:

> MALVOLIO: My masters, are you mad? or what
> are you? Have you no wit, manners, nor honesty,
> but to gabble like tinkers at this of night? Do ye
> make an ale-house of my lady's house, that ye

squeak out your cosiers' catches without any miti-
gation or remorse of voice?   Is there no respect
of place, persons, nor time, in you?
--Wm. Shakespeare: Twelfth Night (1601); Act II,
    Scene 3.

CRACCUS, CRACUS: A kind of tobacco.   The origin of the
word is unknown, but it may be a corruption of the name of
the city of Caraccas, in Venezuela, where tobacco is grown.
John Fletcher used it in 1625 in The Woman's Prize.

> CHOUGH: Content. --I'faith, Trim, we'll roar the
> rusty rascal out of his tobacco.
> TRIMTRAM: Ay, and he had the best craccus in
> London.
> --Thomas Middleton & William Rowley: A Fair
>   Quarrel (1617); Act IV, Scene 1.

CROCK: A name for a little, low stool.   The origin is unknown; but perhaps it is related to the word cricket, a type
of low wooden footstool.   (Also, the history of cricket is unknown, too).

> I then inquired for the person that belonged to the
> petticoat; and, to my great surprise, was directed
> to a very beautiful young damsel, with so pretty a
> face and shape, that I bid her come out of the
> crowd, and seated her upon a little crock at my
> left hand.
> --Joseph Addison in The Tatler, No. 116 (1709);
>   paragraph 1.

CROODLE: To nestle close to something or someone; to
crouch down; to draw together, as for warmth or protection.
Of unknown derivation, perhaps a diminutive of the verb
"crowd."

> "There," said Lucia, as she clung croodling to
> him, "there is a pretty character of you, sir!
> Make the most of it, for it is all those Yankees
> will ever send you."
> --Charles Kingsley: Two Years Ago (1857); chap-
>   ter 10.

CROWD: An old ancient Celtic musical instrument somewhat
like the violin, but having originally three strings, then six,
four of which were played with a bow, the other two being

plucked with the fingers. Through later usage, the word
has come to mean a fiddle, and also has a verb form associated with it. It originates in the Welsh <u>crwth</u>, "fiddle;
swelling body or box. "

> 'Tis strange how some men's tempers suit
> (Like bawd and brandy) with dispute;
> That for their own opinions stand fast
> Only to have them claw'd and canvass'd;
> That keep their consciences in cases,
> As fiddlers do their crowds and bases,
> Ne'er to be used but when they're bent
> To play a fit for argument.
> --Samuel Butler: <u>Hudibras</u>, Part Second (1664);
>   Canto II, lines 1-8.

> GNOTHO: Fiddlers, crowd on, crowd on; let no
> man lay a block in your way. --Crowd on, I say.
> --Thomas Middleton & William Rowley: <u>The Old
>   Law</u> (1599); Act V, Scene 1.

<u>CUCK</u>: To punish by setting in a cuck-stool (see the follow-
ing word).

> MOLL: Here be the angels, gentlemen; they were
>   given me
> As a musician: I pursue no pity;
> Follow the law, and you can cuck me, spare not;
> Hang up my viol by me, and I care not.
> --Thomas Dekker & Thomas Middleton: <u>The Roar-
>   ing Girl</u> (1611); Act V, Scene 2.

<u>CUCK-STOOL, CUCKING-STOOL</u>: Known by various names
(trebucket, tumbrel, castigatory), the cuck-stool was a kind
of chair used as a device of punishment, in which the offenders, such as prostitutes, pimps, ill-tempered wives,
dishonest merchants, etc. , were tied and exposed to public
ridicule. Originally, the instrument was shaped like a toilet
seat to add to the occasion; it was also used like a ducking-
stool for dunking people in ponds, lakes, or heaps of filth.
The word apparently is from the old verb <u>cuck</u>, "to defile
with excrement, " from the Old Norse <u>kūka</u>.

> "That thou art, noble sir, " said the same forward
> dame, who had before expressed her admiration so
> energetically; 'I will uphold thee worthy of her
> presence, and whatever other grace a lady can do

> thee. "
>   'Now hold thy tongue, with a wanion!" said the
> monk; while in the same breath the Fleming ex-
> claimed, "Beware the cucking-stool, Dame Scant-
> o'-Grace!" while he conducted the noble youth
> across the court.
>   --Sir Walter Scott: The Betrothed (1825); chapter
>   9.

CUDDEN: A numbskull; a clown; a dolt; "a stupid rustic"
(Johnson). The history of this word is uncertain, but perhaps it is related to the word "cuddy," meaning "a donkey
or ass," from which the figurative uses were taken.

> MONSIEUR: Ha! ha! ha! turn out. --Lord, that
> people should be such arrant cuddens! ha! ha! ha!
>   --William Wycherley: The Gentleman Dancing-
>   Master (1672); Act IV, Scene 1.

CURNEY: A company; a number; a group; a lot. A diminutive form of "curn," "a few; a small quantity." The etymology is obscure, but perhaps it is related to "kern," meaning
"to granulate, to grind up." Principally Scottish.

> "He foretold that all my sister's children would die
> some day; and he foretold it in the very hour that
> the youngest was born, and that is this lad Quen-
> tin--who, no doubt, will one day die, to make up
> the prophecy--the more's the pity--the whole cur-
> ney of them is gone but himself."
>   --Sir Walter Scott: Quentin Durward (1823); chap-
>   ter 31.

CURTAIN-LECTURE: A talking-to that a wife gives to her
husband in bed; a reproof.

> I was no sooner got into another bed-chamber, but
> I heard very harsh words uttered in a smooth,
> uniform tone. I was amazed to hear so great a
> volubility in reproach, and thought it too coherent
> to be spoken by one asleep; but upon looking near-
> er, I saw the head-dress of the person who spoke,
> which showed her to be a female with a man lying
> by her side broad awake, and as quiet as a lamb.
> I could not but admire his exemplary patience, and
> discovered by his whole behaviour, that he was
> then lying under the discipline of a curtain-lecture.

--Joseph Addison in The Tatler, No. 243 (1710);
    paragraph 4.

CUTTY-STOOL: Originally, in Scotland, a particular seat
in the parish church, reserved for offenders against chastity,
or other delinquents, who had to sit there during the ser-
vices and be subjected to public rebuke from the parson,
and were exposed to the public view; a stool of repentance.
Later, in the Scottish dialects, a low stool, similar to a
crock.

> "Fie, fie, cummer," said the matron of Glendearg,
> hitching her seat of honor, in her turn, a little
> nearer to the cuttie-stool on which Tibb was
> seated.
> --Sir Walter Scott: The Monastery (1820); chapter
> 4.

Also used by Robert Fergusson and by Keats, and by
Charles Gibbon in his For Lack of Gold (1871), chapter 8.

-D-

DADDLE: An old word in use since the 18th century meaning "hand" or the "ball of the fist." The origin is unknown,
but perhaps it is related to paddle.

> "Adzooks!" exclaimed the bailiff--"sure Harry
> Wakefield, the nattiest lad at Whitson Tryste,
> Wooler Fair, Carlisle Sands, or Stagshaw Bank,
> is not going to show white feather? Ah, this
> comes of living so long with kilts and bonnets--
> men forget the use of their daddles."
> --Sir Walter Scott: The Two Drovers (1827).

DANDIPRAT, DANTIPRAT: A very small coin minted in
England in the 16th century by Henry VII; thus, a small or
insignificant person; also, a dwarf. The word is also used
to apply to a young boy or (rarely) a young girl. The origin is unknown. William Camden used the word in the coin-
sense in 1605 in his Remains, as did William Prynne in
1641 in The Antipathy of the English Lordly Prelacie both to
Regall Monarchy and Civil Unity. John Heywood in 1556 and
Joshua Sylvester in his translation of Du Bartas (1606) used
the sense of a dwarf. The last sense was employed by
Stanyhurst in 1583 and by Richard Estcourt in his comedy,

Fair Example (1706). The rare use of the word in reference
to a young girl is illustrated in Act I of Thomas Heywood's
The Wise Woman (1638):

> YOUNG CHARTLEY: There is a fair, sweet, mod-
> est rogue, her name is Luce; with this dandiprat,
> this pretty little ape's face, is yon blunt fellow in
> love; and no marvel, for she hath a brow bewitch-
> ing, eyes ravishing, and a tongue enchanting; and,
> indeed, she hath no fault in the world but one, and
> that is, she is honest.
> --Thomas Heywood: The Wise Woman of Hogsdon
>   (1638); Act I, Scene 1.

> "It is even so," he said, with a thundering sound
> of exultation--"it is even so, my little dandieprat."
> --Sir Walter Scott: Kenilworth (1821); chapter 26.

DANSKER: A nautical slang word for a Dane. From the
Danish adjective, spelled identically. The principal usage
of this word was the late 19th and early 20th centuries,
though it was employed much earlier, as in the following:

> POLONIUS: Look you, sir,
> Inquire me first what Danskers are in Paris;
> And how, and who, what means, and where they
>   keep,
> What company, and what expense.
> --William Shakespeare: Hamlet (1600); Act II,
>   Scene 1.

DARBY: Ready money; cash that can be spent immediately
and for any purpose. Also, handcuffs. The word can be
found in Hickeringill and in Richard Estcourt's interlude,
Prunella (1712). It comes from a certain pronunciation of
the English shire of Derby, and was once spelled this way;
but the association of it with the meaning of the word is un-
clear.

> BELFOND SENIOR: How much cole, ready, and
> rhino shall I have?
> CHEATLY: Enough to set thee up to spark it in
> thy brother's face: And e're thou shalt want the
> ready, the darby, thou shalt make thy fruitful
> acres in reversion to fly, and all thy sturdy oaks
> to bend like switches!
> --Thomas Shadwell: The Squire of Alsatia (1688);
>   Act I, Scene 1.

DARKMANS: Night-time; a thieves' word for the night or
twilight. It is a common formation of certain cant words,
in which a noun or adjective is prefixed to the suffix -mans,
which is of uncertain origin. Examples are crackmans, a
hedge, and lightmans, the daylight. This word was principally in use from the 16th to the 19th centuries, and can be
found in Harman's Caveat for Vagabonds (1567) and in Dekker & Middleton's The Roaring Girl (1611).

> 'The times are sair altered since I was a kitchen-
> mort. Men were men then, and fought other in
> the open field, and there was nae milling in the
> darkmans. "
> --Sir Walter Scott: Guy Mannering (1815); chapter
>   28.

DEGAMBOY: A kind of musical instrument, either the violin
or the bass-viol. The Italian word for "leg" is gamba; this
word is short for viola-da-gamba, so-called because the bass
is placed next to the legs rather than in the arm.

> ANTONIO: Take heed, fiddler;
> I'll dance ye, by this hand; your fiddle-stick
> I'll grease of a new fashion, for presuming
> To meddle with my de-gamboys.
> --John Fletcher: The Chances (1627); Act IV,
>   Scene 2.

DELL: A young, vagabond girl; the mistress of a rogue or
vagabond; also, a virgin. Principally a thieves' word, also
spelled dill, it was in use from the 16th to the 19th centuries, and can be found in Harman's Caveat for Vagabonds
(1567); in John Taylor's works; in Holme's The Academy of
the Armoury (1688); and, more recently, in William Harrison Ainsworth's novel, Rookwood (1834).

> MINSTREL: Sweet doxies and dells,
> My Roses and Nells,
> Scarce out of the shells,
> Your hands, nothing else.
> --Ben Jonson: The Gypsies Metamorphos'd (1620);
>   lines 803-806.

DEVIL'S COACH-HORSE: A popular name for the large rove-
beetle (Goerius olens), taken from the fact that, when
threatened or disturbed, it rears up in a "furious" or "de-
fiant" manner; often, any cock-tailed beetle.

As this atrocious tale of lies turned up joint by
joint before her, like a "devil's coach-horse,"
mother was too much amazed to do any more than
look at him, as if the earth must open.
--R. D. Blackmore: Lorna Doone (1869); chapter
   4.

DIAN, DIANA: A trumpet blast or a drumroll at break of
day. The word comes through the French diane and Spanish
diana from the Italian diana, described by Florio as "a kind
of march sounded by trumpetters in a morning to their gen-
erall and captaine." Diana is constructed from the Italian
dia, ultimately from the Latin dies, "day." The word can
be located in William Garrard's The Arte of Warre (1591)
and in Thomas Urquhart's Jewel (1652).

       When in the East the Morning Ray
       Hangs out the Colours of the Day,
       The Bee through these known Allies hums,
       Beating the Dian with its Drumms.
       --Andrew Marvell: Upon Appleton House (1678);
          stanza 37.

DIMBLE, DUMBLE, DRUMBLE: A deep and shady dell or
hollow, ravine; a deep, quiet dell, often with a stream run-
ning through it. Specifically, a dumble is a wooded valley,
or a stretch of trees along the sides of a stream. A drumble is a coarse, wooded dip or hole in the ground. The
origin of these forms is unknown, but possibly they are connected with the word dim, as is suggested in their meanings.
Connection with dingle has also been suggested. Actually,
dimble and dimple are versions of the same word, meaning
essentially "a hole." The words were used principally in
the 16th to 18th centuries; Ben Jonson employed dimble in
his Sad Shepherd (1637).

       The Sylvans in their songs their mirthful meeting
          tell;
       And Satyrs, that in slades and gloomy dimbles
          dwell,
       Run whooting to the hills to clap their ruder hands.
       --Michael Drayton: Polyolbion (1612); Song 2.

DING-DING, DING-A-DING, DING-DONG: A very old term
of endearment, of unknown origin. William Bulleyn used it
in his Dialogue, bothe plesaunte and pietifull; wherein is
shewed a goodlie Regimente against the Fever of Pestilence
(1564).

CAPTAIN: Let Philaster
Be deeper in request, my ding-a-dings,
My pairs of dear indentures, kings of clubs,
Than your cold water-camlets, or your paintings
Spitted with copper.
--Francis Beaumont & John Fletcher: Philaster
(1611); Act V, Scene 4.

DISCANDY, DISCANDER: To dissolve or to melt away out
of a solid or "candied" condition, as with butter or choco-
late. The verb candy, meaning "to sugar," comes through
the French se candir from the Italian candire, the Arabic
qand, "sugar," and qandi, "composed of sugar."

CLEOPATRA:
Dissolve my life! The next Caesarion smite!
Till, by degrees, the memory of my womb,
Together with my brave Egyptians all,
By the discandying of this pelleted storm,
Lie graveless,--till the flies and gnats of Nile
Have buried them for prey!
--William Shakespeare: Antony and Cleopatra
(1607); Act III, Scene 13.

DITCH-CONSTABLE: An expression of reproach or of dis-
like, directed toward a worthless scoundrel, making use of
"ditch" as representing anything dirty or filthy.

FOLLYWIT: I'll make you an example for all ditch
constables, how they abuse justice.--Here, bind
him to the chair.
--Thomas Middleton: A Mad World, My Masters
(1608); Act V, Scene 2.

DOBBIE, DOBBY, "MASTER DOBBS": A household spirit or
sprite that was believed to haunt certain places, such as
groves, walks, or houses, and that apparently was attached
to the families that lived in the area rather than to the area
itself. Grose gives us a good description of the dobbie:
'Dobbies correspond to the brownies in Scotland; demons
attached to particular houses and farms. Though naturally
lazy, they are said to make incredible exertions for the
family in cases of trouble or difficulty, such as to stack all
the hay, or house all the corn in one night. The farmer's
horses are left to rest, and stags or other wild animals are
supposed to fulfill the orders of the demon. They are believed to follow the person or family to one place or another

on removal.   One kind of them differs from the domestic
Dobbies, by inhabiting bridges, old towers, etc. instead of
the kitchen; and instead of working, doing only mischief, by
frightening travellers, by jumping behind them on horseback,
and squeezing them so as to impede their breathing. " The
origin of the word dobbie is not known, but it may be an
adaptation of the proper name Dobbie, a variation of Robbie,
Rob, in the same fashion that dobbin, "a farm-horse," was
created.   The word can be found in Washington Irving's
Bracebridge Hall (1822), and in the following:

> But when the peasant-boy, her companion, who had
> hitherto followed her, whistling cheerily, with a
> hedge-bill in his hand, and his hat on one side,
> perceived that she turned to the stile which en-
> tered to the Dobby's Walk, he showed symptoms
> of great fear, and at length, coming to the lady's
> side, petitioned her, in a whimpering tone, 'Don't
> ye now--don't ye now, my lady--don't ye go yon-
> der. "
> --Sir Walter Scott: Peveril of the Peak (1823);
>   chapter 10.

DODDYPOLL: A stupid idiot; a fool; a simpleton; a blockhead.   The word is related to the verb dote, "to be silly,"
and to dod, "to clip, to lop off" (to clip the poll, or "head,"
i. e. to cut the hair).   Found in Thomas Hoccleve's Story of
Jonathan (1422); in the old play Hickscorner, where the form
is Doctor Doddypoll; in the Towneley Mystery Plays, and in
Brome.   Here is an example of a more recent application:

> And here without staying for my reply, shall I be
> called as many blockheads, numskulls, doddypoles,
> dunderheads, ninnyhammers, goosecaps, joltheads,
> nincompoops, sh-t-a-beds ... And I'll let them do
> it, as Bridget said, as much as they please.
> --Laurence Sterne: Tristram Shandy (1767); Book
>   IX, chapter 25.

DODMAN, HODMANDOD, HODDYDODDY: An old name for
a snail.   The origin is totally unknown; perhaps it is connected with dod, "something rounded," in reference to the
shell of the snail?   It has been used by John Bale and by
Lisle; Francis Bacon employed it in his Sylva Sylvarum
(1626).

"My house ain't much for to see, sir, but it's

hearty at your service if ever you should come
along with Mas'r Davy to see it. I'm a reg'lar
Dodman, I am," said Mr. Peggotty, by which he
meant snail, and this was in allusion to his being
slow to go, for he had attempted to go after every
sentence, and had somehow or other come back
again; "but I wish you both well, and I wish you
happy!"
--Charles Dickens: David Copperfield (1850); chapter 7.

DOG-BOLT: A term of contempt for a person of low moral
character. Dr. Johnson sheds some light on this word:
"Of this word I know not the meaning, unless it be, that
when meal or flower is sifted or bolted to a certain degree,
the coarser part is called dogbolt, or flower for dogs."
The exact origin cannot be ascertained, but there is the possibility of a connection with a type of blunt or "soft" arrow-
head that was of little use except for shooting at dogs. The
word was used principally from the 15th to 17th centuries,
and can be found in the Paston Letters for 1465; in Ulpian
Fulwell's Ars Adulandi (1579); in John Lyly, in Beaumont &
Fletcher and in Shadwell, as well as more recently in Sir
Walter Scott's Peveril of the Peak (1823).

> LYSANDER: I am old, you say,
> Yes, parlous old, kids, an you mark me well!
> This beard cannot get children, you lank suck-eggs,
> Unless such weasels come from court to help us.
> We will get our own brats, you letcherous dog-
>   bolts!
> --Thomas Middleton & William Rowley: The Old
>   Law (1599); Act III, Scene 2.

DOG-LEECH: (1) A veterinarian; a doctor who treats dogs
and other animals. Seen in Thomas Nabbes (1640) and in
Thomas Carlyle (1831).

> SECCO: The young whelp is mad; I must slice the
> worm out of his breech. I have noosed his neck
> in the collar; and I will once turn dog-leech:
> stand from about me, or you'll find me terrible
> and furious.
> --John Ford: The Fancies, Chaste and Noble
>   (1635); Act IV, Scene 1.

(2) A derogatory name for a quack doctor; an idiot

physician. Thomas More used this word, as did Brome in
1652. Once again for a quotation we turn to Ford:

> RHETIAS: Thou art an excellent fellow. Diabolo!
> O these lousy close-stool empirics, that will un-
> dertake all cures, yet know not the causes of any
> disease! Dog-leeches! By the four elements I
> honour thee; could find in my heart to turn knave,
> and be thy flatterer.
> --John Ford: The Lover's Melancholy (1628); Act
>   IV, Scene 2.

DONZEL: A young nobleman not yet a knight; a page or
squire, or merely a youth or servant. The word comes
from the Italian donzello, the Spanish doncel; from the late
Latin domnicellus, "little lord," from dominus, "master,
lord." It can be found in Nashe's Pierce Pennilesse (1592),
Butler's Hudibras, and Bulwer-Lytton's The Last of the
Barons (1843).

> Donzel, methinks you look melancholic,
> After your coitum, and scurvy: truly,
> I do not like the dulness of your eye;
> It hath a heavy cast, 'tis upsee Dutch,
> And says you are a lumpish whore-master.
> --Ben Jonson: The Alchemist (1610); Act IV,
>   Scene 4.

DOODLE: A silly nitwit; a little fool. The exact origin is
unknown, but perhaps there is a connection with the Low
German dudeltopf, "simpleton." Used by Samuel Foote in
The Mayor of Garrat (1764) and by Richard Cobden (1845).
Once again, we are indebted to John Ford:

> CORAX: No quarrels, good Whiske! lay by your
> trumperies, and fall to your practice: instructions
> are ready for you all. Pelias is your leader, fol-
> low him; get credit now or never. Vanish, doodles,
> vanish!
> --John Ford: The Lover's Melancholy (1628); Act
>   III, Scene 1.

A different word is the verb doodle, meaning "to play
on the bagpipes," from dudelsack, "bagpipe." The use here
is principally in the Scottish; it is also spelled doudle. Scott
used it in Redgauntlet and in the following:

'I am wearied wi' doudling the bag o' wind a' day. "
--<u>Old Mortality</u> (1816); chapter 3.

<u>DOR</u>: A fool or nitwit. The origin is uncertain, but per-
haps it comes from the Old Norse <u>dári</u>, same meaning.
Jonson used it in <u>Cynthia's Revels</u>:

>   MERCURY: It is our purpose, Crites, to correct,
>   And punish, with our laughter, this night's sport,
>   Which our court-dors so heartily intend:
>   And by that worthy scorn, to make them know
>   How far beneath the dignity of man
>   Their serious and most practised actions are.
>   --Ben Jonson: <u>Cynthia's Revels</u> (1600); Act V,
>   Scene 1.

<u>DORP</u>: A Dutch village; a thorp. The word came into Eng-
lish from the Dutch of the same spelling, which became
"thorp" and "dorp" in variations. Also cf. the German
<u>dorf</u>, "village. " Stanyhurst used it in his Aeneid in 1583;
as did Thomas Fuller in <u>A Pisgah-Sight of Palestine</u> (1650),
and John Dryden.

>   Tailors then were none of the Twelve Companies.
>   Their Hall, that now is larger than some dorps
>   among the Netherlands, was then no bigger than a
>   Dutch butcher's shop.
>   --Thomas Dekker: <u>The Gull's Horn-Book</u> (1609);
>   chapter 1.

<u>DROMOND, DROMOUND</u>: A very large medieval sailing-
ship, "a great vessel of the class of long ships" (Jal). It
was used both for shipping and for raiding during wartime;
many rowers propelled it on its course, and, in older
times, it had but one sail. By the 16th century the word
had gone out of use, except in historical senses. It can be
found in <u>Guy Warwick, Coeur de Lion,</u> and <u>King Alisaunder;</u>
also in Caxton's <u>Chronicle of England</u> (1480), and in John
Speed's <u>History of Great Britain</u> (1611).

>   But for one moment--could I see once more
>   The grey-roofed sea-port sloping towards the shore
>   Or note the brown boats standing in from sea,
>   Or the great dromond swinging from the quay.
>   --William Morris: <u>The Earthly Paradise</u> (1870);
>   Prologue, stanza 8.

DRY-FAT: A large container for holding dry things; a great
wooden crate or vessel. The word comes from the old
noun fat, meaning "a vat or vessel." In 1558 it appears in
Hakluyt; it is in Holished, and in Andrew Yarranton's England's Improvement by Sea and Land (1677).

> PENNYBOY SENIOR:
> I am a broken vessel, all runs out:
> A shrunk old dryfat.
> --Ben Jonson: The Staple of News (1626); Act III,
>   Scene 2.

DRY-FIST: A stingy person or miser; pennypincher. The
origin of this word is not known, but the adjective dry,
"stingy, miserly," is probably related. The word was principally used in the 17th and 18th centuries, and can be found
in Thomas Dekker's The Honest Whore (1604), as well as in
Ford:

> FERENTES: You again! nay, an if you be in that
> mood, shut up your fore-shop, I'll be your journey-
> man no longer. Why, wise madam Dry-fist, could
> your mouldy brain be so addle, to imagine I would
> marry a stale widow at six-and-forty?
> --John Ford: Love's Sacrifice (ca. 1627); Act III,
>   Scene 1.

DUNDERWHELP: A detestable numbskull or idiot; literally,
a "dunderheaded whelp." The origin of the element dunder
is not known, but it perhaps is connected with the verb
dunner, "to make a loud noise." It can be found often in
Fletcher:

> MIRABEL:
> What a purblind puppy was I! now I remember him;
> All the whole cast on's face, though it were um-
>   bered,
> And masked with patches: what a dunder-whelp,
> To let him domineer thus! how he strutted,
> And what a load of lord he clapt upon him!
> Would I had him here again! I would so bounce
>   him,
> I would so thank his lordship for his lewd plot!
> --John Fletcher: The Wild-Goose Chase (1621);
>   Act III, Scene 1.

-E-

<u>EA</u>: A river; in marshland, a drainage channel. Also, any marshy or boggy land or meadow; an island. Sometimes spelled <u>eau</u>, because of association with the French word for water, <u>eau</u>, <u>ea</u> is the modern form of the Middle English word for river, <u>ae</u>.

> And they rowed away for Crowland, by many a mere and many an ea; through narrow reaches of clear brown glassy water.
> --Charles Kingsley: <u>Hereward the Wake</u> (1866); chapter 20.

<u>EAR-SPECTACLE</u>: The ear-trumpet, an aid in hearing, which was trumpet-shaped and held with the smaller end close to the ear.

> Let it be tried, for the help of the hearing, (and I conceive it likely to succeed,) to make an instrument like a tunnel ... let the narrow end of it be set close to the ear: and mark whether any sound, abroad in the open air, will not be heard distinctly from further distance than without that instrument; being (as it were) an ear-spectacle.
> --Francis Bacon: <u>Sylva Sylvarum</u> (1626); paragraph 285.

<u>EARTH-BATH</u>: An old type of supposedly beneficial treatment for certain illnesses, in which the sick person was buried up to the neck in the ground for a period of time. In later usage, the word came to be a synonym for a grave!

> He advises a new pit to be dug, if it should be necessary to repeat the earth-bath, and observes that it may be used with safety only from the end of the month of May to the month of October.
> --Gerard van Swieten in <u>The Annual Register for 1765</u>; section on Natural History, page 108.

<u>EARTH-BOB</u>: The larva of certain beetles; a maggot or small worm; grub. <u>Bob</u> is an old word of approximately the same meaning, but its origin is uncertain. This word appeared in many books on fishing because of the use of the earth-bob as bait, including Thomas Best's <u>Treatise on Angling</u>, and in the following:

The earth-bob or white-grub is a worm with a red
head.
--Richard Brookes: The Art of Angling, Rock and
   Sea Fishing, With the Natural History of River,
   Pond, and Sea Fish (1740).

EARTH-MAD: An old name for the common earthworm,
Lumbricus terrestris. The word comes from the Old English eorthmata, from eorthe "earth" and matha, "maggot,
worm."

The earth-mads and all the sort of worms & grubs,
are without eies.
--Philemon Holland, trans.: Pliny's Historie of
   the World (1601); I. 334.

EDER, EDERA: An old name for ivy. It comes from the
Latin word for same, hedera, edera.

The Lord God made redy an eder, and it styede
up on the hed of Jonas.
--John Wycliffe's Bible (1382): Jonah iv, 6.

EGYPTIAN: A humorous name for a gypsy. Gypsy is a
corruption of the Middle English Egypcien, "Egyptian," ultimately from the Greek word for Egypt, Aiguptos.

The people then assembled in this barn were no
other than a company of Egyptians or, as they are
vulgarly called, gypsies, and they were now celebrating the wedding of one of their society.
--Henry Fielding: Tom Jones (1747); Book XII,
   chapter 12.

EISEL: An old name for vinegar; later, any acid substance.
Through the Old French aisil, the word is derived from the
Latin word for vinegar, acetum. Many spellings exist, include eisell, eysell, aisille, etc. Tobie Venner used it in
1620 in his Via Recta ad Vitam Longam.

HAMLET: 'Swounds, show me what thou'lt do:
Woo't weep? woo't fight? woo't fast? woo't tear
   thyself?
Woo't drink up eisel? eat a crocodile?
--William Shakespeare: Hamlet (1600); Act V,
   Scene 1.

EMBEDLAM: To drive insane; to "put into bedlam," a hospital for the insane, originally St. Mary of Bethlehem, incorporated in 1547 by King Henry VIII. Bedlam is merely a corruption of Bethlehem.

> HALA: A work that no age dares
> Allow, yet none conceal, I must attempt.
> Fury! then spur thyself, embedlam wit;
> Poison my thoughts, to make my reason see
> Pleasure in cruelty, Glory, in spite:
> Rage to exceed examples doth delight.
> --Sir Fulke Greville: Alaham (1628); Act II, Scene
>   2.

EME: An extremely ancient word for a maternal uncle or a close companion. It appears in Beowulf; the Old English form, éam, is believed to be related to the Latin avus, "grandfather," and avunculus, "little grandfather," i. e. uncle. Originally it meant strictly the maternal uncle, but later it came to be used in reference to the father's brother also. It appears in Arthur and Merlin (ca. 1330); in Barbour's Bruce (1375); much later, in Allan Ramsay and in Scott's Heart of Midlothian (1818).

> 'I choose the battle next of Shrewsbury to chant,
> Betwixt Henry the Fourth, the son of John of
>   Gaunt,
> And the stout Percies, Henry Hotspur and his eame
> The earl of Wor'ster, who the rightful diadem
> Had from king Richard reft, and heav'd up to his
>   seat."
> --Michael Drayton: Polyolbion (1612); song 22.

EMMET: An old name for the ant. The original Old English, aemete, formed two pronunciations, amete and emete. The former contracted and evolved into our present word ant; the latter retained the middle vowel as emmet. Scottish forms of the word include emmot, emmock, emock, and emmack. It can be located in Barclay's Ship of Folys of the World (1509), Johnson's Life of Pope (1779), and in Singleton's Virgil (1855).

> You must remember that he is an emmet of quality, and has better blood in his veins than any pismire in the mole-hill.
> --Joseph Addison: The Guardian, No. 153 (1713);
>   paragraph 7.

ENAUNTER: Lest by chance; in case it should happen that. From the French en aventure, same sense; adventure has a similar construction. It can be found very early in English literature, as in Coeur de Lion (1307).

> Anger nould let him speake to the tree,
> Enaunter his rage mought cooled bee.
> --Edmund Spenser: The Shepherds Calendar (1579);
> lines 199-200.

ENCAVE: To hide in an underground place, such as a cavern or cellar. This word is adopted from the Old French encaver, "to store in a cellar," constructed from en, "in," and cave, "cellar."

> IAGO: Do but encave yourself,
> And mark the fleers, the gibes, and notable
> scorns,
> That dwell in every region of his face.
> --William Shakespeare: Othello (1604); Act IV,
> Scene 1.

ENEW: A word used in reference to a hunting-bird, such as a hawk, in driving other fowl into water. Through the Old French enewer, same sense, from eau, "water," and the Provencal aigua, the word is derived from the Latin word for water, aqua. It can be located as early as 1486 in the Book of St. Albans; in George Turbervile's Book of Falconrie (1575); Gervase Markham's Country Contentments (1611); and in Drayton:

> But when the whizzing bells the silent air do
> cleave,
> And that their greatest speed, them vainly do de-
> ceive;
> And the sharp cruel hawks, they [fowls] at their
> backs do view,
> Themselves for very fear they instantly ineaw.
> --Michael Drayton: Polyolbion (1612); song 20.

ENGLISH: To speak in words that any layman can understand; to render understandable to common ears. Used by Milton in 1649, and earlier by Shakespeare:

> SIR JOHN FALSTAFF: Briefly, I do mean to make
> love to Ford's wife: I spy entertainment in her;
> she discourses, she carves, she gives the leer of

invitation: I can construe the action of her familiar style; and the hardest voice of her behaviour,
to be English'd rightly, is, 'I am Sir John Falstaff's. "
--William Shakespeare: The Merry Wives of Windsor (1601); Act I, Scene 3.

ENLARD: To fill up with lard or fat. Lard comes through
the Old French from the Latin lardum, "bacon, lard, " and
largus, "large. " It is also related to the Greek larinos,
"fat. " It can be found in Burton's Anatomy of Melancholy
(1621), and in Shakespeare:

> ULYSSES:
> No, this thrice-worthy and right-valiant lord
> Must not so stale his palm, nobly acquired;
> Nor, by my will, assubjugate his merit,
> As amply titled as Achilles is,
> By going to Achilles:
> They were to enlard his fat-already pride,
> And add more coals to Cancer when he burns
> With entertaining great Hyperion.
> --William Shakespeare: Troilus and Cressida (ca.
> 1600); Act II, Scene 3.

ENSKY: A principally poetic word, meaning "to place in the
sky, " the use being restricted to the passive mood. Sky
comes through the Middle English from the Old Norse skȳ,
"cloud, " and is ultimately related to the Latin obscurus,
"dark. " It can be found in William Shenstone's Odes (1763),
as well as in Shakespeare:

> LUCIO:
> I hold you as a thing ensky'd and sainted;
> By your renouncement, an immortal spirit;
> And to be talk'd with in sincerity,
> As with a saint.
> --Wm. Shakespeare: Measure For Measure (1604);
> Act I, Scene 4.

A more recent example can be seen in Coventry Pat-
more's The Angel in the House (1858).

ESCARGATOIRE: An establishment for the cultivation of
snails for food. The word is an error for escargotière, the
French form, from escargot, "snail. "

At the Capuchins I saw the escargatoire, which I
took the more notice of, because I do not remember to have met with anything of the same in other
countries. It is a square place boarded in, and
filled with a vast quantity of large snails, that are
esteemed excellent food when they are well dressed.
The floor is strewed about half a foot deep with
several kinds of plants, among which the snails
nestle all the winter season. When Lent arrives
they open their magazines, and take out of them
the best meagre food in the world, for there is no
dish of fish that they reckon comparable to a rag-
out of snails.
    --Joseph Addison: Remarks On Several Parts of
        Italy: Fribourg, Berne, etc. (1703).

ESPRINGAL: A medieval military machine or catapult for
hurling of missiles, usually stones or bolts. Also spelled
springald, the word later, as springal, came to refer to a
noble youth. It is from the Old French espringale, and the
Spanish espingarda. It can be found in Camden in 1605, and,
more recently, in Leitch Ritchie's Windsor Castle and its
Environs (1840).

                    Nor the Gallic host remit
    Their eager efforts; some, with watery fence,
    Beneath the tortoise roof'd, with engines apt
    Drain painful; part, laden with wood, throw there
    Their buoyant burdens, labouring so to gain
    Firm footing: some the mangonels supply,
    Or charging with huge stones the murderous sling,
    Or petrary, or in the espringal
    Fix the brass-winged arrows.
    --Robert Southey: Joan of Arc (1796); Book VIII,
        lines 243-251.

ETIST: A scholar who pronounces the Greek letter eta with
an ē rather than with an ī.

    Reuchlin's school, of which Melanchthon was one,
    adhered to this, and were called Itacists, from the
    continual recurrence of the sound of Iota in mod-
    ern Greek, being thus distinguished from the Etists
    of Erasmus's party.
    --Henry Hallam: Introduction to the Literature of
        Europe (1839): Chapter V, Paragraph 25 of
        Volume I.

EVITE: A humorous name for a woman who wears scanty clothing; the male counterpart is known as an Adamite.

> "You know, sir, that in the beginning of the last century, there was a sect of men among us who called themselves Adamites, and appeared in public without clothes. This heresy may spring up in the other sex, if you do not put a timely stop to it, there being so many in all public places, who show so great an inclination to be Evites."
> --Joseph Addison: The Guardian, No. 134 (1713); paragraph 6.

EXCRUSTATION: The act of removing the covering from a book, the covering usually being made of some valuable metal, such as gold. The word is from the Latin excrustationem, from crusta, "crust, covering."

> Of course, various things--charity and need, as well as cupidity,--were likely to produce what was then termed excrustation, and to risk, if not almost to ensure, the destruction of the manuscript itself.
> --Rev. S. R. Maitland: The Dark Ages (1844); essay #13.

EYE-GLASS: An old formation, referring to the clear lens of the eye.

> LEONTES:
> Ha'not you seen, Camillo,--
> But that's past doubt, you have, or your eye-glass
> Is thicker than a cuckold's horn,--or heard,--
> For, to a vision so apparent, rumour
> Cannot be mute,--or thought,--for cogitation
> Resides not in that man that does not think,--
> My wife is slippery?
> --William Shakespeare: The Winter's Tale (1610); Act I, Scene 2.

-F-

FACY: Impudent, bold, or insolent: having the quality of "face" or "a bold front, unashamed." It refers also to the characteristic of courage to "face" the music.

> VOLPONE: These turdy-facy-nasty-paty-lousy-
> fartical rogues, with one poor groat's-worth of un-
> prepared antimony, finely wrapt up in several
> scartoccios, are able, very well, to kill their
> twenty a week, and play; yet, these meagre,
> starved spirits, who have half stopt the organs of
> their minds with earthy oppilations, want not their
> favourers among your shrivell'd sallad-eating arti-
> zans, who are overjoyed that they may have their
> half-pe'rth of physic; though it purge them into
> another world, it makes no matter.
> --Ben Jonson: Volpone (1606); Act II, Scene 1.

FADGE: A short, fat, lumpy-looking person, usually a man,
but occasionally a woman. The origin of this word is unknown; but it may be related with the verb fadge, meaning
"to be suitable," or with the noun fadge, meaning "a flat
bundle of sticks." The history of the verb form is also unknown, having appeared in literature in the 16th century.

> "Her oxen may die i' the house, billie,
>   And her kye into the byre,
> And I shall hae nothing to mysell
>   But a fat fadge by the fire."
> --Lord Thomas and Fair Annet in Child's Ballads;
>   stanza 8.

FAMBLE: A ring. The original meaning is "a hand," and
thus a ring came to be known as a famble also because it is
worn on the hand. The origin is unknown, but it may be
connected with the verb famble, "to fumble, to grope."
Used principally from the 17th to 19th centuries; a fambler
is another related word, meaning "a glove."

> BELFOND SENIOR: Look on my finger sirrah,
> look here; here's a famble, putt, putt; you don't
> know what a famble, a scout, or a tatler is, you
> putt.
> --Thomas Shadwell: The Squire of Alsatia (1688);
>   Act II, Scene 1.

FAMELIC: Appetizing; exciting the appetite; appealing to the
salivary senses; having the ability to cause hunger. This
word comes from the Latin famelicus, "hungry," formed
from the noun for "hunger," fames. cf. famine.

RABBI BUSY: And it were a sin of obstinacy, great obstinacy, high and horrible obstinacy, to decline or resist the good titillation of the famelic sense, which is the smell.
--Ben Jonson: Bartholomew Fair (1614); Act III, Scene 1.

FAP: Drunk. The origin is totally unknown; Dr. Johnson says that the word was most prevalent during Shakespeare's era.

SIR JOHN FALSTAFF: What say you, Scarlet and John?
BARDOLPH: Why, sir, for my part, I say the gentleman had drunk himself out of his five sentences--
SIR HUGH EVANS: It is his five senses: fie, what the ignorance is!
BARDOLPH: And being fap, sir, was, as they say, cashiered; and so conclusions passed the careires.
SLENDER: Ay, you spake in Latin then too; but 'tis no matter: I'll ne'er be drunk whilst I live again, but in honest, civil, godly company, for this trick: if I be drunk, I'll be drunk with those that have the fear of God, and not with drunken knaves.
--William Shakespeare: The Merry Wives of Windsor (1601); Act I, Scene 1.

FAT-SAGG: An old adjective meaning "having fat hanging down in large quantities." Sag comes through many influences, such as the Danish, Swedish, German, and Icelandic, and its basic meaning was "to sink."

And so between thundering and lightening, the bawd rose, first putting the snuff to an untimely death, a cruel and a lamentable murder, and then, with her fat-sagg chin hanging down like a cow's udder, lay reeking out at the window, demanding the reason why they did summon a parley.
--Thomas Middleton: The Black Book (1604).

FAUCET: An old derogatory name for a tavern-keeper or bartender. The word comes from the association of this individual with the faucet or spigot of the barrels of liquor or ale. It comes from the French fausset, "spigot," but further tracing of it is very uncertain.

> ADAM OVERDO: Dost thou hear, boy? There's
> for thy ale, and the remnant for thee. --Speak in
> thy faith of a faucet, now; is this goodly person
> before us here, this vapours, a knight of the
> knife?
> --Ben Jonson: Bartholomew Fair (1614); Act II,
>   Scene 1.

FAUSE-HOUSE: A vacant space or hollow within a corn-stack, which had one side exposed to the prevailing winds, in order to dry the corn; it was often used as a "play-house" for children, and, indeed, fause is nothing more than the Scottish form of "false," thus, "false-house."

> Nell had the fause-house in her min',
>   She pits hersel an' Rob in;
> In loving bleeze they sweetly join,
>   Till white in ase they're sobbin.
> --Robert Burns: Halloween (1785); stanza 10.

FAZENDA: A large, rambling home on an equally large estate or plantation; also, the estate or plantation itself. The word is taken directly from the Portuguese fazenda, which is related to the familiar Spanish hacienda. It can be located in Alexander Caldcleugh's Travels in South America (1825) and in George Gardner's Travels in the Interior of Brazil (1846).

> On such fazendas as these, I have no doubt the
> slaves pass happy and contended lives. On Satur-
> day and Sunday they work for themselves, and in
> this fertile climate the labour of two days is suf-
> ficient to support a man and his family for the
> whole week.
> --Charles Darwin: The Voyage of the Beagle (1845);
>   chapter 2.

FECKET: A Scottish name for a waistcoat or under-waist-coat; also, a shirt. The form is the same in the Scottish, but further origins are rather uncertain.

> Ye've heard this while how I've been licket,
> And by fell Death was nearly nicket:
> Grim loon! He got me by the fecket,
>   And sair me sheuk;

But by guid luck I lap a wicket,
      And turn'd a neuk.
--Robert Burns: To Collector Mitchell (1795);
      stanza 4.

FEE-FAW-FUM: This word originates in the famous nur-
sery story of Jack and the Beanstalk, in which it was spoken
by the giant when he discovered Jack's presence. The origin cannot be ascertained; but the word has evolved into different meanings, such as "a cry to frighten children, " or
"a bloodthirsty scream, " or, as is illustrated in the quotation, "a murderous person. " The spellings vary considerably; a more recent use can be found in Mary Ferrier's
The Inheritance (1824).

      WOODALL: Limberham must have found me out;
      that fe-fa-fum of a keeper would have smelt the
      blood of a cuckold-maker: They say, he was
      peeping and butting about in every cranny.
      --John Dryden: The Kind Keeper (1678); Act V,
          Scene 1.

FEEZE, FEIZE: To beat or to punish with a stick or whip;
also, to frighten away, to cause to flee. This word comes
through the Old English fésian, "to drive, " but further
sources are uncertain. The threat, "I'll feeze you" was an
extremely popular sentence in older writers, as is illustrated
in the quotation. Other examples of the use of feeze can be
seen in Shakespeare's The Taming of the Shrew (ca. 1595);
Beaumont & Fletcher's The Coxcomb (ca. 1613); Fletcher's
The Chances (1627); and in Massinger's Emperor of the East
(1631).

      LOVEWIT: You lie, boy;
      As sound as you; and I'm aforehand with you.
      KASTRIL: Anon!
      LOVEWIT: Come, will you quarrel? I will feize
      you, sirrah;
      Why do you not buckle to your tools?
      --Ben Jonson: The Alchemist (1610); Act V, Scene
          3.

FELLMONGER: One who trades or deals in the skins and
furs of animals, especially sheep-skin. From the old word
fell, "skin, hide, " and monger, "a merchant. "

      BEAUGARD: As, for example, to endure the

familiarities of a rogue that shall cock his greasy
hat in my face, when he duns me, and at the same
time vail it [take it off] to an over-grown deputy of
the ward, though a frowsy fellmonger.
  --Thomas Otway: The Soldier's Fortune (1681);
    Act IV, Scene 1.

FERNSHAW: A thicket or brush of fern, from shaw, "a
wood. " This word is also known as fernbrake, as in the
old proverb, "It is a blind goose that knows not a fox from
a fernbrake. " Shaw is related to the noun shag.

And so, just giving her a glimpse
Of a purse, with the air of a man who imps
The wing of the hawk that shall fetch the hernshaw,
He bade me take the Gipsy mother
And set her telling some story or other
Of hill or dale, oak-wood or fernshaw,
To wile away a weary hour
For the lady left alone in her bower,
Whose mind and body craved exertion
And yet shrank from all better diversion.
  --Robert Browning: The Flight of the Duchess
    (1845); stanza 13.

FEWMAND: To encrust with filth; to dirty or soil; to cause
to become dirty. A device used by Ben Jonson:

LOREL: Why scorn you me?
Because I am a herdsman, and feed swine!
I am a lord of other geer:--This fine
Smooth bawson cub, the young grice of a gray,
Twa tiny urchins, and this ferret gay.
EARINE: Out on 'em! what are these?
LOREL: I give 'em ye,
As presents, mistress.
EARINE: O the fiend on thee!
Gae, take them hence; they fewmand all the
    claithes,
And prick my coats: hence with 'em, limmer lown,
Thy vermin and thyself, thyself art one!
Ay, lock me up--all's well when thou art gone.
  --Ben Jonson: The Sad Shepherd (1637); Act II,
    Scene 1.

FEWTERER: Originally, one who takes care of greyhounds;
a dog-keeper who takes care of the kennels. Also, often

the name of the animal cared for was prefixed to this word,
as in fox-fewterer, or yeoman-fewterer.   Later, the sense
widened to include any servant.   The word comes through
the Anglo-French veutrier, the Old French veutre, Italian
veltro, from the Latin veltrum, vertragum, "greyhound. "
It is a very old word, and can be found in Sir Gawain and
the Green Knight (ca. 1340) as well as in the following:

> PUNTARVOLO: Stay; who be these that address
> themselves towards us? What Carlo! Now by the
> sincerity of my soul, welcome; welcome, gentle-
> men: and how dost thou, thou Grand Scourge, or
> Second Untruss of the time?
> CARLO BUFFONE: Faith, spending my metal in
> this reeling world (here and there), as the sway of
> my affection carries me, and perhaps stumble upon
> a yeoman-feuterer, as I do now; or one of for-
> tune's mules, laden with treasure, and an empty
> cloak-bag, following him, gaping when a bag will
> untie.
> --Ben Jonson: Every Man Out of His Humour
>   (1599); Act II, Scene 1.

> BIANCA:
> As you acknowledge that young handsome wench,
> That lies by such a bilbo-blade, that bends
> With every pass he makes to th'hilts, most miser-
>   able,
> A dry-nurse to his coughs, a fewterer
> To such a nasty fellow, a robb'd thing
> Of all delights youth looks for.
> --John Fletcher: The Woman's Prize (ca. 1612);
>   Act II, Scene 2.

FEWTRILS: Little, trifling toys; mere trifles.   The etymology of this word is uncertain.

> 'I ha' paid her to keep awa' fra' me.   These five
> year I ha' paid her.   I ha' gotten decent fewtrils
> about me agen.   I ha' lived hard and sad, but not
> ashamed and fearfo' a' the minnits o' my life.
> Last night, I went home.   There she lay upon my
> harstone!   There she IS! "
> --Charles Dickens: Hard Times (1854); Book I,
>   chapter 11.

FIDDLECOME: Silly, foolish, full of nonsense; flighty.   The

word is short for fiddle-come-faddle, a form of fiddle-faddle.
Fiddle-faddle comes from the old verb fiddle, "to dawdle. "
The origins are unknown for certain, but tracing reveals
German, Danish, and Norse influences.   In 1777 Richard
Brinsley Sheridan used the word in his A Trip to Scarbor-
ough.

> HOYDEN: Prithee, Nurse, don't stand ripping up
> old stories to make one ashamed before one's love.
> Do you think such a fine proper gentleman as he
> cares for a fiddlecome tale of a draggle-tailed
> girl?   If you have a mind to make him have a
> good opinion of a woman, don't tell him what one
> did then, tell him what one can do now.
> --Sir John Vanbrugh: The Relapse (1696); Act IV,
>   Scene 1.

FIDIBUS: A match of paper used to light a pipe.   The im-
mediate source of this word is in the German, but further
tracing is uncertain.

> I strolled into an adjoining room after dinner,
> which looked out upon the principal street.   A lit-
> tle knot of smokers stood at the door.   I was just
> lighting my pipe, when one remarked to a friend
> at his elbow, "Hast du das Spectakel gesehen?"
> (Hast thou seen the show?)   I paused to catch the
> reply, for my heart misgave me, and the "fidibus"
> fell from my hand.
> --Samuel Longfellow, ed.: The Life of Henry
>   Wadsworth Longfellow (1891); Volume I, chapter
>   11.

FIG OF SPAIN, FIGO, FICO: An old gesture of contempt,
in which the thumb was thrust between two of the closed
fingers, or was stuck in the mouth.   Very popular in the
16th and 17th centuries, the word comes through the French
figue from the Italian fica, "fig. " It has been suggested that
"to give the fig of Spain" referred to a poisoned fig that was
used to eliminate a person who was considered undesirable;
but perhaps the origin is obscene.   In Spanish, to give this
gesture was known as dar la higa, and was spelled in many
ways which gave rise to the varied spellings also in English.

> PISTOL: Die and be damn'd! and figo for thy
> friendship!
> FLUELLEN: It is well.

PISTOL: The fig of Spain!   (EXIT)
FLUELLEN: Very goot.
GOWER: Why, this is an arrant counterfeit rascal; I remember him now; a bawd, a cutpurse.
FLUELLEN: I'll assure you, a' utter'd as prave
'ords at the pridge as you shall see in a summer's
day.   But it is very well; what he has spoke to
me, that is well, I warrant you, when time is
serve.
--William Shakespeare: King Henry The Fifth
    (1599); Act III, scene 6.

FILCH: An old device consisting of a wooden staff hooked
at one end, used by robbers for "filching" certain articles
from atop hedges, window ledges, etc., similar to the
curved staff used to remove untalented performers from the
stage.   The verb filch is of unknown origin.   It can be
found in Dekker, and in the following:

HIGGEN:
That thou art chosen, venerable Clause,
Our kind and sovereign, monarch o' the maunders,
Thus we throw up our nab-cheats first, for joy,
And then our filches.
--John Fletcher: Beggars' Bush (1622); Act II,
    Scene 1.

FILIBEG, PHILIBEG: The short plaid kilt worn by the
Scottish Highlanders.   Also, when used in the plural form,
long drawers.   The word comes from the Gaelic feileadh-
beag, "kilt," constructed of feileadh, "a fold," and beag,
"little"; hence, "little fold, little plait. "

With his philibeg, an' tartan plaid,
An' guid claymore down by his side,
The ladies' hearts he did trepan,
My gallant, braw John Highlandman.
--Robert Burns: The Jolly Beggars (1794); Air
    IV, Chorus stanza 2.

FILLIP: Originally, the small motion of casting a pebble by
placing it next to the thumb and cocking one finger behind
that thumb, and suddenly releasing the finger to propel the
pebble away.   As the word evolved, it came to mean a
small tap given in this manner; then anything small or
trifling; and, more recently, a short, smart, stinging blow
given in boxing.   It was very widely used, principally in the

17th and 18th centuries, and can be found in the writings of
Thomas Jefferson. The origin is unknown, but it is prob-
ably an onomatopoeic word from the sound of the nail hit-
ting the object. It can be located in Sir Hugh Platt's The
Jewell-House of Art and Nature (1594) and in The Irish
Hubbub (1619) of Capt. Barnaby Rich.

> DON JOHN:
> Sir, he is worth your knowledge, and a gentleman
> (If I that so much love him may commend him),
> Of free and virtuous parts; and one, if foul play
> Should fall upon us (for which fear I brought him),
> Will not fly back for fillips.
> --John Fletcher: The Chances (1627); Act III,
>   Scene 4.

FIPPLE: The underlip, when loose and dangling, as in certain grazing-animals; hence, "the plug at the mouth of a
wind-instrument, by which its volume was contracted"
(N.E.D.). The verb form of this word means "to whimper"
or "to drool." The exact origin is unknown; but there are
certain similar words, such as the Icelandic flipi, "lip of a
horse," to which it might be related. In the Scottish, it is
spelled faiple, and can also refer to the crest of a turkey.

> Let there be a recorder made with two fipples, at
> each end one: the trunk of it of the length of two
> recorders, and the holes answerable towards each
> end; and let two play the same lesson upon it, at
> an unison; and let it be noted whether the sound be
> confounded, or amplified, or dulled.
> --Francis Bacon: Sylva Sylvarum (1626); para-
>   graph 161.

FIRE-DOG: One of the andirons before a fireplace. Perhaps it comes from the French chenet, same sense, which
is the diminutive form of chien, "dog," through meaning-
association rather than through word-form.

> He was none of your flippant young fellows, who
> would call for a tankard of mulled ale, and make
> themselves as much at home as if they had or-
> dered a hogshead of wine ... none of your free-
> and-easy companions, who would scrape their
> boots upon the firedogs in the common room, and
> be not at all particular on the subject of spittoons.
> --Charles Dickens: Barnaby Rudge (1841); chap-
>   ter 10.

FIRK, FERK: 1) A sudden, sharp blow, often with a whip; a sword-thrust. 2) A trick, a ploy; subterfuge. 3) Any loud commotion or disturbance. 4) A dancing-partner. 5) As a verb, to play the fiddle or violin. The Old English form of the word was fercian; perhaps it comes from an old verb of the same spelling which meant "to support, to feed"; but the exact origin is unknown. Earl Orrery used sense 1 in 1679; sense 2 can be found in Barrey's Ram-Alley (1611) and in the quotation below; sense 4 is probably used in James Shirley's Hyde Park (1632); and the verb sense is illustrated in the second quote below.

THWACK:
Why, this was such a firk of piety,
I ne'er heard of: bury her gold with her!
'Tis strange her old shoes were not interr'd too,
For fear the days of Edgar should return,
When they coin'd leather.
--Sir William Davenant: The Wits (1636); Act V,
    Scene 2.

DON JOHN: Come, sir, dispatch; for brevity is as convenient in posset as it is in speech. I'll give you a song if you will call for music.
SANCHO: Firk your fiddles!
--Sir William Davenant: The Man's The Master
    (1668); Act III, Scene 2.

FLAPDOODLE: Nonsense; a trifle; talk with little truth in it; a pretty toy of no use to anyone. The origin is unknown, but perhaps it is related to fadoodle, also meaning "nonsense." It originated in the nineteenth century.

Well, by and by the king he gets up and comes forward a little, and works himself up and slobbers out a speech, all full of tears and flapdoodle, about its being a sore trial for him and his poor brother to lose the diseased, and to miss seeing diseased alive after the long journey of four thousand mile, but it's a trial that's sweetened and sanctified to us by this dear sympathy and these holy tears, and so he thanks them out of his heart and out of his brother's heart, because out of their mouths they can't, words being too weak and cold, and all that kind of rot and slush, till it was just sickening; and then he blubbers out a pious goody-goody Amen, and turns himself loose and

goes to crying fit to bust.
--Mark Twain: The Adventures of Huckleberry
Finn (1884); chapter 25.

FLAP-DRAGON: A game in which raisins were caught from
burning brandy and extinguished and cooled on the tongue;
hence, the raisins that were used were called flap-dragons.
Further senses include trifles, and a derogatory name for
a German or a Dutchman.   The word comes from the verb
flap, "to toss," and from dragon, in reference to the fire-
breathing variety.   Snapdragon is a related form.   In both
of the quotations, the sense is raisin:

> MOTH (aside to COSTARD): They have been at a
> great feast of languages, and stolen the scraps.
> COSTARD: O, they have lived long on the alms-
> basket of words.   I marvel thy master hath not
> eaten thee for a word; for thou art no so long by
> the head as honorificabilitudinitatibus; thou art
> easier swallow'd than a flap-dragon.
> --William Shakespeare: Love's Labour's Lost (ca.
> 1595); Act V, Scene 1.

> SECOND COURTIER: What, so quick, sir?
> Will you not allow yourself a breathing-time?
> LYSANDER:
> I've breath enough at all times, Lucifer's musk-
> cod,
> To give your perfumed worship three venués;
> A sound old man puts his thrust better home
> Than a spiced young man; there I.   (They fence).
> SECOND COURTIER: They have at you, four-
> score.
> LYSANDER: You lie, twenty, I hope, and you
> shall find it.
> SIMONIDES: I'm glad I miss'd this weapon, I'd
> had an eye
> Popt out ere this time, or my two butter-teeth
> Thrust down my throat instead of a flap-dragon.
> --Thomas Middleton & William Rowley: The Old
> Law (1599); Act III, Scene 2.

FLAWN: A type of flat cheesecake or custard; often, a
pancake.   Also, the village festival at which flawns were
sold.   The word is descended through the Old French flaon
from the West Germanic flapon-, basically meaning "flat."

"He that looks on death, lady," answered Dryfes-
dale, "as that which he may not shun, and which
has its own fixed and certain hour, is ever prepared for it. He that is hanged in May will eat
no flaunes in midsummer--so there is the moan
made for the old serving-man. "
--Sir Walter Scott: The Abbot (1820); chapter 33.

FLEAK: Some type of derogatory expression directed toward
a woman; its origin is unknown, but it may be related to
fleak, "flake, a splinter, a little bit. "

> MISTRESS SNORE:
> I will not forbear; you might ha'let your house
> To honest women, not to bawds. Fie upon you!
> QUEASY:
> Fie upon me! 'tis well known I'm the mother
> Of children! scurvy fleak! 'tis not for naught
> You boil eggs in your gruel: and your man Samp-
> son
> Owes my son-in-law, the surgeon, ten groats
> For turpentine, which you have promis'd to pay
> Out of his Christmas box.
> --Sir William Davenant: The Wits (1636); Act III,
> Scene 1.

FLEG: A Scottish word for a terrible fright or a scare; also, when used as a verb, to drive away by fright. The
word comes from the Old English fleczan, same sense, but
further origins are uncertain. Allan Ramsay used it, as
well as did Scott:

> 'I got a fleg, and was ready to jump out o' my
> skin, though naebody offered to whirl it aff my
> body as a man wad bark a tree. "
> --Sir Walter Scott: Rob Roy (1817); chapter 18.

FLIBBERTIGIBBET: A name referring to a fiendish devil.
Also, a light, frivolous, gossiping person, or a little urchin.
The origin is unknown, but it is probably mere doubletalk.
The earliest form is flibbergib, which Dr. Murray believes
to be the original; the second element probably entered by
association with gibbet, "the gallows. "

> EDGAR: This is the foul fiend Flibbertigibbet: he
> begins at curfew, and walks till the first cock; he
> gives the web and the pin, squints the eye, and

makes the hare-lip; mildews the white wheat, and
hurts the poor creature of earth.
--William Shakespeare: King Lear (ca. 1606);
   Act III, Scene 4.

FLICKERMOUSE, FLITTERMOUSE: A bat; the word is imi-
tated from a similar German construction, fledermaus, same
sense. Also spelled flindermouse.

COL. TIPTO: Come, I will see the flickermouse, my Fly.
--Ben Jonson: The New Inn (1628); Act III, Scene
1.

ALKEN: Green-bellied snakes, blue fire-drakes
   in the sky,
And giddy flitter-mice with leather wings!
--Ben Jonson: The Sad Shepherd (1637); Act II,
   Scene 2.

FLIX: The down of various animals, such as the beaver or
the rabbit. The origin is unknown, but it may be related
to the verb fly. Uses can be found in Dryden; in John Dy-
er's The Fleece (1757); and in Henry Hart Milman's Samor,
Lord of the Bright City (1818).

Hair, such a wonder of flix and floss,
   Freshness and fragrance--floods of it, too!
Gold, did I say? Nay, gold's mere dross:
   Here, Life smiled, "Think what I meant to do!"
And Love sighed, "Fancy my loss!"
--Robert Browning: Gold Hair (1863); stanza 4.

FLOATING ISLAND: A delicious dessert, made of a type of
custard with whipped cream or egg-white "floating" on top,
resembling islands. Benjamin Franklin remarked about it
in his letters.

Nor was that most wonderful object of domestic
art called trifle wanting, with its charming con-
fusion of cream and cake and almonds and jam and
jelly and wine and cinnamon and froth; nor yet the
marvellous floating-island,--name suggestive of all
that is romantic in the imaginations of youthful
palates.
--Oliver Wendell Holmes: Elsie Venner (1860);
   chapter 7.

FLOCCI-NAUCI-NIHILI-PILI-FICATION: An estimation of an object with regard to its worthlessness; an accounting of something as being totally without merit of any kind. It is formed from four Latin words, flocci, nauci, nihili, and pili, all synonyms for "at a very small price," in imitation of a rule in the famous Eton Latin Grammar book. It was used by Southey in 1816, and by Scott in his Journal for 1829.

> I loved him for nothing so much as his flocci-
> nauci-nihili-pili-fication of money.
> --William Shenstone: Letters (1741); letter 22.

FODGEL: A Scottish word, which, when used as an adjective, signifies something "fat" or "plump," and when used as a noun, refers to a "fat, jolly person." It comes from fodge, which is a variation on fadge (see fadge).

> If in your bounds ye chance to light
> Upon a fine, fat, fodgel wight,
> O' stature short but genius bright,
>   That's he, mark weel:
> And wow! he has an unco sleight
>   O' cauk and keel.
> --Robert Burns: On the Late Captain Grose's
>   Peregrinations Thro' Scotland (1789); stanza 2.

The word was also employed by Allan Ramsay, another Scottish poet.

FOIST: A mean trick; also, the one who is responsible for the act: a rogue, a pickpocket. Principally used in the 16th, 17th, and 18th centuries, it comes from the verb foist, "to cheat," which was a dicing term for using false dice. The origin is uncertain, but the word probably comes from the Dutch vuisten, "to take in hand," from vuist, "hand" or "fist." This also referred to gaming, where one person grasped a certain number of objects, such as coins, pebbles, etc., in one hand, and others were required to guess how many he had. As could be expected, Robert Greene made use of this word, as did Dekker & Middleton in The Roaring Girl (1611).

> VOLTORE: Scarce,
> To the discovery of your tricks, I fear.
> You are his, only? and mine also, are you not?
> MOSCA: Who? I, sir?

VOLTORE: You, sir. What device is this
About a Will?
MOSCA: A plot for you, sir.
VOLTORE: Come,
Put not your foists upon me; I shall scent them.
--Ben Jonson: Volpone (1606); Act III, Scene 5.

FONDA: In Spanish-speaking lands, a word for an inn or a
hotel. It comes through the Spanish fonda from the Arabic
funduq, same sense, and is also related to the Greek pan-
dokos, "innkeeper." Used by Sir Francis Bond Head in
Rough Notes taken during some Rapid Journeys across the
Pampas and among the Andes (1826).

> By the time he reached the highway of the town it
> was quite dark, and he plunged into the first fonda
> at the wayside, and endeavored to forget his woes
> and his weariness in aguardiente.
> --Bret Harte: The Story of a Mine (1877); chapter
>   3.

FOOKER: A word of uncertain origin and meaning; it probably refers to a banker or financier, possibly from Fugger,
the name of a famous banking family of Augsburg during the
15th and 16th centuries.

> PURSENET: Pist! a supply;--carry't closely, my
> little fooker,--how much?
> BOY: Three pound, sir.
> PURSENET: Good boy! take out another lesson.
> --How now, gentlemen?
> TAILBY: Devil's in't, did you e'er see such a
> hand?
> PURSENET: I set you these three angels.
> BOY: My master may set high, for all his stakes
> are drawn out of other men's pockets.
> --Thomas Middleton: Your Five Gallants (ca.
>   1606); Act II, Scene 3.

FOOT-LICKER: A toadying slave, a fawner, one who "licks
the foot" of his beloved master. Used principally from the
17th to 19th centuries.

> CALIBAN:
> Prithee, my kind, be quiet. See'st thou here,
> This is the mouth o' the cell: no noise, and enter.
> Do that good mischief which may make this island

Thine own for ever, and I, thy Caliban,
For aye thy foot-licker.
--William Shakespeare: The Tempest (1611); Act
    IV, Scene 1.

FOPDOODLE: A silly fool or simpleton; numbskull, ninny-
hammer. Dr. Johnson says: "A fool, an insignificant
wretch." Principally a 17th-century word, it comes from
fop, "a fool," and doodle, "to dawdle, to trifle."

> Quoth he, This scheme of th'Heavens set,
> Discovers how in fight you met
> At Kingston with a May-pole idol,
> And that y' were bang'd, both back and side well;
> And though you overcame the Bear,
> The Dogs beat you at Brentford fair;
> Where sturdy butchers broke your noddle,
> And handled you like a fop-doodle.
> --Samuel Butler: Hudibras (1664); Part Second,
>   Canto III, lines 991-998.

FOU: An old Scottish word meaning variously "drunk,"
"fat," or "conceited." It comes from the common adjective
full, and can be found in Ross's Helenore (1768) and Scott's
The Monastery (1820), as well as in Burns:

> The clachan [village] yill had made me canty,
> I was na fou, but just had plenty.
> --Robert Burns: Death and Dr. Hornbook (1785);
>   stanza 3.

FOURGON: A wagon or van for carrying luggage or other
articles for transportation. From the French fourgon, same
meaning, it can be found in Mrs. Henry Wood's novel St.
Martin's Eve (1866), and in Thackeray:

> There was Sir John's great carriage that would
> hold thirteen people; my Lord Methuselah's car-
> riage, my Lord Bareacres' chariot, britzka, and
> fourgon, that anybody might pay for who liked.
> --William Makepeace Thackeray: Vanity Fair
>   (1848); chapter 62.

FOX: An old sword, which possibly obtained its name from
the fact that the head of a wolf was often engraved on the
hilt--but the "wolf" became mistaken for a "fox." It can be
found in John Ford's Love's Sacrifice (1633), and in Scott:

"Come, come, comrade," said Lambourne, "here
is enough done, and more than enough--put up your
fox, and let us be jogging--The Black Bear growls
for us."
--Sir Walter Scott: Kenilworth (1821); chapter 4.

FRAMPOLD: Cross, vile-tempered, disagreeable. "Peevish, boisterous, rugged, cross-grained" (Johnson). Also,
when referring to a horse: Spirited, lively. The origin is
unknown, but perhaps it has descended from the Scots
frample, "to cause to be in disarray, to disorder." It can
be found in Jonson and Bunyan, in Dekker & Middleton's
The Roaring Girl (1611), and in Scott's Peveril of the Peak
(1823).

MISTRESS QUICKLY: Marry, she hath received
your letter; for the which she thanks you a thousand times: and she gives you to notify, that her
husband will be absence from his house between
ten and eleven.
SIR JOHN FALSTAFF: Ten and eleven?
MISTRESS QUICKLY: Ay, forsooth; and then you
may come and see the picture, she says, that you
wot of;--Master Ford, her husband, will be from
home. Alas, the sweet woman leads an ill life
with him! he's a very jealousy man: she leads a
very frampold life with him, good heart.
--William Shakespeare: The Merry Wives of Windsor (1601); Act II, Scene 2.

FRANION: A fellow of gay, free, loose behavior; a reckless
lover. Also, a loose woman; a good friend. The origin is
unknown, but perhaps it is related to the Old French fraig-
nant, "breaking, shattering." It can be found in Turberville,
in Spenser's Faerie Queene, and in Edward IV.

Fine merry franions,
Wanton companions,
My days are ev'n banyans
   With thinking upon ye!
--Charles Lamb: Going Or Gone (1810); stanza 1.

FRICATRICE: A lewd, indecent woman; a mistress, harlot.
From the Latin fricare, "to rub."

SIR POLITICK WOULD-BE: The gentleman, I believe it, is of worth,

And of our nation.
LADY POLITICK WOULD-BE: Ay, your White-
   friars nation.
Come, I blush for you, master Would-be, I;
And am asham'd you should have no more forehead,
Than thus to be the patron, or St. George,
To a lewd harlot, a base fricatrice,
A female devil, in a male outside.
--Ben Jonson: Volpone (1606); Act IV, Scene 1.

FRIPPERY: Old clothes which are no longer worn; also,
fine garments, perhaps too fine; or, the place where such
clothes are sold. In a figurative sense, the word can mean
"joy, frivolity." It comes from the Old French freperie,
same meaning, from frepe, ferpe, "rag." Examples of its
use can be located in Ford's Fancies (1638), in Horace Walpole's correspondence, and in Washington Irving.

FOIBLE: Humh (says he) I hear you are laying
   designs against me too (says he) and Mrs. Milla-
   mant is to marry my uncle; (he does not suspect
   a word of your Ladiship;) but (says he) I'll fit you
   for that, I warrant you (says he) I'll hamper you
   for that (says he) you and your old frippery too
   (says he) I'll handle you--
LADY WISHFORT: Audacious villain! handle me,
   wou'd he durst--frippery? old frippery! Was there
   ever such a foul-mouth'd fellow? I'll be marry'd
   to morrow, I'll be contracted to night.
--William Congreve: The Way of the World (1700);
   Act III, Scene 5.

FROWZE, FRUZ-TOWER, FROWES: An old type of wig
worn in the 16th and 17th centuries by women, made of
frizzled hair. The origin of the word is not known, but it
may come from frounce, "wrinkle," in association with friz
or fuzz. Also spelled frouze, frowze-tower.

BELINDA: Why, the father bought a powder-horn,
   and an almanack, and a comb-case; the mother, a
   great fruz-towr, and a fat amber-necklace; the
   daughters only tore two pair of kid-leather gloves,
   with trying 'em on--oh gad, here comes the fool
   that din'd at my Lady Freelove's t'other day.
--William Congreve: The Old Bachelor (1693);
   Act IV, Scene 8.

FUD: Principally a Scottish form meaning "the buttocks, the seat." Also, the tail or scut of a rabbit, or a pony-tail. The origin of this word is unknown, but may be related to the old Sanskrit word for buttocks, putau.

> They toom'd their pocks, they pawn'd their duds,
> They scarcely left to coor their fuds.
> --Robert Burns: The Jolly Beggars (1794); reci-
> tativo VIII.

> Do you cock your fud at me, you tiny thief you?--
> he struck at it with his stick. Tip the duck dived
> and did not rise again.
> --Michael Scott: Tom Cringle's Log (1859); page
> 459.

FULHAM, FULLUM, FULLAM, FULLAMS: A term in dic-ing which referred to a die loaded at one corner; a throw of 4, 5, or 6 was known as the "high fulham," and a toss of 1, 2, or 3 was called the "low fulham." The word also referred in general to false dice. The origin is uncertain; it has been suggested that it refers to the place Fulham, in southwest London, which was once a notorious gambling spot. But it may also be related to fullan, meaning "full one," in reference to the die. Perhaps a combination of both senses? Butler used it in Hudibras, and more recently it was employed by Sir Arthur Conan Doyle in Micah Clarke (1889).

> PISTOL: Let vultures gripe thy guts! for gourd
>   and fullam holds,
> And high and low beguiles the rich and poor:
> Tester I'll have in pouch when thou shalt lack,
> Base Phrygian Turk!
> --William Shakespeare: The Merry Wives of Wind-
>   sor (1601); Act I, Scene 3.

FUNK: To smoke; to annoy someone by blowing smoke in his face; also, to stink, to have a terrible odor. The ori-gin is uncertain; perhaps through the Old French funkier from the Latin fumicare, from fumus, "smoke." The word appears in many writers: in William King (1699); D'Urfey's Pills to Purge Melancholy (1719); Tobias Smollett's Count Fathom (1753); Thomas Bridges' travesty of Homer (1764); George Huddesford's Salmagundi: Original Poems (1791); and in Frederick Marryat's Jacob Faithful (1835).

But there my triumph's straw-fire flared and
    funked;
Their betters took their turn to see and say:
The Prior and the learned pulled a face
And stopped all that in no time.
--Robert Browning: Fra Lippo Lippi (1855); lines
    172-175.

FUSTY: A word of uncertain meaning and origin. It is believed to mean "damp, ill-tempered, peevish, stale, " etc.,
possibly formed from fust, "a strong odor. " It may be related to foisty, "moldy. "

    At noon home to dinner, where my wife still in a
    melancholy, fusty humour, and crying, and do not
    tell me plainly what it is.
    --Samuel Pepys' Diary: June 18th, 1668.

-G-

GABLOCK, GAVELOCK, GAFF: An old word of several
meanings: (1) a metallic spur placed around the leg of a
fighting cock; (2) a large fork for farm use; (3) a lever;
(4) a crowbar. Also spelled gaffle, gafflet. The word
comes through the Old English gafeluc, from gafel, "fork, "
and is related to and often synonymous with gavelock, "a
spear. "

    Gablocks are spurs made of iron, or brass, or
    silver and are fixed on the legs of such cocks as
    want their natural spurs, some call them gaffs.
    --Randle Holme: The Academy of the Armoury
        (1688); pg. 252.

GADE, GAID: A metal crossbar; in Scotland, the metal bar
which extended across a prison cell and to which the handcuffs and shackles of the prisoners were fastened. The exact origin of the word is uncertain, but it is related to gad,
"a nail, " from the Old Norse word for same, "gaddr. "

    This mode of securing prisoners was universally
    practiced in Scotland after condemnation. When a
    man received sentence of death, he was put upon
    the Gad, as it was called, that is, secured to the
    bar of iron ... The practice subsisted in Edin-
    burgh till the old jail was taken down some years

since, and perhaps may be still in use.
--Sir Walter Scott: Guy Mannering (1815); chapter
57, footnote.

GAMASH: Bootleggings worn for protection in inclement
weather or in hostile surroundings to keep water, mud, etc.,
from splashing on the legs. It comes through the French
gamache, the Italian gamascia, the Provencal garamacha,
and the Portuguese guadamecim, "leather," probably derived
from the Arabic ghadāmasī, from the proper name Ghadā-
mas, a center of the leather trade in Tripoli. Uses of this
word can be found in Nashe, John Marston, and in Randle
Holme's Academy of the Armoury (1688).

> He threw himself as he spoke upon a chair, and
> indolently, but gracefully, received the kind offices
> of Albert, who undid the coarse buttonings of the
> leathern gamashes which defended his legs.
> --Sir Walter Scott: Woodstock (1826); chapter 21.

GANCANACH, GANCANAGH: A type of sprite, very well
defined by Yeats:

> Irish gean-canach--i. e., love-talker, a kind of
> fairy appearing in lonesome valleys, a dudeen
> (tobacco-pipe) in his mouth, making love to milk-
> maids, etc.
> --William Butler Yeats, ed.: Irish Fairy & Folk
> Tales (1888); Loughleagh.

GANCH, GAUNCH: A deep wound caused by the tusk of a
wild boar; also, to snarl, to snap the teeth, to impale.
From the French gancher, and the Italian ganciare, "to impale," from gancio, "hook." The word can be found in
Sandys' translation of Ovid, in Dryden, and in Scott:

> "I have heard my father say, who was a forester
> at the Cabrach, that a wild boar's gaunch is more
> easily healed than a hurt from the deer's horn,
> for so says the old woodman's rhyme--
>> If thou be hurt with horn of hart, it brings thee
>>   to thy bier;
>> But tusk of boar shall leeches heal, thereof
>>   have lesser fear. "
> --Sir Walter Scott: The Bride of Lammermoor
> (1818); chapter 9.

GARDYLOO: In old Edinburgh, a shout of warning given before throwing slop, garbage, or dirty water out of a window
and into the street.   Roughly, "Look out!" the origin of this
appears to be in a corruption of the French phrase gare
l'eau ("beware the water!") into gare de l'eau.   It is also
spelled garde loo, gardiloo, jordeloo, etc.   Used principally
in the 18th and 19th centuries, the word can be found in
Laurence Sterne's A Sentimental Journey (1768) and in Tobias
Smollett's Humphrey Clinker (1771), as well as in Scott:

> "But the other night comes a Highland quean of a
> lass, and she flashes, God kens what, out at the
> eastmost window of Mrs. MacPhail's house, that's
> the superior tenement.   I believe the auld women
> wad hae greed, for Luckie MacPhail sent down
> the lass to tell my friend Mrs. Crombie that she
> had made the gardyloo out of the wrang window,
> out of respect for twa Highlandmen that were
> speaking Gaelic in the close below the right ane. "
> --Sir Walter Scott: The Heart of Midlothian (1818);
>   chapter 27.

GAZEHOUND: A type of hunting dog which relies on its
eyes to hunt down its prey rather than on its nose.   It can
be found in Folkingham's Epitome of Surveying Methodised
(1610) and in Scott's Marmion (1808), as well as in the following:

> At this very moment, who should come into the
> end of the passage upon them but the heavy writer
> of these doings, I, John Ridd, myself, and walk-
> ing the faster, it may be, on account of the noise
> I mentioned.   I entered the house with some wrath
> upon me at seeing the gaze-hounds in the yard;
> for it seems a cruel thing to me to harass the
> birds in the breeding time.
> --R. D. Blackmore: Lorna Doone (1869); chapter
>   22.

GELT: An insane person or lunatic.   From the Irish geilt,
"a mad, frothing individual. "

> Which when as fearefull Amoret perceived,
> She staid not the utmost and thereof to try,
> But like a ghastly gelt, whose wits are reaved,
> Ran forth in hast with hideous outcry,
> For horrour of his shamefull villany.

--Edmund Spenser: The Faerie Queene, Book IV
(1596); Canto VII, stanza 21.

GENERALESS: A general's wife; or, rarely, a female general. Carlyle used the latter sense in 1837, and the former
is illustrated in the following quotation:

My service and dear affections to the General and
Generaless. I hear she is very kind to thee; it
adds to all other obligations. My love to all. I
am
Thy dear Father,
OLIVER CROMWELL;
October 25, 1646
London.
--Oliver Cromwell to his daughter, Bridget Ireton,
at Cornbury, the General's Quarters.

GIBUS-HAT: The tall, collapsible opera hat or crush hat,
usually made of black silk. Gibus is from the surname of
the first maker of the hat.

Ask little Tom Prig, who is there in all his glory,
knows everybody, has a story about everyone; and,
as he trips home to his lodgings in Jermyn Street,
with his gibus-hat and his little glazed pumps,
thinks he is the fashionablest young fellow in town,
and that he really has passed a night of exquisite
enjoyment.
--William Makepeace Thackeray: The Book of
Snobs (1848); chapter 18.

GILLIAN: A term for a girl, especially one of flirtatious
tendencies, similar to jill. The origin of the word is in the
Latin proper name Juliana, from the masculine Julius.

ALATHE: What will become on's, sir?
LURCHER'S MISTRESS:
She is cold, dead-cold. --D'ye find your conscience?
D'ye bring your Gillians hither? Nay, she's punish'd,
Your conceal'd love's cas'd up.
--John Fletcher & James Shirley: The Night-
Walker (1625); Act II, Scene 3.

GILT: A thief, robber, or burglar, or the pick-lock or
skeleton key employed by such people. The origin of the

word is unknown; it can be found in Head's Canting Academy
(1673) and in John Melton's Astrologaster (1620). Francis
Grose tells us: "A thief who picks locks, so called from
the gilt or picklock key: many of them are so expert, that,
from the lock of a church door to that of the smallest cabinet, they will find means to open it: these go into reputable
public houses, where, pretending business, they contrive to
get into private rooms, up stairs, where they open any
bureaus or trunks, they happen to find there."

> "We shall have the whole village upon us while
> you're striking the jigger. Use the gilt, man!"
> --W. Harrison Ainsworth: Jack Sheppard (1839);
>   chapter 18.

GIPON: A medieval under-garment resembling a tunic, usually worn beneath the mail or under the hauberk. The word
comes from the Old French gipon, jupon, "tunic," from
gipe, jupe, "cassock." This is a very old word, and can
be found in Chaucer (1386) and Lydgate (1420), and more
recently in James' Forest Days (1843).

> Fair was his manly form, and fair
> His keen dark eye, and close curl'd hair,
> When, all unarm'd, save that the brand
> Of well-proved metal graced his hand,
> With nought to fence his dauntless breast
> But the close gipon's under-vest,
> Whose sullied buff the sable stains
> Of hauberk and of mail retains,
> Roland De Vaux upon the brim
> Of the broad moat stood prompt to swim.
> --Sir Walter Scott: The Bridal of Triermain
>   (1813); Canto III, Stanza 18.

GIRANDOLA: A revolving spray of water, or a series of
them, in a large fountain of intricate design. Principally a
17th century word, it comes through the Italian girandola,
from girare, "to revolve," derived from the Latin gyrare,
gyrus, and the Greek guros, "circle." It can be found in
John Ray's Journey through Part of the Low Countries (1673),
and in the following:

> The parterre ... 'Tis divided into four squares,
> and as many circular knots, having in the centre
> a noble basin of marble near thirty feet diameter
> (as I remember), in which a Triton of brass holds

>a dolphin, that casts a girandola of water near
>thirty feet high, playing perpetually, the water be-
>ing conveyed from Arceuil by an aqueduct of stone,
>built after the old Roman magnificence.
>--John Evelyn's Diary: Paris, April 1st, 1644.

GIRD: A nasty or sneering remark made against someone,
usually for the purpose of calumny. Dr. Johnson tells us:
"To break a scornful jest. " The origin is unknown; but the
word is very prevalent, and can be located in Drant (1566),
Andrew Marvell (1676), North (1734), in Henry Taylor's
Philip Van Artevelde: A Dramatic Romance (1834), and in
the following:

>Dry tobacco with my leaves, you good dry-brained
>polypragmonists, till your pipe-offices smoke with
>your pitifully stinking girds shot out against me.
>--Thomas Dekker: The Gull's Horn-Book (1609);
>proemium, paragraph 2.

GIZZ, JIZ: Some type of old wig. The origin of the word
is unknown, but it was employed by Robert Fergusson in his
collection of Poems in 1774, as well as by Burns:

>And auld John Trot wi' sober phiz,
>   As braid and braw's a Bailie,
>His shouthers and his Sunday's jiz
>   Wi' powther and wi' ulzie
>   Weel smear'd that day.
>--Robert Burns: A Mauchline Wedding (1785);
>stanza 5.

GLEEK: An old game of cards in which three persons par-
ticipated, employing forty-four cards from the deck, each
player receiving twelve; the eight cards left over formed the
common deck. This word also refers to a set of three
court cards of the same rank in a single hand while playing
this game; hence, the meaning of "a trio, three. " This
last sense is illustrated in the quotation. The exact origin
of gleek is not known, but it comes through the Old French
glic possibly from the Middle Dutch ghelic, "like, similar, "
in reference to the three cards of the same rank. It was
very prevalent in literature, and can be seen in many writers: in Sir Thomas Elyot (1533); in Rev. John Northbrooke's
A Treatise on Dicing, Dauncing, Vain Playes, etc. (1577);
in Ben Jonson's The Devil is an Ass (1616) and The Staple
of News (1625); in Richard Brathwait's English Gentleman

(1630); in Marvell (1671); Samuel Butler (1680); Thomas Shadwell (1680); Oliver Goldsmith (1762), and in Sir Walter Scott's The Fortunes of Nigel (1822). Another form, gleeker, "one who plays gleek, " is in Etherege's Man of Mode (1676).

> TRINCALO:
> Call Armellina: for this day we'll celebrate
> A gleek of marriages: Pandolfo and Flavia,
> Sulpitia and my self, and Trincalo
> With Armellina.
> --Thomas Tomkis: Albumazar (1615); Act IV,
>   Scene 10.

GLENLIVET: An old kind of Scotch whisky, named after its place of distillation, Glenlivet, in Banffshire, on the North Sea in northeastern Scotland.

> Each was well known as an excellent shot; and the captain offered a bet to Jekyl of a mutchkin of Glenlivat, that both would fall by the first fire.
> --Sir Walter Scott: St. Ronan's Well (1823); chapter 39.

The word can also be found in Charles James Lever's Charles O'Malley, the Irish Dragoon (1841).

GLIMFLASHY: Angry; in a rage. Principally used in the 17th, 18th, and 19th centuries, the word is constructed from glim, "a light, an eye, " and flashy, "showy. " Thus, "flashy-eyed. "

> "And this is what you call well! " said Clifford, angrily. "No, captain, don't be glimflashey! you have not heard all yet! "
> --Edward George Bulwer-Lytton: Paul Clifford (1830); chapter 31.

GLUNCH: To look sulky, moody, or sad; also, a sour glare, angry stare. The word is constructed from glum, and clunch, "Lumpy, a lump. " Allan Ramsay employed it in 1719, and it was also used by Burns:

> May gravels round his blather wrench,
> An' gouts torment him, inch by inch,
> What twists his gruntle wi' a glunch
>   O' sour disdain,

> Out owre a glass o' whisky-punch
> Wi' honest men!
> --Robert Burns: Scotch Drink (1786); stanza 17.

GOLILLA: A kind of starched and plaited pasteboard collar, covered over with white muslin, worn originally in Spain by businessmen, but later only by attorneys. The word comes through the Spanish golilla, from gola, "throat," from the Latin word for same, gula. Principally a 17th and early 18th century word, it appears in the Freethinker No. 94 (1718), as well as in the following:

> MONSIEUR de PARIS: Will you have no mercy, no pity? alas! alas! alas! Oh! I had rather put on the English pillory, than that Spanish golilla, for 'twill be all a case, I'm sure: for when I go abroad, I shall soon have a crowd of boys about me, peppering me with rotten eggs and turnips. Hélas! hélas!
> --William Wycherley: The Gentleman Dancing-
>   Master (1672); Act IV, Scene 1.

> There came up another witness, who spoke much to the reputation of Count Tariff. This was a tall black, blustering person dressed in a Spanish habit, with a plume of feathers on his head, a Golillio about his neck, and a long Toledo sticking out by his side: his garments were so covered with tinsel and spangles, that at a distance he seemed to be made up of silver and gold.
> --Joseph Addison: The Late Trial and Conviction
>   of Count Tariff (1713); paragraph 22.

GOLL, GOL: The hand. Principally used in the 16th through 19th centuries, the word is of unknown origin; it can be located in Sidney's Arcadia (1586), Ben Jonson's The Poetaster (1601), and Philip Massinger's The City Madam (1632). Dr. Johnson tells us: 'Hands; paws; claws. Used in contempt, and obsolete."

> SOSIA: Bless me, what an arm and fist he has, with great thumbs too: and gols and knuckle-bones of a very butcher.
> --John Dryden: Amphitryon (1690); Act II, Scene
>   1.

GOME: A man. A very ancient word, appearing in Beowulf,

King Horn, Sir Ferumbras, and the Destruction of Troy. It
comes through the Old English guma and the Old Saxon gumo
from the Old High German gumo, gomo, a form cognate with
the familiar Latin synonym, homo, hominis. This word is
actually still used very frequently today, as the second element in "bridegroom."

> "Christian knight," quoth Ferumbras, "thou art a
> wonder gome."
> --Sir Ferumbras (ca. 1380); line 402.

GOOSE-CAP: A silly numbskull; a fool or simpleton; a
dumbbell. Grose says, "A silly fellow or woman." The
origin is unknown; it was used principally from the 16th to
the 19th centuries, and can be located in Thomas Nashe
(1589); Thomas Dekker's The Honest Whore (1604); John
Ford's Fancies, Chaste and Noble (1638); in Jonathan Swift
(1711); in Samuel Foote's The Mayor of Garrat (1764), and
in Scott:

> "Alas, father!" replied the crestfallen lover,
> "there is that written on her brow, which says
> she loves me well enough to be my Valentine, es-
> pecially since you wish it,--but not well enough to
> be my wife."
>   "Now, a plague on thee for a cold, down-hearted
> goose-cap," answered the father. "I can read a
> woman's brow as well, and better than thou; and
> I can see no such matter on hers."
> --Sir Walter Scott: The Fair Maid of Perth (1828);
>   chapter 5.

GORBELLY: A person with a fat belly; a plump, good-na-
tured individual; a jolly fellow. The origin of this word is
not known, but it may be related to gore, "dirt, filth, dung."

> My gorbelly host, that in many a year could not
> without grunting crawl over a threshold but two foot
> broad, leaped half a yard from the corpse (it was
> measured by a carpenter's rule) as nimbly as if
> his guts had been taken out by the hangman.
> --Thomas Dekker: The Wonderful Year (1603).

GRAIP: A large fork used in farming and gardening for dig-
ging or for constructing dunghills; also, a handful, or a
piece of something. This word comes through the Old Norse
greip, "grip, grasp," and the Danish greb, "fork": but its

exact origins are uncertain. Burns used it, as is seen in
the quotation, and it was also employed by Scott in The
Pirate (1822).

> He marches thro' amang the stacks,
>   Tho' he was something sturtin;
> The graip he for a harrow taks,
>   An' haurls at his curpin.
> --Robert Burns: Halloween (1785); stanza 18.

GREW: A greyhound, shortened form of grew-hound, which
was probably an alteration meaning "Greek hound. " It can
be found in George Macdonald's Richard Falconer (1868), as
well as in the following:

> "A bonny terrier that, sir--and a fell chield at the
> vermin, I warrant him--that is, if he's been weel
> entered, for it a' lies in that. "
>   "Really, sir, " said Brown, "his education has
> been somewhat neglected, and his chief property
> is being a pleasant companion. "
>   "Ay, sir? that's a pity, begging your pardon--
> it's a great pity that--beast or body, education
> should aye be minded. I have six terriers at
> hame, forbye twa couple of slow-hunds, five grews,
> and a wheen other dogs. "
> --Sir Walter Scott: Guy Mannering (1815); chapter
>   22.

GRIFF: An old word for a claw; taken directly from the
French synonym, griffe. It can be found in Bulwer-Lytton's
Harold, or the Last of the Saxon Kings (1848), and in the
following:

> And a northern whirlwind, wandering about
> Like a wolf that had smelt a dead child out,
> Shook the boughs thus laden, and heavy and stiff,
> And snapt them off with his rigid griff.
> --Percy Bysshe Shelley: The Sensitive Plant
>   (1820); Part Third, lines 110-113.

GRIG: An old word of unknown origin; Dr. Johnson says it
means "anything below the natural size. " Hence, among
other senses, it has come to mean a cricket, grasshopper,
or young eel.

> "But Philip chatter'd more than brook or bird,

Old Philip; all about the fields you caught
His weary daylong chirping, like the dry
High-elbow'd grigs that leap in summer grass. "
--Alfred, Lord Tennyson: The Brook (1855); lines
   51-54.

GRISY, GRIESY: Terrible; horrible; ghastly; grisly. This
word is from the Middle English grisen, and Old English
grîsan (same base as "grisly"), meaning, "to tremble with
horror, " "to be frightened to death. " It can be found in
Wycliffe (1382) and in William Shakespeare's A Midsummer
Night's Dream (1594), as well as in Spenser:

So she him lefte, and did her selfe betake
Unto her boat again, with which she clefte
The slouthfull wave of that great griesy lake.
--Edmund Spenser: The Faerie Queene, Book II
   (1590); Canto VI, stanza 18.

GRUMBLEDORY: A heavy, clumsy idiot; a clod. This word
is a variation of drumbledory, which is from dromedary,
from the Greek dramein, "to run. "

MACILENTE: Pork! heart, what dost thou with
such a greasy dish? I think thou dost varnish thy
face with the fat on't, it looks so like a glue-pot.
CARLO: True, my raw-boned rogue, and if thou
wouldst farce thy lean ribs with it too, they would
not, like ragged laths, rub out so many doublets
as they do; but thou know'st not a good dish, thou.
O, it's the only nourishing meat in the world.
No marvel though that saucy, stubborn generation,
the Jews, were forbidden it; for what would they
have done, well pamper'd with fat pork, that durst
murmur at their Maker out of garlick and onions?
'Slight! fed with it, the whoreson strummel-
patch'd, goggled-eyed grumbledories would have
gigantomachised--!
--Ben Jonson: Every Man Out of His Humour
   (1599); Act V, Scene 4.

GRUMPHIE: A Scottish familiar name for the pig, from
grumph, "to grunt, " in imitation of the animal's sound. It
can be found in Michael Scott's Cruise of the Midge (1834),
and in Burns:

He roar'd a horrid murder-shout,

> In dreadfu' desperation!
> An' young an' auld come rinnin out,
>   An' hear the sad narration:
> He swoor 't was hilchin Jean M'Craw,
>   Or crouchie Merran Humphie--
> Till stop! she trotted thro' them a';
>   An' wha was it but grumphie
>   Asteer that night?
> --Robert Burns: Halloween (1785); stanza 20.

GULCH: One who either drinks or eats to excess; drunkard or glutton. From the verb gulch, "to devour rapaciously." It is probably an echoic word, similar to the German gulken and the Norwegian gulka, same meanings.

> PANTILIUS TUCCA: Come we must have you turn fiddler again, slave, get a base viol at your back, and march in a tawny coat, with one sleeve, to Goose-fair; then you'll know us, you'll see us then, you will, gulch, you will.
> --Ben Jonson: The Poetaster (1601); Act III, Scene 1.

GUNDY-GUT(S): Says Grose: "A fat, pursy fellow." Thus, a fat, voracious glutton; a big-bellied slob. Principally used in the 17th, 18th, and 19th centuries, the origin of this word is not known; but it may be related to gound, "pus-like matter in the eye," from the Old English gund, "pus, filth." Gorbelly may also be a connection. It can be seen in John Arbuthnot's History of John Bull (1712), and in Bridges' travesty of Homer:

> Slice after slice you'll see him cut,
> And stuff within his gundy-gut.
> --Thomas Bridges: New Translation of Homer's Iliad, Adapted to the Capacity of Honest English Roast Beef and Pudding Eaters (1764); volume II, page 292.

GYRE-CARLINE: A Scottish name for an old hag or witch; also, a scarecrow or hobgoblin; a spook. The first element is from the Old Norse gýgr and the Norwegian gjure, "witch, ugly woman," and the second is the feminine form of carl (see CARLOT), from ancient sources, meaning simply "woman."

> "Aweel, Ellangowan," she said, "wad it no hae

been a bonnie thing, an the leddy had been brought-
to-bed, and me at the fair o' Drumshourloch, no
kenning, nor dreaming a word about it? Wha was
to hae keepit awa the worriecows, I trow? Ay,
and the elves and gyre-carlings frae the bonny
bairn, grace be wi' it?"
--Sir Walter Scott: Guy Mannering (1815); chapter
    3.

Scott also employed it in his novel The Pirate, pub-
lished in 1822.

GYTRASH: A word of unknown origin, referring to a ghost
or spirit that takes the outward appearance of an animal.

As this horse approached, and as I watched for it
to appear through the dusk, I remembered certain
of Bessie's tales, wherein figured a North-of-
England spirit, called a "Gytrash"; which, in the
form of horse, mule, or large dog, haunted solitary ways, and sometimes came upon belated
travellers, as this horse was now coming upon
me.
--Charlotte Bronte: Jane Eyre (1847); chapter 12.

-H-

HABERGEON, HAUBERGEON, HABURION: A short sleeve-
less coat of plate or chain-mail, usually with a high neck to
protect the breast and throat, worn over the gambeson and
under the jupon; originally it was lighter than the hauberk,
but sometimes the word refers to that also. It is from the
French haubegeon, diminutive of hauberc, "hauberk," and
can be located in John Bourchier, Lord Berners' translation
of Froissart's Chronicles, and in Milton:

Then put on all thy gorgeous arms, thy helmet
And brigandine of brass, thy broad habergeon,
Vant-brace and greaves, and gauntlet; add thy
    spear,
A weaver's beam, and seven-times-folded shield.
--John Milton: Samson Agonistes (1671); lines
    1119-1122.

HAFFET, HAFFIT: The sides of the head; the temples or
cheeks. From the Anglo-Saxon heafod, "head," it can be

located in Allan Ramsay's The Gentle Shepherd (1725); David
Davidson's Thoughts on the Seasons (1789); Scott's Heart of
Midlothian (1818); the poetry of Robert Nicoll (1842); in
Samuel Rutherford Crockett (1893), and in the following:

> "Are ye distraught, lassie?" shouted Dorothy, as
> Catharine made past her towards the street door.
> "You would not gang into the street with the hair
> hanging down your haffets in that guise, and you
> kenn'd for the Fair Maid of Perth?"
> --Sir Walter Scott: The Fair Maid of Perth (1828);
>   chapter 19.

HA-HA, HAW-HAW: A fence or wall bounding a garden or
park, set in a trench, the inner side of which is faced with
stone, and which does not obscure the view from within; a
sunk fence, not perceived until approached at close range.
It may be a reduplication of haw, "hedge," or a cry of sur-
prise (emitted when coming upon the fence). Examples of
its use can be seen in Daniel Defoe's Tour of Great Britain
(1769); R. S. Surtees' Sponge's Spanish Tour (1852), and in
the following:

> O let the Muse attend thy march sublime,
> And, with thy prose, caparison her rhyme;
> Teacher her, like thee, to gild her splendid song,
> With scenes of Yven-Ming, and sayings of Li-
>   Tsong;
> Like thee to scorn dame Nature's simple fence;
> Leap each ha-ha of truth and common sense.
> --William Mason: An Heroic Epistle to Sir Wil-
>   liam Chambers (1772); lines 7-12.

> The writer wished to be set up in honest business;
> he wished 250£ to be put in a bag, and taken,
> "unseen by mortal eye," to the Ha-ha ditch in
> Kensington Gardens, and deposited in a hole in the
> wall under a water-spout which would there be
> found.
> --"Singular Attempt at Extortion" in the Annual
>   Register For 1849; Chronicle section, page 106,
>   column 2.

HALF-SHIRT: A little shirt-front worn by men and women,
popular in the 17th century.

> Did not stir out all day, but rose and dined below.

And this day left off half-shirts and put on a
wastecoate and my false taby waistcoat with gold
lace.   And in the evening there comes Sir W.
Batten to see me and sat and supped very kindly
with me; and so to prayers and to bed.
--Samuel Pepys' Diary: October 13th, 1661.

HALLANSHAKER: A low, shabby, ragged beggar or vagabond, usually of a rascally character; a dirty rogue.   It
comes from hallan, a word of unknown origin referring to
the mud walls of cottages, and can be found in Allan Ramsay (1721); in Archibald Thom's Amusements of Solitary
Hours (1812); in James Hogg (1838), and in these:

'I just ken this about it, that about twenty years
syne, I, and a wheen hallenshakers like mysell,
and the mason-lads that built the lang dike that
gaes down the loaning, and twa or three herds
maybe, just set to wark, and built this. "
--Sir Walter Scott: The Antiquary (1816); chapter
4.

"Lassie, I bear you no grudge; will you not tell
me who you are?"
"Only a puir gypsy, your honour, " said the
girl, becoming mischievous now that she had gained
her point; "only a wandering hallen-shaker. "
--J. M. Barrie: The Little Minister (1891); chapter 13.

HALTERSACK: A scoundrel rogue, one who will hang from
the halter (gallows) like a sack.

CITIZEN: If he were my son, I would hang him
up by the heels, and flay him, and salt him,
whoreson halter-sack.
--Francis Beaumont: The Knight of the Burning
Pestle (ca. 1610); Act I, Scene 4.

SECOND SHOP-MAN: Away, away! all's done.
THIRD SHOP-MAN: Content. --Farewell, Philip.
FIRST CITIZEN'S WIFE: Away, you halter-sack,
you!
--Francis Beaumont & John Fletcher: King and
No King (1611); Act II, Scene 2.

HANAP: An old silver or golden goblet, also known as the

hanaper, used for state functions. It comes through the
Low Latin hanaperium, "vessel for keeping cups in," the
Old French hanap, the Anglo-Saxon hnoep, Dutch nap, and
the Old High German hnap.

> He positively declined to take back the silver cup.
> It was none of his, he said, but Maitre Pierre's,
> who had bestowed it on his guest. He had, in-
> deed, four silver hanaps of his own, which had
> been left him by his grandmother, of happy memory,
> but no more like the beautiful carving of that in
> his guest's hand.
> --Sir Walter Scott: Quentin Durward (1823); chap-
> ter 4.

HARRATEEN, HARATEEN: An old fabric made of linen,
used in furniture decoration, bedding, and curtains. The
origin is not known. It can be seen in William Shenstone
and Horace Walpole, and in the following:

> The day was close, the window-shutters were fas-
> tened; a huge fire blazed in the chimney; thick
> harateen curtains were close drawn round the bed,
> where the wretched squire lay extended under an
> enormous load of blankets.
> --Tobias Smollett: The Adventures of Sir Launce-
> lot Greaves (1762); chapter 16.

HEARTSPOON, HEARTSPONE: The pit of the stomach, or
depression found at the termination of the breast-bone.
Found in George Meriton's Praise of Yorkshire Ale (1683),
and in Scott:

> "To Varney and Leicester!--two more noble mount-
> ing spirits--and more dark-seeing, deep-diving,
> high-flying, malicious, ambitious miscreants--
> well, I say no more, but I will whet my dagger
> on his heart-spone, that refuses to pledge me!"
> --Sir Walter Scott: Kenilworth (1821); chapter 20.

HECCO: A name for the woodpecker, of unknown origin.
Used by Drayton:

> The Crow is digging at his breast amain;
> The sharp-neb'd Hecco stabbing at his brain;
> That had the Falcon not by chance been near,
> That lov'd the Owl, and held him only dear,

Come to his rescue at the present tide,
The honest Owl undoubtedly had dy'd.
--Michael Drayton: <u>The Owl</u> (1604); lines 205-210.

And of these chaunting fowles, the goldfinch not
    behind,
That hath so many sorts descending from her kind,
The tydie for her notes as delicate as they,
The laughing hecco, then the counterfetting jay,
The softer, with the shrill (some hid among the
    leaves,
Some in the taller trees, some in the lower
    greaves)
Thus sing away the morne, untill the mounting
    sunne,
Through thick exhaled fogs, his golden head hath
    runne,
And through the twisted tops of our close covert
    creeps
To kisse the gentle shade, this while that sweetly
    sleeps.
--Michael Drayton: <u>Polyolbion</u> (1612); Song 13,
    lines 77-86.

<u>HEDGE-BORN</u>:   A person of low or humble birth, "born un-
der a hedge."

LORD TALBOT:
He, then, that is not furnisht in this sort
Doth but usurp the sacred name of knight,
Profaning this most honourable order,
And should--if I were worthy to be judge--
Be quite degraded, like a hedge-born swain
That doth presume to boast of gentle blood.
--William Shakespeare: <u>King Henry The Sixth,</u>
    <u>Part I</u> (ca. 1591); Act IV, Scene 1.

<u>HEELTAP</u>:   The remains of liquor left at the bottom of the
glass following drinking; dregs.   Grose tells us: "A peg in
the heel of a shoe, taken out when it is finished.   A person
leaving any liquor in his glass, is frequently called upon by
the toast-master to take off his heel-tap."   It can be located
in James Boswell (1803); Charles James Lever's <u>Arthur</u>
<u>O'Leary</u> (1844); R. D. Blackmore (1890), and in <u>Dickens</u>:

"Drink that," said the dwarf, who had by this time
heated some more.   "Toss it off, don't leave any

> heeltap, scorch your throat and be happy!"
> --Charles Dickens: The Old Curiosity Shop (1840);
>   chapter 62.

HENCHMAN, HENCHBOY: A male attendant or servant; a
page, groom, squire; follower. The origin is probably in
the Anglo-Saxon hengest, "horse," and man, "man," close
to the "groom" sense. Examples of its use can be located
in the following:

> OBERON:
> Do you amend it, then; it lies in you:
> Why should Titania cross her Oberon?
> I do but beg a little changeling boy,
> To be my henchman.
> --William Shakespeare: A Midsummer Night's
>   Dream (1594); Act II, Scene 1.

> PIERO: I present you
> My service for a farewell; let few words
> Excuse all arts of compliment.
> FUTELLI: For my own part,
> Kill or be kill'd, (for there's the short and long
>   on't,)
> Call me your shadow's hench-boy.
> --John Ford: The Lady's Trial (1638); Act I,
>   Scene 1.

> Pantler and serving-man, henchman and page,
> Stand sniffing the duck-stuffing (onion and sage),
>   And the scullions and cooks,
>   With fidgety looks,
> Are grumbling, and mutt'ring, and scowling as
>   black
> As cooks always do when the dinner's put back.
> --R. D. Barham: The Ingoldsby Legends (1842):
>   The Lay of St. Cuthbert.

HEWT, HEWTE: An orchard, grove, or copse, from the
Old English hiewet, "a hewing, a chopping down." It can
be found in George Turbervile's The Noble Art of Venerie,
or Hunting (1576); Stanyhurst's Aeneis (1583), and in the following:

> Hewts, or springs [are] the places where the Deer
> feeds; taken for the small groves or copyes: and
> the springs the greater groves.

--Randle Holme: <u>The Academy of the Armoury</u>
(1688); Volume II, page 188.

HIGHLONE: Totally alone, solitary, often said of a young
baby learning to walk. It can be located in the following:

NURSE:
Shake, quoth the dove-house: 'twas no need, I trow,
To bid me trudge:
And since that time it is eleven years;
For then she could stand high-lone; nay, by th'
    rood,
She could have run and waddled all about.
--William Shakespeare: <u>Romeo and Juliet</u> (ca.
    1594); Act I, Scene 3.

ANTONIO:
Thou gav'st her me, as some weak-breasted dame
Giveth her infant, puts it out to nurse;
And when it once goes high-lone, takes it back.
She was my vital blood; and yet, and yet,
I'll not blaspheme.
--John Marston: <u>Antonio's Revenge</u> (ca. 1600);
    Act IV, Scene 2.

Mulatto Jack returned home with the Mares he was
sent for, but so poor were they, and so much
abusd had they been by my Rascally Overseer
Hardwick that they were scarce able to go high-
lone, much less to assist in the business of the
Plantations.
--George Washington's <u>Diary</u>: March 13th, 1760.

HISTIE: An old Scottish word of uncertain origin: "Barren,
chapped, dry." Used by Burns:

The flaunting flow'rs our gardens yield,
High shelt'ring woods and wa's maun shield:
But thou, beneath the random bield
        O' clod or stane,
Adorns the histie stibble-field,
        Unseen, alane.
--Robert Burns: <u>To a Mountain Daisy</u> (1786);
    stanza 4.

HOG-RUBBER: A clownish fool; a low, coarse, untidy person; used as a term of reproach.

PORTER: Must I carry this great fiddle to your chamber, Mistress Mary?
MOLL: Fiddle, goodman hog-rubber? Some of these porters bear so much for others, they have no time to carry wit for themselves.
PORTER: To your own chamber, Mistress Mary?
MOLL: Who'll hear an ass speak? whither else, goodman pageant-bearer? They're people of the worst memories!
--Thomas Dekker & Thomas Middleton: <u>The Roaring Girl</u> (1611); Act II, Scene 2.

LEATHERHEAD:
You are angry, goodman Cole; I believe the fair maid
Came over with you a' trust: tell us, sculler, are you paid?
COLE: Yes, goodman Hogrubber of Pickthatch.
--Ben Jonson: <u>Bartholomew Fair</u> (1614); Act V, Scene 3.

SANITONELLA:
That I could not think of this virtuous gentleman
Before I went to'th other Hogg-rubber!
Why, this was wont to give young clerks half fees,
To help him to clients.
--John Webster: <u>The Devil's Law-Case</u> (ca. 1620); Act IV, Scene 1.

HOLT-FELSTER: A woodcutter, one who "fells" a "holt," or grove (related to the German <u>holz</u>, "wood."). Used by Marvell:

But most the hewel's wonders are,
Who here has the holt-felsters care.
He walks still upright from the root,
Meas'ring the timber with his foot,
And all the way, to keep it clean,
Doth from the bark the wood-moths glean.
--Andrew Marvell: <u>Upon Appleton House</u> (1678); stanza 68.

HORSE-GODMOTHER: A large, tall, coarse, masculine woman; "a gentlemanlike kind of a lady," says Grose. Used since the late 16th century, it can be found in Dr. John Wolcot ("Peter Pindar"), and in Thackeray:

"How do, Pitt? How do, my dear? Come to see
the old man, hay? 'Gad--you've a pretty face,
too. You ain't like that old horse-godmother,
your mother. Come and give old Pitt a kiss, like
a good little gal. "
--William Makepeace Thackeray: <u>Vanity Fair</u>
    (1848); chapter 39.

<u>HOUDIE, HOUDY</u>: An old word for a midwife. The origin
is unknown, but it may be related to the Icelandic <u>huga</u>, "to
care for, " and <u>deigja</u>, "a dog, a servant. " It can be located in Allan Ramsay"s <u>The Gentle Shepherd</u> (1725), and
in Scott:

"And ye'll be come in the canny moment, I'm
thinking, for the laird's servant--that's no to say
his body-servant, but the helper like--rade express by this e'en to fetch the houdie, and he just
staid the drinking o' twa pints o' tippenny, to tell
us how my leddy was ta'en wi' her pains. "
--Sir Walter Scott: <u>Guy Mannering</u> (1815); chap-
    ter 1.

<u>HOW</u>: An old word of many spellings, referring to a little
hill or knoll. It comes from the Old Norse <u>haugr</u>, "mound, "
and can be seen in Thomas Shadwell (1682), and in the following:

There's George Fisher, Charles Fleming, and
    Reginald Shore,
Three rosy-cheeked school-boys, the highest not
    more
Than the height of a counsellor's bag;
To the top of Great How did it please them to
    climb:
And there they built up, without mortar or lime,
A Man on the peak of the Crag.
--William Wordsworth: <u>Rural Architecture</u> (1800);
    stanza 1.

<u>HUCKABACK</u>: An old kind of coarse, stout linen with a
very rough surface with raised figures, somewhat like
damask, that was used for towels and table-cloths. It
comes through the Low German <u>hukkebak</u> of uncertain origins, and can be found in Scott:

The rich smoke of the rasher, and the eggs with

which it was flanked, already spread itself through
the apartment; and the hissing of these savoury
viands bore chorus to the simmering of the pan,
in which the fish were undergoing a slower decoction.   The table was covered with a clean hucka-
back napkin, and all was in preparation for the
meal, which Julian began to expect with a good
deal of impatience, when the companion who was
destined to share it with him entered the apartment.
--Sir Walter Scott: Peveril of the Peak (1823);
     chapter 21.

HUFF-CAP: A swaggering braggart or bully; a blustering
swashbuckler. It comes from huff, "to swell up," and
Nares tells us: "From inducing people to set their caps in
a bold and huffing style." Found in Hall's Satires, and in
the following:

> KING: Is our lord mayor of London such a gal-
>   lant?
> NOBLEMAN: One of the merriest madcaps in
>   your land.
> Your grace will think, when you behold the man,
> He's rather a wild ruffian than a mayor.
> Yet thus much I'll ensure your majesty,
> In all his actions that concern his state
> He is as serious, provident, and wise,
> As full of gravity amongst the grave,
> As any mayor hath been these many years.
> KING: I am with child [in suspense] till I behold
>   this huffcap.
> --Thomas Dekker: The Shoemaker's Holiday
>   (1600); Act V, Scene 3.

HUISHER: A court doorman, or official servant or attendant.
Coming through the French huissier, the Latin ostium,
"door," from os, "mouth," this word is an early form of
the modern word "usher." Used by Jonson in A Tale of a
Tub (1633), and in the following:

> FITZDOTTREL: O, bird,
> Could you do this? 'gainst me! and at this time
>   now!
> When I was so employ'd, wholly for you,
> Drown'd in my care (more than the land, I swear,
> I have hope to win) to make you peerless, studying

For footmen for you, fine-paced huishers, pages,
To serve you on the knee.
--Ben Jonson: The Devil Is an Ass (1616); Act II,
   Scene 3.

HUNGARIAN: Beggarly; thievish; stealing. Used principally
in the 17th century, it comes from hungarian, "a hungry
person, " obviously a play also on the nationality.

SIR JOHN FALSTAFF: Bardolph, follow him. A
tapster is a good trade: an old cloak makes a new
jerkin; a wither'd serving-man a fresh tapster.
Go; adieu.
BARDOLPH: It is a life that I have desired: I
will thrive.
PISTOL: O base Hungarian wight! wilt thou the
spigot wield? (EXIT BARDOLPH).
NYM: He was gotten in drink: is not the humour
conceited? His mind is not heroic, and there's
the humour of it.
--William Shakespeare: The Merry Wives of Windsor (1601); Act I, Scene 3.

HUNKS: A term of contempt for a surly miser or niggardly
person; stingy fellow. Grose: "A covetous miserable fellow. " Johnson: "A covetous sordid wretch. " The origin
is unknown. Used principally from the 17th century, it can
be located in Charles Kingsley (1857); Anthony Trollope
(1857), and in the following:

GOMEZ: Go on--Colonel--have you no other marks
of her?
LORENZO: Thou hast all her marks; but she has
an husband; a jealous, covetous, old huncks:
speak; canst thou tell me news of her?
GOMEZ: Yes, this news, Colonel; that you have
seen the last of her.
--John Dryden: The Spanish Friar (1680); Act I.

'He is the most stupid of all my mother's children: he knows nothing of his book: when he
should mind that, he is hiding or hoarding his
taws and marbles, or laying up farthings ... so
within these two months the close hunks has
scraped up twenty shillings, and we will make him
spend it all before he comes home. "
--Sir Richard Steele: The Tatler No. 30 (1709);
   paragraph 1.

HURLEY-HOUSE: A word of unknown origin for a large rambling house that has fallen very much into disrepair or nearly into ruins. Used by Scott:

> 'I now wish (his eyes fixed on a part of the roof which was visible above the trees) that I could have left Rose the auld hurley-house, and the riggs belonging to it. --And yet, " said he, resuming more cheerfully, "it's maybe as weel as it is. "
> --Sir Walter Scott: Waverley (1814); chapter 67.

> "Nothing, " he said, "my lord, now seems to remain in which I can render any assistance; permit me to look after a duty of humanity--the Knight of Ardenvohr, as I am told, is our prisoner, and severely wounded. "
> "And well he deserves to be so, " said Sir Dugald Dalgetty, who came up to them at that moment, with a prodigious addition of acquired importance, "since he shot my good horse at the time that I was offering him honorable quarter, which, I must needs say, was done more like an ignorant Highland cateran, who has not sense enough to erect a sconce for the protection of his old hurley-house of a castle, than like a soldier of worth and quality. "
> --Sir Walter Scott: A Legend of Montrose (1819); chapter 20.

HYTE: Crazy; insane; raging; mad. The origin is uncertain; it can be located in the poetry of Andrew Shirrefs (1790); of Picken (1813); in John Galt's Sir Andrew Wylie (1822), and in Burns:

> The witching, curs'd, delicious blinkers
> Hae put me hyte.
> --Robert Burns: To Major Logan (1786); stanza 10.

-I-

ICHOGLAN, ITCHEOGLAN: The name of a servant-boy or page in the service of a sultan; from the obsolete Turkish ïch oglän, from ïch, "interior, " and oglän, "page. " It can be found in Richard Pococke's Description of the East and some other Countries (1745), and in Thackeray:

> About the door lads and servants were lolling,
> ichoglans and pages, with lazy looks and shabby
> dresses; and among them, sunning himself sulkily
> on a bench, a poor old fat, wrinkled, dismal white
> eunuch, with little fat white hands, and a great
> head sunk into his chest, and two sprawling little
> legs that seemed incapable to hold up his bloated
> old body.
>> --William Makepeace Thackeray: Notes of a Jour-
>>   ney From Cornhill to Grand Cairo (1845); chap-
>>   ter 7.

ICKER, ECHER: The Scottish form of an "ear" of corn.
The exact origin is unknown.

> I doubt na, whyles, but thou may thieve;
> What then? poor beastie, thou maun live
> A daimen icker in a thrave
>   'S a sma' request;
> I'll get a blessin wi' the lave,
>   An' never miss't!
>> --Robert Burns: To a Mouse (1785); stanza 3.

IER-OE, HEIR-OYE: The Scottish word for great-grandchild.
It comes from the Gaelic iar-ogha, constructed from iar,
"after," and ogha, "grandchild." It can be seen in John
Brand's Description of Orkney, Zetland, Pightland, Firth,
and Caithness (1701), and in Burns:

> "May Health and Peace, with mutual rays,
> Shine on the ev'ning o' his days;
> Till his wee, curlie John's ier-oe,
> When ebbing life nae mair shall flow,
> The last, sad, mournful rites bestow!"
>> --Robert Burns: A Dedication to Gavin Hamilton,
>>   Esq. (1786): stanza 14.

INCH, INSCHE: A small island or outcrop of land, principally in Scotland and Ireland, frequently used in Scottish
place-names. It comes from the Gaelic innis, "island,"
and can be found in Henry the Minstrel's Wallace (ca. 1470),
as well as in the following:

> ROSS: That now
> Sweno, the Norways' king, craves composition;

> Nor would we deign him burial of his men
> Till he disbursed, at Saint Colme's-inch,
> Ten thousand dollars to our general use.
> --William Shakespeare: <u>Macbeth</u> (1606); Act I,
>   Scene 2.

> 'The blackening wave is edged with white;
>   To inch and rock the sea-mews fly;
> The fishers have heard the Water Sprite,
>   Whose screams forebode that wreck is nigh. "
> --Sir Walter Scott: <u>The Lay of the Last Minstrel</u>
>   (1805); Canto VI, stanza 23.

<u>INCHPIN, INCHIPIN</u>: The lower guts or the sweetbread of a deer. Dr. Johnson says: "Some of the inside of a deer, " and Randle Holme in his <u>Armoury</u> (1688) relates: "Inchpin are the sweet-breds or sweet gut in the deer. " The origin is unknown; perhaps it is from some lost popular expression. It can be found in Turbervile's <u>Venerie</u> (1576), and in Stany-hurst, and in Jonson:

> MARIAN:
> How hath this morning paid me for my rising!
> First, with my sports; but most with meeting you.
> I did not half so well reward my hounds,
> As she hath me to-day; although I gave them
> All the sweet morsels call'd tongue, ears, and
>   dowcets!
> ROBIN: What, and the inch-pin?
> MARIAN: Yes.
> ROBIN: Your sports then pleased you?
> MARIAN: You are a wanton.
> --Ben Jonson: <u>The Sad Shepherd</u> (1637); Act I,
>   Scene 2.

<u>INCONY</u>: A word of many different spellings and of uncertain origins, referring to "sweet, delicate, pretty, fair, nice, etc. " Dr. Johnson says: "Unlearned; artless ... In Scotland it denotes mischievously unlucky: as, he's an <u>incony</u> fellow. This seems to be the meaning in Shakespeare. " It was principally a 17th century word; and it has been suggested that it originates in the French <u>inconnu</u>, "unknown, " hence, "pretty, rare. " But it also may be a variation of <u>uncanny</u> or of <u>unco</u>, "strange"; or it may be a rhyme-word with "money. " It can be found in Henry Porter's <u>The Pleasant Historie of the two Angrie Women of Abington</u> (1599), and in the following:

BELLAMIRA: Come, gentle Ithamore, lie in my
   lap.
ITHAMORE:
"Love me little, love me long": let music rumble,
Whilst I in thy incony lap do tumble.
--Christopher Marlowe: The Jew of Malta (1587);
   Act IV, Scene 6.

COSTARD:
My sweet ounce of man's flesh! my incony Jew!
--William Shakespeare: Love's Labour's Lost (ca.
   1595); Act III, Scene 1.

IMPERIA: In good troth, if I be not sick, I must
be melancholy then. This same gown never comes
on but I am so melancholy and so heart-burnt!
'tis a strange garment: I warrant, Simperina, the
foolish tailor that made it was troubled with the
stitch when he composed it.
SIMPERINA: That's very likely, madam; but it
makes you have, O, a most incony body!
--Thomas Middleton: Blurt, Master-Constable
   (1602); Act II, Scene 2.

METAPHOR:
O super-dainty Canon! Vicar incony,
Make no delay, Miles, but away.
And bring the wench, and money.
--Ben Jonson: A Tale of a Tub (1633); Act IV,
   Scene 1.

INCORNISHED: Having a cornice. From the Italian incorni-
ciare, "to put a cornice or frame upon (a building)." Ultimately from probably the Latin coronis, "curved line," and
the Greek korōnis, "wreath."

> The outer walls of the house are encrusted with
> excellent antique bass-relievos, of the same mar-
> ble, incornished with festoons and niches set with
> statues from the foundation to the roof.
> --John Evelyn's Diary: April 11th, 1645.

INCORPSED: Incorporated; gathered into one locality or
body. From the Latin word for "body," corpus.

CLAUDIUS:
Here was a gentleman of Normandy, --

I've seen myself, and served against, the French,
And they can well on horseback: but this gallant
Had witchcraft in't; he grew unto his seat;
And to such wondrous doing brought his horse,
As he had been incorpsed and demi-natured
With the brave beast.
   --William Shakespeare: Hamlet (1600); Act IV,
     Scene 7.

ING, ENGE, YNGE: A swampy meadow in the north of England, usually beside a river.   From the Old Norse enge,
"meadow"; but the word cannot be found in Old English.

How different had this scene looked when I viewed
it laid out beneath the iron sky of winter, stiffened
in frost, shrouded with snow!--when mists as chill
as death wandered to the impulse of east winds
along those purple peaks, and rolled down "ing"
and holm till they blended with the frozen fog of
the beck!
   --Charlotte Bronte: Jane Eyre (1847); chapter 9.

INGAN: The Scottish form of the word "onion. " Through
the Old French oignon from the Latin unio, "unity, " from
unus, "one, " referring to "single onion" or "single bulb. "
Used by Allan Ramsay, and by Scott:

"There's the kingdom of Fife, frae Culross to the
East Nuik, it's just like a great combined city--
sae mony royal boroughs yoked on end to end, like
ropes of ingans, with their hie-streets and their
booths, nae doubt, and their kraemes, and houses
of stane and lime and fore-stairs--Kirkcaldy, the
sell o't, is langer than ony town in England. "
   --Sir Walter Scott: Rob Roy (1817); chapter 14.

"There was an unco difference between an anointed
king of Syria and our Spanish colonel, whom I
could have blown away like the peeling of an ingan. "
   --Sir Walter Scott: A Legend of Montrose (1819);
     chapter 2.

INGRAM, UNGRUM: Probably a corrupted form of ingrant,
"ignorant. " It can be seen in Sir Thomas Wilson's Art of
Rhetorike for the Use of all Suche as are studious of Elo-
quence (1553); in Thomas Nashe, John Taylor, and in the
following:

LADY HEARTWELL: You drowsy slave, nothing
but sleep and swilling!
SHORTHOSE: Had you been bitten with bandog-
fleas as I have been,
And haunted with the night-mare--
LADY HEARTWELL: With an ale-pot!
SHORTHOSE: You would have little list to morning
prayers.
Pray, take my fellow, Ralph; he has a psalm-book:
I am an ingrum man.
--Francis Beaumont & John Fletcher: Wit Without
Money (1614); Act V, Scene 1.

INJELLY: To cover or to enclose with jelly. From the
Latin gelare, "to freeze."

There, on a slope of orchard, Francis laid
A damask napkin wrought with horse and hound,
Brought out a dusky loaf that smelt of home,
And, half-cut-down, a pasty costly-made,
Where quail and pigeon, lark and leveret lay,
Like fossils of the rock, with golden yolks
Imbedded and injellied.
--Alfred, Lord Tennyson: Audley Court (1842);
lines 19-25.

INKLE: An old type of inferior, coarse, linen tape, used
for various purposes. The origin is uncertain; but perhaps
it is related to the Dutch enkel, "single," with reference to
the size of the tape. It can be found in Harman's Caveat
for Vagabonds (1567), in John Ray, and in the following:

SAVIL: If you consider me in little, I
Am, with your worship's reverence, sir, a rascal;
One that, upon the next anger of your brother,
Must raise a sconce by the highway, and sell
switches.
My wife is learning now, sir, to weave inkle.
--Francis Beaumont & John Fletcher: The Scorn-
ful Lady (ca. 1610); Act V, Scene 3.

Also, variations of meaning can be found in Shakespeare's Winter's Tale, Act IV, and Pericles, Act V.

INLAPIDATE: To petrify, to turn into stone. From the
Latin word for stone, lapis.

It is already found that there are some natural
spring-waters, that will inlapidate wood; so as
you shall see one piece of wood, whereof the part
above the water shall continue wood, and the part
under the water shall be turned into a kind of
gravelly stone.
--Francis Bacon: Sylva Sylvarum (1626); para-
    graph 85.

INTUSE: A scratch or dark bruise; from the Latin synonym,
from the verb "to bruise," intundere.

The flesh therewith shee suppled and did steepe,
T' abate all spasme and soke the swelling bruze,
And after having searcht the intuse deepe,
She with her scarf did bind the wound from cold
    to keepe.
--Edmund Spenser: The Faerie Queene, Book III
    (1590); Canto V, Stanza 33.

IZZARD, IZZET, UZZARD, IZARD: The old name for the
letter Z, spelled in many various and sundry ways. It was
originally identical with zed, now still used, from the Greek
zeta. It can be found in Jonathan Swift, Robert Southey,
Thomas Hood, John Moultrie, and in the following:

TONY: A damned up-and-down hand, as if it was
disguised in liquor. (Reading). "Dear Sir"--ay,
that's that. Then there's an M, and a T, and an
S; but whether the next be an izzard or an R, con-
found me, I cannot tell.
MRS. HARDCASTLE: What's that, my dear? Can
I give you any assistance?
CONSTANCE: Pray, aunt, let me read it. No-
body reads a cramp hand better than I.
--Oliver Goldsmith: She Stoops to Conquer (1773);
    Act IV.

-J-

JACK-A-LENT: An old English sport in which the image of
a man, the jack-a-lent, was erected during Lenten weeks, at
which the people of the village would cast stones, missiles,
rocks, etc.; hence, the word has come to mean any thing
which serves as the "target" or "butt" of anything, such as
a practical joke. It can be found in Churchyard (1575), in

Breton's Fantasticks (1626), and in Francis Quarles (1646), as well as in the following:

> SIR JOHN FALSTAFF: And these are not fairies?
> I was three or four times in the thought they were
> not fairies: and yet the guiltiness of my mind, the
> sudden surprise of my powers, drove the gross-
> ness of the foppery into a received belief, in de-
> spite of the teeth of all rhyme and reason, that
> they were fairies. See now how wit may be made
> a Jack-a-Lent, when 'tis upon ill employment!
> --William Shakespeare: The Merry Wives of Wind-
> sor (1601); Act V, Scene 5.

> HILTS:
> Thou, that when last thou wert put out of service,
> Travell'dst to Hamstead-heath on an Ash-We'nesday
> Where thou didst stand six weeks the Jack of Lent,
> For boys to hurl, three throws a penny, at thee,
> To make thee a purse: seest thou this bold bright
> blade?
> This sword shall shred thee as small unto the
> grave,
> As minced meat for a pye.
> --Ben Jonson: A Tale of a Tub (1633); Act IV,
> Scene 3.

> These Factious Few, for bitter scourges fit,
> (To shew Addressing and Abhorring Wit)
> Set up a Jack of Lent, and throw at it.
> --Thomas Shadwell: The Medal of John Bayes
> (1682); lines 293-295.

Another use of the word is that of "a small person, a dwarf, a little puppet, an insignificant individual," as illustrated in the following:

> ROBIN: My master, Sir John, is come in at your
> back-door, Mistress Ford, and requests your com-
> pany.
> MISTRESS PAGE: You little Jack-a-Lent, have
> you been true to us?
> ROBIN: Ay, I'll be sworn. My master knows not
> of your being here, and hath threaten'd to put me
> into everlasting liberty, if I tell you of it; for he
> swears he'll turn me away.
> --William Shakespeare: The Merry Wives of

Windsor (1601); Act III, Scene 3.

Additional examples of this sense of the word can be found in Vanbrugh's False Friend (1702) and in "Interlopers at the Knap," in Thomas Hardy's Wessex Tales (1884).

JACK NASTY: A word of unknown origin, but probably merely descriptive, meaning "a person who is lazy or sneaky, or both."

> And Tom and his younger brothers, as they grew up, went on playing with the village boys, without the idea of equality or inequality (except in wrestling, running, and climbing,) ever entering their heads, as it doesn't till it's put there by Jack Nastys or fine ladies' maids.
> --Thomas Hughes: Tom Brown's School Days (1857); Part I, chapter 3.

JACK-PUDDING: A boisterous clown or fool, usually the assistant or cohort of a charlatan, quack, or mountebank; a "merry Andrew." It can be located in Clement Walker's History of Independency (1648), in Fielding (1752), and in the following:

> FOOT-BOY: Sir, in a word, he was Jack-pudding to a mountebank, and turn'd off for want of wit: my master pick'd him up before a puppet-show, mumbling a half-penny custard, to send him with a letter to the post.
> --Sir George Etherege: The Comical Revenge (1664); Act III, Scene 4.

> Everard exclaimed angrily to Wildrake: "Is this your friendship? In Heaven's name, what make you in that fool's jacket, and playing the pranks of a jack-pudding?"
> --Sir Walter Scott: Woodstock (1826); chapter 28.

JACK-SAUCE: A rude, impudent, uncourteous individual; a "saucy" person, used contemptuously. Found in Vanbrugh (1702), and in the following:

> FLUELLEN: Though he be as goot a gentleman as the tevil is, as Lucifer and Belzebub himself, it is necessary, look your Grace, that he keep his vow and his oath: if he be perjured, see you

now, his reputation is as arrant a villain and a
Jack-sauce, as ever his plack shoe trod upon
Got's ground and his earth, in my conscience, la.
--William Shakespeare: King Henry The Fifth
   (1599); Act IV, Scene 7.

JADE: An old, useless, worn-out horse, later applied in a
somewhat playful sense to a woman of loose moral standards.
Dr. Johnson tells us: "A sorry woman. A word of contempt noting sometimes age, but generally vice."

   "Better a lean jade than an empty halter."
   --Old proverb.

   BIANCA: Sir, there's no learning
   An old stiff jade to trot; you know the moral.
   --John Fletcher: The Woman's Prize (ca. 1612);
      Act I, Scene 3.

   From this noun comes a verb usage, meaning "to deceive, to fool."

   MALVOLIO: I do not now fool myself, to let
   imagination jade me; for every reason excites to
   this, that my lady loves me.
   --William Shakespeare: Twelfth Night (1601); Act
      II, Scene 5.

   EARL OF SURREY: My lords,
   Can ye endure to hear this arrogance?
   And from this fellow? If we live thus tamely,
   To be thus jaded by a piece of scarlet,
   Farewell nobility; let his Grace go forward,
   And dare us with his cap like larks.
   --William Shakespeare & John Fletcher: King
      Henry The Eighth (1613); Act III, Scene 2.

JAMBEE, JUMBEE: An old type of cane, popular in the
18th century, made from wood found along the river Djambi
in Sumatra.

   "'Lord! Sir Timothy,' says Charles, 'I am concerned that you, whom I took to understand canes
   better than any baronet in town, should be so over-
   seen! Why, Sir Timothy, your's is a true Jambee, and 'Squire Empty's only a plain Dragon.'"
   --Sir Richard Steele: The Tatler, No. 142 (1710):
      paragraph 5.

JANNOCK: A word of unknown origin and many spellings,
referring to a type of leavened bread made from oats. Examples of its usage can be found in Thomas Cogan's The
Haven of Health made for the Comfort of Students (1584);
Edwin Waugh's Sketches of Lancashire Life and Localities
(1855); and, earlier, in Ralph Thoresby's Diary (1694).

> "Bide a wee--bide a wee; you southrons are aye
> in sic a hurry, and this is something concerns
> yoursell, an ye wad take patience to hear't--Yill?
> --deil a drap o' yill did Pate offer me: but Mattie
> gae us baith a drap skimmed milk, and ane o' her
> thick ait jannocks, that was as wat and raw as a
> divot.   O for the bonnie girdle cakes o' the north!"
> --Sir Walter Scott: Rob Roy (1817); chapter 14.

JARK, JACK: An old cant-word of unknown origin, meaning
"a seal, a safe-conduct pass. " Used principally from the
16th to the 19th centuries, it has been suggested that this
word originates in the Romany jarika, "apron," but no con-
clusive evidence has been forthcoming.   It can be found in
John Awdeley (1561), and in Richard Head's Canting Academy
(1673), as well as in Scott:

> "Stay, gentlemen, " Ratcliffe's pass suddenly occur-
> ring to her; "perhaps you know this paper. "
>   "What the devil is she after now, Frank?" said
> the more savage ruffian--"Do you look at it, for,
> d--n me if I could read it, if it were for the bene-
> fit of my clergy. "
>   "This is a jark from Jim Ratcliffe, " said the
> taller, having looked at the bit of paper.   "The
> wench must pass by our cutter's law. "
> --Sir Walter Scott: The Heart of Midlothian (1818);
>   chapter 29.

JASEY, JAZY: A word of many spellings, meaning "a wor-
sted, flaxen perriwig; a bob-wig. " It has been suggested
that jasey is a corruption of jersey, "flax. " It can be found
in George Parker (1780), in Thackeray's Vanity Fair (1848),
and in the following:

> "Faith, broadbrim, I believe thou art right, and
> the old gentleman in the flaxen jazy shall have no
> more of the comforter.   Besides, we have business
> in hand to-day, and this fellow, for as mad as he
> looks, may have a nose on his face after all.

Harkye, father, what is your name, and what
brings you into such an out-of-the-way corner?"
--Sir Walter Scott: Redgauntlet (1824); chapter
    20.

JAVEL: A word of many spellings, referring to a mean,
worthless, insignificant person; a rascal.   The origin is uncertain, but it may be related to cavel, "a piece of wood. "
It can be found in William Dunbar's poetry; in Thomas More
(1534); in Richard Brathwait's Barnabee's Journall (1650).
Says Dr. Johnson: "A wandering fellow"; perhaps also a
vagabond.   A very old word, used since the 14th century.

Now whenas Time, flying with winges swift,
Expired had the terme, that these two javels
Should render up a reckning of their travels
Unto their master, which it of them sought,
Exceedingly they troubled were in thought,
Ne wist what answere unto him to frame,
Ne how to scape great punishment, or shame,
For their false treason and vile theeverie.
--Edmund Spenser: Prosopopoia: Or Mother
    Hubberds Tale (1591); lines 308-315.

JAZERANT, JESSERANT: A word of many spellings, referring to a type of armor coat which was made by attaching
many tiny metal plates to a strong underlying base material.
It comes through the Old French jaseran, the Provencal
jazeran, the Portuguese jazerao, and the Spanish jazarino,
"Algerian, " from the Arabic jazīrah, "island. " Al-jazāir,
meaning "the islands, " is the origin of the proper name of
the city of Algiers.   This word is very old, and can be
found in the Morte d'Arthur (ca. 1400); in Malory's Arthur
(1470); in Holinshed, and in the Paston Letters.

On the other hand towered Conrade.   Firmly
    fenced,
A jazerent of double mail he wore,
Beneath whose weight one but of common strength
Had sunk.
--Robert Southey: Joan of Arc (1796); Book VII,
    lines 183-186.

...the Scotsman observed that he concealed a
jazeran, or flexible shirt of linked mail, which,
as being often worn by those, even of peaceful
professions, who were called upon at that perilous

period to be frequently abroad, confirmed the
young man in his conjecture, that the wearer was
by profession a butcher, grazier, or something of
that description, called upon to be much abroad.
--Sir Walter Scott: <u>Quentin Durward</u> (1823); chapter 2.

JENNETING, JUNEATING, GENITON: A word of many
spellings, referring to a kind of apple. Originally, the word
came about from the French name <u>Jean</u>, with reference to
the "St. John's apple"; but later it became associated with
the month <u>June</u>, during which it was eaten; hence, "<u>Juneat-
ing</u>." It can be found in Holland's <u>Pliny</u> (1601) and in Francis Bacon, as well as in the following:

> Yet, tho' I spared thee all the spring,
> Thy sole delight is, sitting still,
> With that gold dagger of thy bill
> To fret the summer jenneting.
> --Alfred, Lord Tennyson: <u>The Blackbird</u> (1833);
>   stanza 3.

JERRY-COME-TUMBLE, JERRY-GO-NIMBLE: An old slang
expression for an acrobat, a tumbler, or a clown, similar
to a jack-pudding.

> "Well. Be as churlish as you list--I never quarrel
> with my customers--my jerry-come-tumbles, my
> merry dancers, my little playfellows. "
> --Sir Walter Scott: <u>Quentin Durward</u> (1823); chap-
>   ter 14.

> "They took me to Greenhill Fair, and into a great
> large jerry-go-nimble show, where there were
> women-folk riding around--standing upon horses,
> with hardly anything on but their smocks. "
> --Thomas Hardy: <u>Far From the Madding Crowd</u>
>   (1874); chapter 8.

JESTING-STOCK: A laughing-stock; the butt of a joke.

> HOLDFAST: The world's well alter'd.
> He's your kind brother now; but yesterday
> Your slave and jesting-stock.
> --Philip Massinger: <u>The City Madam</u> (1632); Act
>   IV, Scene 4.

JIGGUMBOB: A word of many spellings, referring to something wonderful or new, something fanciful; a trinket; a toy;
a funny little thing. Dr. Johnson says: "A trinket; a knick-
knack; a slight contrivance in machinery." Similar to
thingumbob. It comes as a humorous formation from the
dance called the jig. Used principally from the 17th century, the word can be located in Massinger's The Picture
(1629); in Richard Brome's The Antipodes (1638); in Butler's
Hudibras (1678), and in the following:

> MOTHER: What jiggumbob have we here? Pray
> God, you have not pilfered this somewhere.
> Thou'rt such a puling thing! wipe your eyes, and
> rise; go your ways.
> --Francis Beaumont & John Fletcher: The Coxcomb
>   (1613); Act IV, Scene 7.

> FABRITIO: 'Twas a use her mother had
> When she was invited to an early wedding;
> She'ld dress her head o'ernight, sponge up her-
>   self,
> And give her neck three lathers.
> GUARDIANO: Ne'er a halter?
> FABRITIO: On with her chain of pearl, her ruby
>   bracelets,
> Lay ready all her tricks and jiggambobs.
> --Thomas Middleton: Women Beware Women (ca.
>   1621); Act II, Scene 2.

> LADY LOVEYOUTH: How am I confounded with
> this disaster; yet I have it in my head to be re-
> veng'd on 'em both.
> SIR RICHARD LOVEYOUTH: Your ladyship was
> too credulous to trust him so soon.
> LADY LOVEYOUTH: And Robin, he's a dirty per-
> son thus to desert me; but I'll be quit with him,
> and that Jig-em-bob my niece.
> --Thomas Shadwell: The Humorists (1671); Act V.

JILLET: A familiar term for a young girl, especially one
who is light-headed and flighty. From the proper name
Jill. Found in Robert Burns and in the following:

> "Thou hast not many of the tender sex in thy
> household, I take it, Ramorny?"
>   "Faith, none--except the minstrel wench--but a
> household drudge or two whom we may not dispense

with. By the way, she is anxiously inquiring after
the mistress your Highness promised to prefer
her to.--Shall I dismiss her, to hunt for her new
mistress at leisure?"
    "By no means, she will serve to amuse Cather-
ine--And, hark you, were it not well to receive
that coy jillet with something of a mumming?"
--Sir Walter Scott: The Fair Maid of Perth (1828);
    chapter 31.

JOAN: In the second part of the 18th century, a tight-fitting
cap worn by women. The word is from the female name,
but the exact reason for the connection is not known.

    "In some lesser borough towns, the contest, I
    found, lay between three or four black and green
    bibs and aprons: at one, a grocer's wife attracted
    our eyes, by a new-fashioned cap, called a Joan;
    and at another, they were wholly taken up by a
    mercer's daughter, in a Nun's Hood. "
    --William Cowper: The Connoisseur, No. 134
        (1756); paragraph 7.

        Then of late you're so fickle, that few people
            mind you;
        For my part, I never can tell where to find you:
        Now dress'd in a cap, now naked in none,
        Now loose in a mob, now close in a Joan.
        --Beauty and Fashion: A Repartee in The Annual
            Register (1762); Poetry section, page 208.

JOCKEY: Formed from the Scottish name Jock, from Jack,
this word referred to a strolling or traveling minstrel or
beggar, or a vagabond or tinker. It can be found in George
Sinclair's Satan's Invisible World discovered; or, A Choice
Collection of Relations anent Devils, Spirits, Witches, and
Apparitions (1685), and in the following:

    The tribes of gipsies, jockies, or cairds,--for by
    all these denominations such banditti were known,
    --became few in number, and many were entirely
    rooted out.
    --Sir Walter Scott: Guy Mannering (1815); chapter
        7.

JOCKTELEG, JOCTALEG, JACK-O-LEGS: A word of many
varied spellings, referring to a type of large knife which

was worn attached to the leg. Used principally in the 17th,
18th, and 19th centuries, the origin is uncertain; it may be
from the legend that there once was an old type of knife cut
by a man named Jacques de Liege, who inscribed his name
on his blades. However, this has never been proven, nor
has any such knife or even a record of one been discovered.
It has also been suggested that, since jack was a common
name applied to instruments or tools, the word merely refers to a jack worn at the leg. Uses of the word can be
found in Allan Ramsay and Robert Burns, as well as in the
following:

> "The deil be in my feet," said Andrew, without
> either having respect to the presence in which he
> stood, or waiting till I replied--"the deil be in
> my feet, if I gang my tae's length. Do the folk
> think I hae another thrapple in my pouch after
> John Highlandman's snecked this ane wi' his jocta-
> leg? or that I can dive doun at the tae side of a
> Highland loch and rise at the tother, like a shell-
> drake? Na, na--ilk ane for himsell, and God for
> us a'."
> --Sir Walter Scott: Rob Roy (1817); chapter 32.

JOHN-A-DREAMS: One who wastes his time in idle day-
dreams or fancies; a dreamy, lazy fellow. Found in Armin's A Nest of Ninnies (1608).

> HAMLET: Yet I,
> A dull and muddy-mettled rascal, peak,
> Like John-a-dreams, unpregnant of my cause,
> And can say nothing; no, not for a king,
> Upon whose property and most dear life
> A damn'd defeat was made.
> --William Shakespeare: Hamlet (1600); Act II,
>   Scene 2.

JORDAN: A very old word of uncertain origin, referring
originally to a type of flask used by medieval alchemists,
and later coming to mean a chamber-pot or bedpan. It may
be related to Jordan-bottles, which contained water collected
from the river Jordan by pilgrims to the Holy Land; or it
may be an association with the baptismal name Jordan,
which was very common in older times. Used since the
14th century, it can be found in Chaucer, Jonson, Pope,
Smollett, and Goldsmith, as well as in Shakespeare:

SECOND CARRIER: I think this be the most vil-
lainous house in all London road for fleas: I am
stung like a tench.
FIRST CARRIER: Like a tench! by the mass,
there is ne'er a king christen could be better bit
than I have been since the first cock.
SECOND CARRIER: Why, they will allow us ne'er
a jordan, and then we leak in the chimney; and
your chamber-lie breeds fleas like a loach.
--William Shakespeare: King Henry The Fourth,
Part I (1597); Act II, Scene 1.

JOSEPH: A large, old-fashioned woman's great-coat, often
worn when riding; it had a row of buttons down the front,
and sometimes was equipped with a hood or a cape. The
origin has been disputed; some believe it comes from the
reference to Joseph in the Bible and his coat of many colors;
others see the origin in the fictitious name Joseph Gay,
(used by Curl in his pamphlets to make them look as though
they were written by John Gay), satirized by Alexander Pope
in his Dunciad:

Curl stretches after Gay, but Gay is gone:
He grasps an empty Joseph for a John.

Found in Goldsmith, Crabbe, and the following:

BELFOND JUNIOR: Ounds! Who's here? my
father? Lolpoop, Lolpoop, hide me: give me my
Joseph. Let's sneak into the next room.
--Thomas Shadwell: The Squire of Alsatia (1688);
Act II, Scene 1.

Some women, I grant, would not appear to advantage seated on a pillion, and attired in a drab
joseph and a drab beaver bonnet, with a crown resembling a small stew-pan; for a garment suggest-
ing a coachman's greatcoat, cut out under an
exiguity of cloth that would only allow of miniature
capes, is not well adapted to conceal deficiencies
of contour, nor is drab a color that will throw
sallow cheeks into a lively contrast.
--George Eliot: Silas Marner (1861); chapter 11.

JUMP: To risk or to hazard something. Of unknown origin,
known only since the 16th century.

MACBETH:
If it were done--when 'tis done--then 'twere well
It were done quickly: if th'assassination
Could trammel up the consequence, and catch,
With his surcease, success; that but this blow
Might be the be-all and the end-all here,
But here, upon this bank and shoal of time,
We'ld jump the life to come.
--William Shakespeare: Macbeth (1606); Act I,
   Scene 7.

FIRST GAOLER: Your death has eyes in's head,
then; I have not seen him so pictured: you must
either be directed by some that take upon them to
know, or to take upon yourself that which I am
sure you do not know; or jump the after-inquiry
on your own peril: and how you shall speed in
your journey's end, I think you'll never return to
tell one.
--William Shakespeare: Cymbeline (1611); Act V,
   Scene 4.

JUSTAUCORPS: Not "just a corpse" but a kind of tight-fitting jacket which appeared about 1650 in Paris, worn by
women. The name is a corruption of the French juste au
corps, literally "close to the body."

This done Sir W. Batten and I back again to London, and in the way met my Lady Newcastle going
with her coaches and footmen all in velvet: herself, whom I never saw before, as I have heard
her often described, for all the town-talk is now-
a-days of her extravagancies, with her velvet-cap,
her hair about her ears; many black patches, because of pimples about her mouth; naked-necked,
without any thing about it, and a black just-au-
corps.
--Samuel Pepys' Diary: April 26th, 1667.

JUT-WINDOW: A bay-window, from the verb jet, "to pro-
ject outward."

BELINDA: I fansied her like the front of her
father's hall; her eyes were the two jut-windows,
and her mouth the great door, most hospitably
kept open, for the entertainment of travelling flies.
--William Congreve: The Old Batchelor (1693):
   Act IV, Scene 8.

-K-

KAE: A Scottish form from the Middle English co, referring
to a small blackbird or crow; the jackdaw or chough. From
the Old High German chaha, Danish kaa, and Old Norse ká.
Many spellings exist for it: kaa, ca, kay, key, etc. It can
be found in the works of Richard Rolle of Hampole (1340),
Sir John Ballenden (1536), and in Burns:

> God bless your Honors, a' your days,
> Wi' sowps o' kail and brats o' claes,
> In spite o' a' the thievish kaes,
>   That haunt St. Jamie's!
> Your humble Bardie sings an' prays,
>   While Rab his name is.
> --Robert Burns: The Author's Earnest Cry and
>   Prayer (1786); stanza 25.

KEBBUCK: Another old Scottish word with many spelling
variations (cabok, kibbock, cabbac to name a few), kebbuck
can be a general name for cheese or a specific name: "A
huge kebbuck--a cheese, that is, made with ewe-milk mixed
with cow's milk. "--Scott, OLD MORTALITY (1816). The
origin is unknown, but there may be a connection with the
Gaelic word for cheese, càbag. It can be found as early as
1470 in Robert Henryson's Fabils; it appears in Allan Ramsay and in Samuel Rutherford Crockett's The Stickit Minister
(1893), as well as in the following:

> But now the supper crowns their simple board,
>   The healsome parritch, chief o' Scotia's food:
> The soupe their only Hawkie does afford,
>   That 'yont the hallan snugly chows her cood;
> The dame brings forth in complimental mood,
>   To grace the lad, her weel-hain'd kebbuck, fell.
> --Robert Burns: The Cotter's Saturday Night
>   (1785); stanza 11.

> In comes a gaucie, gash Guidwife,
>   An' sits down by the fire,
> Syne draws her kebbuck an' her knife;
>   The lasses they are shyer.
> --Robert Burns: The Holy Fair (1786); stanza 24.

KECKSY, GICKSY, KEXY: A word for the hemlock, or
plants with hollow stems ("kecks" or "kex" as they are also
variously called). The origin is totally unknown; usage can

be found in James Hurdis (1800), in Coleridge (1816), and
in Shakespeare:

> DUKE OF BURGUNDY:
> The even mead, that erst brought sweetly forth
> The freckled cowslip, burnet, and green clover,
> Wanting the scythe, all uncorrected, rank,
> Conceives by idleness, and nothing teems
> But hateful docks, rough thistles, kecksies, burs,
> Losing both beauty and utility.
> --William Shakespeare: King Henry The Fifth
>   (1599); Act V, Scene 2.

Many various spellings of this word also exist.

KEECH: A big clump of mud or hay; or, more specifically,
a lump of the fat of a slaughtered animal rolled up into a
ball. The origin is unknown. In King Henry the Fourth,
Part II (1598), Shakespeare mentions "goodwife Keech, the
butcher's wife," and in another of his works we find the following use:

> DUKE OF BUCKINGHAM:
> The devil speed him! no man's pie is freed
> From his ambitious finger. What had he
> To do in these fierce vanities? I wonder
> That such a keech can with his very bulk
> Take up the rays o' the beneficial sun,
> And keep it from the earth.
> --William Shakespeare & John Fletcher: King
>   Henry The Eighth (1613); Act I, Scene 1.

KENDAL GREEN: An old kind of rough, green woolen cloth,
worn in legend by foresters and men of the Robin Hood variety. It is named for Kendal, in Westmorland, where it was
made. Found in Lydgate (1425), Thomas More (1532),
Charles Cotton (1687), and in the following:

> PRINCE HENRY: Why, how couldst thou know
> these men in Kendal green, when it was so dark
> thou couldst not see thy hand? come, tell us your
> reason: what say'st thou to this?
> --William Shakespeare: King Henry The Fourth,
>   Part I (1597); Act II, Scene 4.

His garb was fashion'd, to express
The ancient English minstrel's dress,

> A seemly gown of Kendal green,
> With gorget closed of silver sheen.
> --Sir Walter Scott: Rokeby (1813); Canto V, stanza
>   15.

KERRY-MERRY-BUFF: A soft, friendly blow or striking on
the back with the open palm; a "love-tap." The origin is
not known; buff is an old word meaning a "hit" or "blow."
It was once suggested to be the name of a kind of material
of which jackets were made; but this explanation has been
almost universally discounted.

> VIOLETTA: If you wonder that I take this strange
> leave, excuse it thus, that women are strange
> fools, and will take any thing.
> HIPPOLITO: Tricks, tricks; kerry merry buff!
> --Thomas Middleton: Blurt, Master Constable
>   (1602); Act I, Scene 1.

KIBBO: A word of unknown derivation, referring to a stout
stick or staff, good for striking hard blows. Found in the
works of John Collier, the "Tim Bobbin" author, and in
Shadwell:

> LOLPOOP: Hawd you, hawd you: And I take kib-
> bo, I'st raddle the bones o' thee; Ise tell a that:
> for aw th'art a Captain mun.
> --Thomas Shadwell: The Squire of Alsatia (1688);
>   Act II, Scene 1.

KIDDY: An old thieves' term for a young bully who dresses
up in the most outrageous or "flashy" style, and who believes himself to be the center of attention and admiration
when he is really the butt of ridicule. It is a formation
from kid, referring to a young thief or scoundrel. It can
be found in Charles Cowden Clarke's Shakespeare Characters,
chiefly those Subordinate (1863), and in the following:

> Poor Tom was once a kiddy upon town,
>   A thorough varmint, and a real swell,
> Full flash, all fancy, until fairly diddled,
> His pockets first and then his body riddled.
> --Lord Byron: Don Juan (1824); Canto XI, stanza
>   17.

KIDNEY: 1) Disposition; nature; temperament. Also, (2)
a certain class or social group. The origin is unknown; it

may possibly be a construction of kid, "young goat, " and ei,
"egg" (i. e. testicle), but no definite proof of this assertion
has been forthcoming. Francis Grose tells us: "Disposition, principles, humour. Of a strange kidney; of an odd
or unaccountable humour. A man of a different kidney; a
man of different principles. " Found in Henry Fielding (1733),
George Colman (1763), and in many other writers, including
the following:

Sense 1:

> SIR JOHN FALSTAFF: ... and then, to be stopt in,
> like a strong distillation, with stinking clothes that
> fretted in their own grease: think of that, --a man
> of my kidney, --think of that, --that am as subject
> to heat as butter; a man of continual dissolution
> and thaw;--it was a miracle to scape suffocation.
> --William Shakespeare: The Merry Wives of Wind-
> sor (1601); Act III, Scene 5.

Sense 2:

> It was a large and rather miscellaneous party, but
> all of the right kidney.
> --Benjamin Disraeli: Endymion (1880); chapter 17.

KILL-COW: A swaggering, murdering, boasting, fighting
bully; one who thinks that he is of the greatest importance,
because he has "killed the cow, " referring to the killing of
the Dun Cow of Dunsmore-Heath by Guy of Warwick in English legend. Also, a butcher; a swashbuckler. Found in
Richard Harvey's Plaine Percevall the Peace-maker of England (1589) and in North's Lives (1734). John Fletcher used
it in Bonduca and in the following:

> MALFORT: The bullet flew close by me,
> Close by my ear: another had a huge sword,
> Flourish'd it thus, but at the point I met him;
> But the rogue, taking me to be your lordship
> (As sure your name is terrible, and we
> Not much unlike in the dark), roar'd out aloud,
> 'It is the kill-cow Dorilaus!" and away
> They ran as they had flown. --Now you must love
> me,
> Or fear me for my courage, wench.
> --John Fletcher: The Lovers' Progress (ca. 1623);
> Act III, Scene 3.

KIMNEL, KEMLIN, KIMLIN: A word of many spellings, referring to a large powdering-tub used for kneading, salting,
brewing, washing, etc. Principally in use from the 16th to
the 19th centuries, it comes through the Middle English
kemelin, from an unknown source; it may be related to the
Old English cumb, "coomb," a large brewing vat. Found as
early as 1386 in Chaucer's The Miller's Tale in The Canterbury Tales.

> ALEXANDER: She's somewhat simple, indeed; she
> knew not what a kimnel was; she wants good nur-
> ture mightily.
> --Francis Beaumont & John Fletcher: The Cox-
>   comb (1613); Act IV, Scene 7.

KINCHIN-LAY: A word used from around 1600, referring to
the act of robbing little children sent on errands by their
mothers. From the German kindchen, "small child."
Charles Dickens gives us a good description:

> "Stop!" said Fagin, laying his hand on Noah's
> knee. "The kinchin lay."
> "What's that?" demanded Mr. Claypole.
> "The kinchins, my dear," said Fagin, "is the
> young children that's sent on errands by their
> mothers, with sixpences and shillings; and the lay
> is just to take their money away--they've always
> got it ready in their hands,--then knock 'em into
> the kennel, and walk off very slow, as if there
> were nothing else the matter but a child fallen
> down and hurt itself. Ha! ha! ha!"
> --Charles Dickens: Oliver Twist (1839); chapter
>   42.

KING'S CUSHION: A ready seat made from the hands of two
people crossed over, used for carrying individuals or for
giving a boost to a higher position. Also known as the
queen's cushion.

> They had suffered the unfortunate Porteous to put
> on his night-gown and slippers, as he had thrown
> off his coat and shoes, in order to facilitate his
> attempted escape up the chimney. In this garb he
> was now mounted on the hands of two of the riot-
> ers, clasped together, so as to form what is called
> in Scotland, "The King's Cushion."
> --Sir Walter Scott: The Heart of Midlothian (1818);
>   chapter 7.

KINGCUP: A common name for the buttercup or the marsh
marigold. Found in Henry Peacham's The Gentleman's Exercise in The Compleat Gentleman (1634), and in Tennyson
(1833), as well as in the following:

> Even in the spring and playtime of the year,
> That calls the unwonted villager abroad
> With all her little ones, a sportive train,
> To gather kingcups in the yellow mead,
> And prink their hair with daisies, or to pick
> A cheap but wholesome salad from the brook,
> These shades are all my own.
> --William Cowper: The Task (1785); Book VI,
>   lines 299-305.

> Pansies, lilies, kingcups, daisies,
> Let them live upon their praises;
> Long as there's a sun that sets,
> Primroses will have their glory;
> Long as there are violets,
> They will have a place in story:
> There's a flower that shall be mine,
> 'Tis the little Celandine.
> --William Wordsworth: To the Small Celandine
>   (April 30th, 1802); stanza 1.

KIPPAGE: A Scottish word for a state of great excitement,
anger, wrath, or passion; a time of irritation or annoyance.
The origin can be seen in the French équipage, "the people
on board a ship, both passengers and crew." This word
was greatly used by Scott, in The Antiquary (1816), The
Bride of Lammermoor (1818), and in the following:

> He entered the room with all the marks of a man
> agitated by a towering passion; and there were few
> upon whose features rage produced a more violent
> effect. The veins of his forehead swelled when he
> was in such agitation: his nostrils became dilated;
> his cheek and eye inflamed; and his look that of a
> demoniac...
> "The Colonel's in an unco kippage," said Mrs.
> Flockhart to Evan, as he descended; "I wish he
> may be weel,--the very veins on his brent brow
> are swelled like whip-cord; wad he no tak some-
> thing?"
> --Sir Walter Scott: Waverley (1814); chapter 53.

KIRN: A churn. Related to the Old Norse kirna, same
sense. Also, a festival celebrating the end of the harvest
(seen in Scott's Marmion). Found in Allan Ramsay, and in
the following:

> Thence, countra wives, wi' toil an' pain,
> May plunge an' plunge the kirn in vain.
> --Robert Burns: Address to the Deil (1785); stanza
>   10.

> "I gave her, " he said, "yester-e'en nae farther
> gane, a yard of that very black sey, to make her
> a couvre-chef; but I see it is ill done to teach
> the cat the way to the kirn. "
> --Sir Walter Scott: The Monastery (1820); chapter
>   35.

KISSING-STRINGS: The strings of a woman's bonnet, fastened
under the chin with the ends dangling loose.

> The trunk, hastily opened, as the reader will not
> doubt, was found to be full of wearing apparel of
> the best quality, suited to Jeanie's rank in life ...
> to name the various articles by their appropriate
> names, would be to attempt things unattempted yet
> in prose or rhyme; besides, that the old-fashioned
> terms of manteaus, sacques, kissing-strings, and
> so forth, would convey but little information even
> to the milliners of the present day.
> --Sir Walter Scott: The Heart of Midlothian (1818);
>   chapter 45.

KIT: 1) an old type of small violin.   2) a dancing-master.
From the Greek kithara, "cithara, " the ancient musical instrument which resembled a lyre and which was an ancestor
of the zither. Also, 3) a fiddler himself. The kit or violin
was usually of a triangular shape, with from seven to eleven
strings. About sense (2), Grose tells us: "A dancing-
master; so called from his kit or cittern, a small fiddle,
which dancing-masters always carry about with them, to
play to their scholars. " Found in Thomas Phaer's Aeneid
(1562), and in the following (all sense 1):

> SLICER: O that endeavouring face!
> When will your costiveness have done, good madam?
> HEARSAY: Do you not hear her guts already squeak
> Like kit-strings?

SLICER: They must come to that within
This two or three years: by that time she'll be
True perfect cat. They practise beforehand.
MISTRESS POTLUCK: I can endure no longer,
    though I should
Throw off my womanhood.
HEARSAY: No need, that's done
Already: nothing left thee that may style thee
Woman, but lust and tongue: no flesh but what
The vices of the sex exact, to keep them
In heart.
--William Cartwright: The Ordinary (ca. 1634);
    Act I, Scene 2.

ROBIN:
I do not know what their sharp sight may see,
Of late, but I should think it still might be
As 'twas, an happy age, when on the plains
The woodmen met the damsels, and the swains
The neat-herds, ploughmen, and the pipers loud,
And each did dance, some to the kit or crowd,
Some to the bag-pipe; some the tabret mov'd,
And all did either love, or were belov'd.
--Ben Jonson: The Sad Shepherd (1637); Act I,
    Scene 2.

To put them to the trial, "Look ye," said I, "I
must not rashly give my judgement in matters of
this importance; pray let me see you dance, I play
upon the kit."
--Sir Richard Steele: The Tatler, No. 34 (1709);
    paragraph 4.

I curtsied to a little blue-eyed fair man of youthful
appearance with flaxen hair parted in the middle
and curling at the ends all round his head. He
had a little fiddle, which we used to call at school
a kit, under his left arm, and its little bow in the
same hand.
--Charles Dickens: Bleak House (1853); chapter
    14.

KITCHEN-FEE: The skimmings or drippings of fat which
roll off roasting meats. From fee, a gratuity or customary
tip, so-called because the kitchen-fee was the "perquisite"
of the cook. Found in Gervase Markham's Cheap and Good
Husbandry (1614), and in the following:

"But will ye not take anither dish of tea, Maister
Francie, and a wee bit of the diet-loaf, raised wi'
my ain fresh butter, Maister Francie, and no wi'
greasy kitchen-fee, like the seedcake down at the
confectioner's yonder, that has as mony dead
flees as carvy in it?"
--Sir Walter Scott: St. Ronan's Well (1823); chapter 2.

KNAPSCALL: A word of many spellings, referring to a
type of old helmet worn by privates or other lowly soldiers.
It comes from knape, related to knave, "a youth," and probably from a variation of skull.

"Take the ribbons from your halberds, ye knaves,
and get on your jacks, plate-sleeves, and knap-
skulls, that your presence may work some terror
if you meet with opposers."
--Sir Walter Scott: The Abbott (1820); chapter 26.

KNITCH: A word of many spellings, such as knucche,
knytche, knohche, etc., referring to a bundle of things, usually wood-cuttings, tied and roped together. Through the
Middle English knücche, from the Old English word for
"bond," related to the Low German knuck, "bundle of flax."
Further derivation is uncertain. Found in John Wycliffe
(1382), John de Trevisa (1398), Holland (1603), and, more
recently, in the following:

"I've got no bread--where should I? I've got no
fire--how can I give one shilling and sixpence a
hundred for coals? And if I did, who'd fetch 'em
home? And if I dared break a hedge for a knitch
o' wood, they'd put me in prison, they would, with
the worst. What be I to do? What be you going
to do? That's what I came here for."
--Charles Kingsley: Alton Locke (1850); chapter
28.

KNITTING-CUP: A cup of wine passed around to the guests
during a wedding feast, with reference to the "knitting" of
the bonds of matrimony.

COMPASS: Have you a license?
PRACTISE: No;
But I can fetch one straight.
COMPASS: Do, do, and mind

The parson's pint, to engage him [in] the business;
A knitting cup there must be.
--Ben Jonson: The Magnetic Lady (1632); Act IV,
   Scene 1.

KNURL, KNURLE, NURL: A squat, thick-set, stout individual; a dumpy dwarf. The exact origin is uncertain, but
it may be in the old word knur, a "knot" or "swelling."

   The miller was strappin, the miller was ruddy,
   A heart like a lord, and a hue like a lady.
   The laird was a widdifu', bleerit knurl--
   She's left the guid fellow, and taen the churl!
   --Robert Burns: Meg O' the Mill (Second Set)
      (1793); stanza 2.

KYTE: An old Scottish word of unknown origin, referring to
a fat belly or stomach. It may possibly be related to the
Middle Low German kût, "entrails," or the Dutch kuit, "calf
of the leg."

   Then, horn for horn, they stretch an' strive:
   Deil tak the hindmost, on they drive,
   Till a' their weel-swall'd kytes belyve
               Are bent like drums;
   Then auld Guidman, maist like to rive,
               "Bethankit!" hums.
   --Robert Burns: Address to a Haggis (1786);
      stanza 4.

   'I sair doubt me, father," she said, "whether
Mysie finds her way back to the Mill in a hurry;
but it was all her father's own fault that let her
run lamping about the country, riding on bare-
backed haigs, and never settling to do a turn of
wark within doors, unless it were to dress dainties
at dinner time for his ain kyte."
   --Sir Walter Scott: The Monastery (1820); chapter
      33.

   A more recent example can be located in Samuel
Rutherford Crockett's The Men of the Moss Hags (1895).

-L-

LADRONE: A word of many varied spellings, including la-
tron, ladren, ladron, latherin, etc., referring to (1) in
Scotland, a contemptuous term for a rogue or scoundrel; or
(2) in Spanish countries, a thief, robber, bandit, or highwayman; a brigand. Through the Spanish ladrón and the Old
French ladron, from the Latin latro, "robber, mercenary."
The Scottish sense can be found in Allan Ramsay (1718) and
in David Davidson's Thoughts on the Seasons (1789); the second sense is seen in James Shirley (1626); in Capt. Mayne
Reid's The Scalp-Hunters (1851); in Alexander Fraser's
Scraps; or, Scenes, Tales, and Anecdotes from Memories of
my Earlier Days (1883); in George Meredith's The Egoist
(1879); and in the following:

> He told us that he had a list of all the robbers in
> the country, and meant to ferret out every mother's
> son of them; he offered us at the same time some
> of his soldiers as an escort. "One is enough to
> protect you, señors; the sight of one is enough to
> spread terror through a whole sierra." We
> thanked him for his offer, but assured him, in his
> own strain, that with the protection of our re-
> doubtable squire, Sancho, we were not afraid of
> all the ladrones of Andalusia.
> --Washington Irving: The Alhambra (1832); chapter
> 1.

LADY'S LONGING, LADY LONGING: A word of unknown
origin, referring to some type of apple. Found in John
Evelyn's Sylva (1664); in Worlidge (1676), and in Lyly:

> EPI: Why in marrying Dipsas, he shall have
> every day twelve dishes of meat to his dinner,
> though there be none but Dipsas with him. Four
> of flesh, four of fish, four of fruit.
> SAMIAS: As how Epi?
> EPI: For flesh these; woodcock, goose, biter,
> and rayle.
> DARES: Indeed he shall not miss, if Dipsas be
> there.
> EPI: For fish these; crab, carp, lumpe, and
> powting.
> SAMIAS: Excellent! for of my word, she is both
> crabbish, lumpish, and carping.
> EPI: For fruit these; fretters, medlers,

hartichockes, and Lady longings. Thus you see he
shall fare like a King, though he be but a beggar.
--John Lyly: Endymion (ca. 1585); Act III, Scene
    3.

LANGOON: A kind of white wine from Langon, a town on
the Garonne, about 22 miles southeast of Bordeaux. E.
Smith, in the Complete Housewife, speaks of "the best langoon white wine," and Shadwell employs it in the following:

> SIR HUMPHREY SCATTERGOOD: Away you cox-
> comb: Let it be your care to keep my cellar
> always full as it is now.
> STEWARD: I am acquainted with my old master's
> merchant, he us'd to let him have very good
> Langoon and Burdeaux.
> SIR HUMPHREY SCATTERGOOD: Porters and
> carriers shall drink that; I'll have Vin d'aye, high
> country wine, Frontiniac; all the delicious wines
> of Italy and Spain; the richer wines of Greece and
> Sicily.
> --Thomas Shadwell: The Woman-Captain (1679);
>   Act I.

LASSOCK: A Scottish diminutive of lass, referring thus to
a little girl. Lass comes from the Old Norse löskr, "idle,"
hence, a girl "idle" or "not wed." Lassock can be seen in
Robert W. Buchanan's The Heir of Linne (1887), and in the
following excerpts from Scott:

> "But tak heed o' the young queans, lad ... I mind,
> when I was a gilpy of a lassock, seeing the Duke,
> that was him that lost his head at London ...
> weel, he had a comely presence, and when a' the
> gentles mounted to show their capers, his Grace
> was as near to me as I am to you; and he said
> to me, 'Tak tent o' yoursell, my bonny lassie
> (these were his very words), for my horse is not
> very chancy.'"
> --Sir Walter Scott: Old Mortality (1816); chapter
>   4.

> "I see how it is--I see how it is. But say naething
> about it--there's a gude callant; and charge that
> lang-tongued, conceited, upsetting servant man o'
> yours, to sae naething neither. I wadna for ever
> sae muckle that even the lassock Mattie ken'd

onything about it. I wad never hear an end o't. "
--Sir Walter Scott: Rob Roy (1817); chapter 36.

LATHE, LAITHE, LATH, LEATH: An old word for a barn,
from the Old Norse hlatha (Danish lade), "to fill up, to
load, to take on. " Found in William Camden (1605); in
James Hutton, the geologist (1781), and in the following excerpts, one very old, and one comparatively recent:

> And as I alther-fastest wente
> Aboute, and dide al myn entente
> Me for to pleye and for to lere,
> And eek a tyding for to here,
> That I had herd of som contree
> That schal not now be told for me;--
> For hit no nede is, redely;
> Folk can singe hit bet than I;
> For al mot out, other late or rathe,
> Alle the sheves in the lathe.
> --Geoffrey Chaucer: The Hous of Fame (ca. 1384);
>   Book III, lines 1041-1050.

> "I would not keep my door barred in the day-time.
> I don't care--I will get in!" So resolved, I
> grasped the latch and shook it vehemently. Vine-
> gar-faced Joseph projected his head from a round
> window of the barn.
>   "What are ye for?" he shouted. 'T' maister's
> down i' t' fowld. Go round by th' end ot' laith,
> if ye went to spake to him. "
> --Emily Bronte: Wuthering Heights (1847); chapter
>   2.

LAUWINE, LAWINE: An avalanche of snow; from the German lawine, from lau, "tepid. " Found in John Nichol's The
Death of Themistocles, and Other Poems (1881), and in Byron:

> The Suabian sued, and now the Austrian reigns--
> An Emperor tramples where an Emperor knelt;
> Kingdoms are shrunk to provinces, and chains
> Clank over sceptred cities; nations melt
> From power's high pinnacle, when they have felt
> The sunshine for a while, and downward go
> Like lauwine loosen'd from the mountain's belt;
> Oh for one hour of blind old Dandolo!
> --Lord Byron: Childe Harold's Pilgrimage (1818);
>   Canto IV, stanza 12.

LAWING: In Scotland, the bill due to a customer at a tavern or inn; inn-reckoning. From the old word law, "an expense," from the Old Norse lag, "market-price." It can be found in George Stuart's Joco-Serious Discourse, in Two Dialogues between a Northumberland Gentleman and his Tenant, a Scotchman, both old Cavaliers (1686); Allan Ramsay (1728); Robert Fergusson (1774), and in the following:

> "Well, I do not blame you for being kind to Darsie Latimer; but it would have done as much good if you had walked with him as far as the toll-bar, and then made your farewells; it would have saved horse-hire--and your reckoning, too, at dinner."
> "Latimer paid that, sir," I replied, thinking to soften the matter; but I had much better have left it unspoken.
> "The reckoning, sir!" replied my father. "And did you sponge upon any man for a reckoning? Sir, no man should enter the door of a public-house without paying his lawing."
> --Sir Walter Scott: Redgauntlet (1824); letter 2.

LESTERCOCK: A type of buoy used by fishing boats, a good description of which is provided in the quotation. The word is from the Old Cornish lester, "ship," and cock, "a small boat."

> Upon the North coast where want of good harbours denieth safe roade to the fisher boats, they have a device of two sticks filled with corks and crossed flatlong, out of whose midst there riseth a thred, and at the same hangeth a saile; to this engine termed a Lestercock, they tie one end of their Boulter.
> --Richard Carew: Survey of Cornwall (1602).

LIARD, LYARD, LIERDE: A kind of small French coin of little worth; hence, any coin that has a small value. From the French liard, "gray," of unknown origin. Also, this word can be used as an adjective meaning "gray." Dr. Johnson says: "Liard in Scotland denotes gray-haired: as, he's a liard old man." The Scottish form is lyart. It can be found in Andrew Borde's The First Boke of the Introduction of Knowledge (1542); in Davenant (1657); in Tobias Smollett's Peregrine Pickle (1751); in Benjamin Disraeli's Tancred (1847), and in the following from Scott:

"The Lady Rowena is desirous to return to Rother-
wood, and must be escorted by a sufficient force.
I should, therefore, ere now, have left this place;
and I waited--not to share the booty, for, so help
me God and Saint Withold! as neither I nor any
of mine will touch the value of a liard, --I waited
but to render my thanks to thee and to thy bold
yeomen, for the life and honour ye have saved. "
--Sir Walter Scott: Ivanhoe (1819); chapter 32.

LIBKEN: A small room; a place in which to sleep, usually
occupied by thieves, robbers, and highwaymen; also, any
place where stolen goods are stored. From lib, "to sleep, "
and ken, "thieves' house, " both of unknown origin. Found
in Ben Jonson's The Gipsies Metamorphos'd (1622), and in
the following:

TRAPDOOR: My doxy stays for me in a bousing
ken, brave captain.
MOLL: He says his wench stays for him in an
alehouse. You are no pure rogues!
TEARCAT: Pure rogues? no, we scorn to be
pure rogues; but if you come to our lib ken or
our stalling ken, you shall find neither him nor
me a queer cuffin.
--Thomas Dekker & Thomas Middleton: The Roaring Girl (1611); Act V, Scene 1.

"Weel, weel, then ye shall be put up like a prince, "
said Mac-Guffog. "But mark ye me, friend, that
we may have nae colly-shangie [quarrel, argu-
ment] afterhend, these are the fees that I always
charge a swell that must have his lib-ken to him-
sell--Thirty shillings a-week for lodgings, and a
guinea for garnish; half-a-guinea a-week for a
single bed, and I dinna get the whole of it, for I
must gie half-a-crown out of it to Donald Laider
that's in for sheep-stealing, that should sleep with
you by rule, and he'll expect clean strae, and
maybe some whiskey beside. "
--Sir Walter Scott: Guy Mannering (1815); chapter
44.

LICKPENNY: Something or someone that "licks up" pennies,
or causes them to be spent rapidly. Thomas Gage, in A
New Survey of the West Indies (1648): "Their Religion is a
dear and lickpenny religion for such poor Indians. " Found

also in John Day's <u>The Blind Beggar of Bednal Green</u> (1659), and in the following:

> WIAT: Sweet musick, gallant fellow-Londiners.
> CLOWN: I'faith we are the mad-caps, we are the lick-pennies.
> WIAT: You shall be all Lord Mayors at least.
> --Thomas Dekker & John Webster: <u>The Famous Historie of Sir Thomas Wyat</u> (1607).

> SANCHO: She has two devils in her eyes, that last ogle was a lickpenny.
> --John Dryden: <u>Love Triumphant</u> (1691); Act I, Scene 1.

> "The circumstances of embarrassment under which you found me at Smyrna were merely temporary-- I am most able and willing to pay my debt; and, let me add, I am most desirous to do so."
>   "Another time--another time," said Mr. Touchwood--"time enough before us, Mr. Tyrrel--besides, at Smyrna, you talked of a lawsuit--law is a lick-penny, Mr. Tyrrel--no counsellor like the pound in purse."
> --Sir Walter Scott: <u>St. Ronan's Well</u> (1823); chapter 28.

LICKSPIGOT: A term of contempt for a tapster or bartender: one who "licks" the "spigot." Also, from this same sense, a parasite, fawner, or flatterer. Spigot is probably related to the word spike, through Middle English.

> COOK: Sir, the mad Greeks of this age can taste their Palermo as well as the sage Greeks did before them. --Fill, lick-spiggot.
> DRAWER: Ad imum, sir.
> --Thomas Middleton & William Rowley: <u>The Old Law</u> (1599); Act IV, scene 1.

> LODOVICO: Who are they Snayle? I hope you do not mean mine uncle her Master; he's mine uncle and I love him well, and I know the old lickspiggot will be nibling a little when he can come to't: but I must needs say he will do no hurt, he's as gentle as an adder that has his teeth taken out.
> --George Chapman: <u>May-Day</u> (1611); Act III.

LIME-TWIG: A branch or little twig of a tree dabbed with
birdlime, a sticky liquid made from holly-bark, used for
catching small birds in flypaper-fashion.   Hence, a second-
ary meaning in a figurative sense: A robber; one who has
birdlime on his fingers and grabs whatever he can.   A very
old word, found in John Lydgate (1400); John Bunyon (1678);
in Dekker & Webster's Historie of Sir Thomas Wyat (1607);
in Thomas Ken (1711); in Samuel Rogers' Italy; a Poem
(1820); in Smollett's Humphrey Clinker (1771), and in the
following:

> CARDINAL BEAUFORT:
> Comb down his hair; look, look! it stands upright,
> Like lime-twigs set to catch my winged soul!
> --William Shakespeare: King Henry The Sixth,
>   Part II (1591); Act III, Scene 3.

> But now I find it true; for by this means
> I knew the foul enchanter though disguised,
> Entered the very lime-twigs of his spells,
> And yet came off.
> --John Milton: Comus (1634); lines 643-646.

> "'T is true, it gets another bright and fresh,
>   Or fresher, brighter; but the year gone through,
> This skin must go the way, too, of all flesh,
>   Or sometimes only wear a week or two;--
> Love's the first net which spreads its deadly mesh;
>   Ambition, Avarice, Vengeance, Glory, glue
> The glittering lime-twigs of our latter days,
> Where still we flutter on for pence or praise. "
> --Lord Byron: Don Juan (1824); Canto V, Stanza
>   22.

LIMMER: A word of many spellings, referring to (1) a
scoundrel or rascal; or (2) a mistress; prostitute; woman of
the evening. The origin of the word is not known. The
first sense can be found in Henryson's Fabils (1470), and in
the following:

> EARINE: O the fiend on thee!
> Gae, take them hence; they fewmand [soil] all the
>   claithes,
> And prick my coats: hence with 'em, limmer lown,
> Thy vermin and thyself, thyself art one!
> Ay, lock me up--all's well when thou art gone.
> --Ben Jonson: The Sad Shepherd (1637); Act II,
>   Scene 1.

"What is the matter, my son Harry?" said Simon,
who now appeared at the window. --"I hear thy
voice in another tone than I expected. --What is
all this noise? and why are the neighbors gather-
ing to the affray?"
     "There have been a proper set of limmers
about to scale your windows, father Simon; but I
am like to prove godfather to one of them, whom
I hold here, as fast as ever vice held iron. "
--Sir Walter Scott: The Fair Maid of Perth (1828);
     chapter 4.

     The second sense can be located in George Borrow
(1851) and Samuel Rutherford Crockett (1897), and in these
excerpts:

     For thae frank, rantin, ramblin billies,
     Fient haet o' them's ill-hearted fellows;
     Except for breaking, o' their timmer,
     Or speaking lightly o' their limmer,
     Or shootin o' a hare or moor-cock,
     The ne'er-a-bit they're ill to poor folk.
     --Robert Burns: The Twa Dogs (1786); lines 179-
          184.

     "As it's near the darkening, sir, wad ye just step
     in by to our house, and tak a dish o' tea? and I
     am sure, if ye like to sleep in the little room, I
     wad tak care ye are no disturbed, and naebody wad
     ken ye, for Kate and Matty, the limmers, gaed aff
     wi' twa o' Hawley's dragoons, and I hae two new
     queans instead o' them. "
     --Sir Walter Scott: Waverley (1814); chapter 63.

LINK-BOY, LINK-MAN: The "link" was a lighted torch that
was carried ahead of pedestrians by this person, to light the
way in the dark of night. The origin of link is unknown.
Examples of usage can be seen in George Farquhar (1698);
in John Mottley's Joe Miller's Jests (1739), and in the following:

     Thence to Sir Harry Wrights; but my Lady not be-
     ing within, I spoke to Mrs. Carter about it, who
     will get one [a hanging Jack to roast birds on]
     against Monday. So with a link-boy to Scotts,
     where Mrs. Ann was in a fit; but I spoke not to
     her but told Mrs. Jem what I had done; and after

that, went home and wrote letters into the country
by the post.
--Samuel Pepys' Diary: February 4th, 1660.

Let constant vigilance thy footsteps guide,
And wary circumspection guard thy side;
Then shalt thou walk, unharm'd, the dangerous
    night,
Nor need th'officious linkboy's smoky light.
--John Gay: Trivia (1716); Book III, lines 111-
    114.

They waited some time, but nobody came.
   "Servants is in the arms o' Porpus, I think,"
said the short chairman, warming his hands at the
attendant linkboy's torch.
--Charles Dickens: The Pickwick Papers (1837);
    chapter 36.

In walking through streets which may have been
gay and polite when ladies' chairmen jostled each
other on the pavement, and link-boys with their
torches lighted the beaux over the mud, who has
not remarked the artist's invasion of those regions
once devoted to fashion and gaiety?
--William Makepeace Thackeray: The Newcomes
    (1855); chapter 17.

Though thou art tempted by the link-man's call,
Yet trust him not along the lonely wall;
In the mid-way he'll quench the flaming brand,
And share the booty with the pilfering band.
--John Gay: Trivia (1716); Book III, lines 139-
    142.

LINSTOCK: A word of many spellings, including lent-stock,
linestoke, limstock, etc., referring to the stick or staff
which had a forked head to hold a gunner's lighted match.
It was usually three to four feet in length, the lower end
being pointed, enabling it to be anchored in the ground.
The origin is seen in the Dutch lontstock, constructed from
lont, "match," and stok, "stick." Found in Churchyard's
Chips Concerning Scotland, being a Collection of his Pieces
relative to that Country (1575); in Scott's Kenilworth (1821),
and in the following authors:

    BOBADILL: Observe me judicially, sweet sir,

they had planted me three demi-culverings, just in
the mouth of the breach; now, sir (as we were to
give on) their master gunner (a man of no mean
skill, and mark, you must think) confronts me
with his linstock, ready to give fire; I spying his
intendment, discharg'd my petronel in his bosom,
and with these single arms, my poor rapier, ran
violently, upon the Moors, that guarded the ordi-
nance, and put 'hem pell-mell to the sword.
--Ben Jonson: Every Man in His Humour (1598);
   Act III, Scene 1.

Suppose th'ambassador from the French comes
     back;
Tells Harry that the king doth offer him
Katharine his daughter; and with her, to dowry,
Some petty and unprofitable dukedoms.
The offer likes not: and the nimble gunner
With linstock now the devilish cannon touches,
And down goes all before them.
--William Shakespeare: King Henry The Fifth
   (1599); Act III, Prologue.

DILDO: The match of fury is lighted, fastened to
the linstock of rage, and will presently set fire
to the touchhole of intemperance, discharging the
double culverin of my incensement in the face of
thy opprobrious speech.
--John Marston: Antonio and Mellida (ca. 1600);
   Act II, Scene 1.

MOLL: A justice in this town, that speaks nothing
but "Make a mittimus, away with him to Newgate,"
used that rogue like a firework to run upon a line
betwixt him and me.
ALL: How, how?
MOLL: Marry, to lay trains of villainy to blow
up my life: I smelt the powder, spied what linstock gave fire to shoot against the poor captain
of the galley-foist [barge with oars], and away
slid I my man like a shovel-board shilling. He
struts up and down the suburbs, I think, and eats
up whores, feeds upon a bawd's garbage.
--Thomas Dekker & Thomas Middleton: The Roaring Girl (1611); Act V, Scene 1.

Minstrels and trumpeters were there,

The gunner held his linstock yare,
    For welcome-shot prepared:--
Entered the train, and such a clang,
As then through all his turrets rang,
    Old Norham never heard.
--Sir Walter Scott: Marmion (1808); Canto I,
    stanza 9.

Hairy-faced Dick understands his trade;
He stands by the breech of a long carronade,
The linstock glows in his bony hand,
Waiting that grim old Skipper's command.
--R. H. Barham: The Ingoldsby Legends (1842):
    "The Legend of Hamilton Tighe."

LOOBY: A word of many spellings, such as loby, lowbie,
lubby, etc., referring to a lazy good-for-nothing; a stupid
clown; a fool; a dull boor. Says Grose: "An awkward,
ignorant fellow." And Dr. Johnson tells us: "A lubber; a
clumsy clown." Used primarily from the 14th to 19th centuries, it is connected with lob, "a rustic, a hillbilly," and
further derivations are not known for certain. It can be
seen in Langland's Piers Plowman (1377); in Stanyhurst
(1577); in Thomas Flatman's poems (1681); in Edmund Hickeringill (1705); Sir Richard Steele (1713); in John Clare's
The Village Minstrel, and Other Poems (1821); in Benjamin
Disraeli's Sybil (1845), and in these:

JOHNSON. "Depend upon it, Sir, a savage when
he is hungry will not carry about with him a
looby of nine years old, who cannot help himself.
They have no affection, Sir." BOSWELL. "I believe natural affection of which we hear so much,
is very small." JOHNSON. "Sir, natural affection is nothing. But affection from principle and
established duty is sometimes wonderfully strong."
--James Boswell: Life of Samuel Johnson, LL.D
    (1791); April 20th, 1783.

Thus while I tell the truth about loobies, my reader's imagination need not be entirely excluded from
an occupation with lords; and the petty sums which
any bankrupt of high standing would be sorry to
retire upon, may be lifted to the level of high
commercial transactions by the inexpensive addition of proportional ciphers.
--George Eliot: Middlemarch (1872); Book IV,
    chapter 35.

LOPEMAN: A runner; also, as in the quote, according to
Dyce, a "rope-dancer." Lope is a provincial form of leap;
hence, "leaping-man." From the Dutch loopman, from
loopen, "to run."

> MADAME MARINE:
> Oh, for a stronger lace to keep my breath,
> That I may laugh the nine days, till the wonder
> Fall to an ebb! the high and mighty duchess!
> The high and mighty! God, what a style is this!
> Methinks it goes like a Dutchy lope-man:
> A ladder of a hundred rounds will fail
> To reach the top on't.
> --John Fletcher: The Noble Gentleman (1625); Act
> III, Scene 4.

LUMPERDEE CLUMPERDEE: To move in an awkward,
clumsy, hulking manner; of unknown origin.

> TALKAPACE: Then shall ye see Tibet, sirs,
>   tread the moss so trim;
> Nay, why said I tread? ye shall see her glide and
>   swim;
> Not lumperdy-clumperdy, like our spaniel Rig.
> TRUEPENNY: Marry, then, prick-me-dainty!
>   come, toast me a fig.
> --Nicholas Udall: Ralph Roister Doister (ca. 1550);
>   Act II, Scene 3.

LURDAN: A word of many spellings, including lurden, lor-
dein, lurdon, lorde dane, lourdain, etc., referring to a
worthless person; a lazy rascal; a sluggard; loafer; rogue;
idiot. Through the Old French lourdin, "sluggard," from
lourd, "heavy." In use from the 13th to 18th centuries, it
can be found in many writers: in Barbour's Bruce (ca.
1375); John Rastell's The Pastyme of the People (1529);
Henry Crosse's Virtue Commonwealth; or the Highway to
Honour (1603); in Milton (1641); Allan Ramsay (1723); Charles
Kingsley (1865); and in the following:

> CONSTABLE: Marry, sir, here's a company of
> rufflers that, drinking in the tavern, have made a
> great brawl, and almost killed the vintner.
> MILES: Salve, doctor Burden! this lubberly lur-
> den,
> Ill-shap'd and ill faced, disdain'd and disgrac'd,
> What he tells unto vobis, mentitur de nobis.

--Robert Greene: Friar Bacon and Friar Bungay
(1591); Act II, Scene 4.

'I will beat him and thee too, " answered Roland,
without hesitation, "an ye look not better after
your business. See how the bird is cast away
between you. I found the careless lurdane feeding
her with unwashed flesh, and she an eyas. "
--Sir Walter Scott: The Abbot (1820); chapter 4.

Then was he ware of three pavilions rear'd
Above the bushes, gilden-peakt. In one,
Red after revel, droned her lurdane knights
Slumbering, and their three squires across their
  feet.
--Alfred, Lord Tennyson: Pelleas and Ettarre
(1859); lines 419-422.

LUXUR: A lecher; "an incontinent man. " The origin is uncertain; it may be a formation from luxurious.

There I heard news out of all countries, in all
languages; how many villains were in Spain, how
many luxurs in Italy, how many perjurds in
France, and how many reel-pots in Germany.
--Thomas Middleton: The Black Book (1604).

Happy art thou, and all thy brothers,
That never feel'st the hell of others!
The torment to a luxur due,
Who never thinks his harlot true;
Although upon her heels he stick his eyes,
Yet still he fears that though she stands she lies.
--Thomas Middleton: "The Nightingale's Canzonet"
in Father Hubburd's Tales (1604).

VENDICE:
Duke! royal lecher! go, grey-haired adultery!
And thou his son, as impious steeped as he:
And thou his bastard, true begot in evil:
And thou his duchess, that will do with devil:
Four excellent characters! O, that marrowless age
Should stuff the hollow bones with damned desires!
And, 'stead of heat, kindle infernal fires
Within the spendthrift veins of a dry duke,
A parched and juiceless luxur.
--Cyril Tourneur: The Revenger's Tragedy (1607);
Act I, Scene 1.

-M-

MACARONI: In the latter half of the eighteenth century, a
term referring to a member of the Macaroni Club, a group
of young Englishmen who had traveled in Europe and acquired
the fashions and tastes of the continental society; hence, any
person gaudily dressed; an exquisite; a fop or dandy. The
name "Macaroni Club" probably originated in the club's
preference for foreign cooking (macaroni was not a common
dish in England). Says Grose: "A fop: which name arose
from a club, called the Maccaroni Club, instituted by some
of the most dressy travelled gentlemen about town, who led
the fashions; whence a man foppishly dressed, was supposed
a member of that club, and by contraction styled a Maccaroni. " The word itself comes through the Italian, possibly
from the Greek makaria, "barley soup. " It can be found in
the letters of Horace Walpole; in Boswell's Life of Johnson
(1773); in Fanny Burney (1783); in Thackeray's The Virginians (1859); and in the following:

>   The cashier at that time was one Evans, a Cam-
>   bro-Briton. He had something of the choleric
>   complexion of his country men stamped on his
>   visage, but was a worthy sensible man at bottom.
>   He wore his hair, to the last, powdered and
>   frizzed out, in the fashion which I remember to
>   have seen in caricatures of what were termed, in
>   my young days, Maccaronies. He was the last of
>   that race of beaux.
>   --Charles Lamb: The South-Sea House (1820);
>   paragraph 8.

MACCOBOY, MACKABAW, MACABAO: Named after an area
of Martinique, this was an old type of snuff, perfumed with
attar of roses. Found in Robert Louis Stevenson's Catriona
(1893), and in the following:

>   My lord ... pocketed his snuff-box, not desirous
>   that Madame Brock's dubious fingers should plunge
>   too frequently into his Mackabaw.
>   --William Makepeace Thackeray: The History of
>   Pendennis (1850); Volume II, chapter 2.

MALISON: A word of many spellings, referring to a curse.
Through the Old French maleison from the Latin maledictio,
"malediction" or "slander. " It is very old, and can be
seen in the Cursor Mundi (1300); Sir Beves (1320); in John

Ray (1691); Allan Ramsay (1721); Charles Kingsley's Hereward the Wake (1865), and in Scott:

> Dun-Edin's Cross, a pillar'd stone,
> Rose on a turret octagon;
> (But now is razed that monument,
>   Whence royal edict rang,
> And voice of Scotland's law was sent
>   In glorious trumpet clang.
> Oh! be his tomb as lead to lead,
> Upon its dull destroyer's head!--
> A minstrel's malison is said.)
> --Sir Walter Scott: Marmion (1808); Canto V,
>   Stanza 25.

MALKIN, MAWKIN, MALKYNE: A word of many spellings,
and many meanings; from the female name-diminutive of
Matilda or Maud. Here are some of the many senses:

1) When used as a proper name: A female devil or
spirit.

> HECATE: Now I go, now I fly,
> Malkin my sweet spirit and I.
> O what a dainty pleasure 'tis
> To ride in the air
> When the moon shines fair,
> And sing and dance, and toy and kiss
> Over woods, high rocks, and mountains,
> Over seas, our mistress' fountains,
> Over steep towers and turrets,
> We fly by night, 'mongst troops of spirits:
> No ring of bells to our ears sounds,
> No howls of wolves, no yelps of hounds;
> No, not the noise of water's breach,
> Or cannon's throat our height can reach.
> --Thomas Middleton: The Witch (ca. 1604); Act
>   III, Scene 3.

> FIRST WITCH: Where the place?
> SECOND WITCH: Upon the heath.
> THIRD WITCH: There to meet with Macbeth.
> FIRST WITCH: I come, Graymalkin!
> SECOND WITCH: Paddock calls:--anon!
> --William Shakespeare: Macbeth (1606); Act I,
>   Scene 1.

2) Proper name for Maid Marian:

> DOROTHEA: You must turn tippet,
> And suddenly, and truly, and discreetly,
> Put on the shape of order and humanity,
> Or you must marry Malkin the May-Lady;
> You must, dear brother.
> --John Fletcher: Monsieur Thomas (ca. 1619);
>   Act II, Scene 2.

3) An untidy, loose woman; a slattern; also, a poorly-dressed servant woman. In Nicholas Breton (1600); Sir John Vanbrugh (1702); Jonathan Swift (1745), and in the following:

> DIONYZA:
> She did distain my child, and stood between
> Her and her fortunes: none would look on her,
> But cast their gazes on Marina's face;
> Whilst ours was blurted at, and held a malkin,
> Not worth the time of day.
> --William Shakespeare: Pericles (ca. 1606); Act
>   IV, Scene 3.

> JUNIUS BRUTUS:
> All tongues speak of him, and the bleared sights
> Are spectacled to see him: your prattling nurse
> Into a rapture lets her baby cry
> While she chats him: the kitchen malkin pins
> Her richest lockram 'bout her reechy neck,
> Clamb'ring the walls to eye him.
> --William Shakespeare: Coriolanus (1608); Act II,
>   Scene 1.

> PETER: I gave her no ill language.
> GILLIAN: Thou liest lewdly;
> Thou took'st me up at every word I spoke,
> As I had been a maukin, a flurt-gillian;
> And thou think'st, because thou canst write and
>   read,
> Our noses must be under thee.
> --John Fletcher: The Chances (1627); Act III,
>   Scene 1.

> At length my sire, his rough cheek wet with tears,
> Panted from weary sides, "King, you are free!
> We did but keep your surety for our son,
> If this be he,--or a draggled mawkin, thou,

That tends her bristled grunters in the sludge;"
For I was drench'd with ooze, and torn with bri-
    ers,
More crumpled than a poppy from the sheath
And all one rag, disprinced from head to heel.
--Alfred, Lord Tennyson: The Princess (1847);
    Part Fifth, lines 22-29.

Then Tristram, ever dallying with her hand,
"May God be with thee, sweet, when old and gray,
And past desire!" a saying that anger'd her.
"'May God be with thee, sweet, when thou art old,
And sweet no more to me!' I need Him now.
For when had Lancelot utter'd aught so gross
Even to the swineherd's malkin in the mast?"
--Alfred, Lord Tennyson: The Last Tournament
    (1859); lines 621-627.

4) A scarecrow; any strange or grotesque object set up in
a public place, or in a field to scare birds. In Thomas
Nabbes' Covent-Garden; a Comedy (1638); in Jonathan Swift
(1710); Horace Walpole (1742); in Samuel Jackson Pratt's
The Pupil of Pleasure (1776); in Charles Lamb (1818), and
in the following:

> SETTER: Oh! I begin to smoak ye: thou art some
> forsaken Abigail, we have dallied with heretofore
> --and art come to tickle thy imagination with re-
> membrance of iniquity past.
> LUCY: No thou pitiful flatterer of thy master's
> imperfections; thou maukin made up of the shreds
> and pairings of his superfluous fopperies.
> --William Congreve: The Old Batchelor (1693);
>   Act III, Scene 6.

> "As I say, you might be grateful to be hired in
> that way to a respectable place; and you knew no
> more o' what belongs to work when you come here
> than the mawkin i' the field. "
> --George Eliot: Adam Bede (1859); chapter 6.

5) A semi-proper name for a cat:

> With that I perceiv'd no excuse would avail,
> And, seeing there was no defence for a flail,
> I said I was ready master may'r to obey,
> And therefore desir'd him to lead me the way.

We went, and ere Malkin could well lick her ear,
(For it but the next door was, forsooth) we were
   there.
  --Charles Cotton: A Voyage to Ireland in Bur-
   lesque (1673); Canto II, lines 178-183.

MAMMOCK: A scrap, shred, fragment, or piece of something; as a verb, to tear up, to rend to pieces.   The origin
is unknown. It can be found in Skelton (1529); in John Day's
The Blind Beggar of Bednal Green (1600); in Walkington
(1607); John Milton's Of Reformation in England (1641); in
Ogilby (1651); Edward Lisle's Observations on Husbandry
(1722); in Sir Walter Scott's The Fair Maid of Perth (1828);
William Morris's The Earthly Paradise (1870), and in the
following:

    VALERIA: I saw him run after a gilded butterfly;
    and when he caught it, he let it go again; and after
    it again; and over and over he comes, and up
    again; catcht it again: or whether his fall enraged
    him, or how 'twas, he did so set his teeth, and
    tear it: O, I warrant, how he mammockt it!
    --William Shakespeare: Coriolanus (1608); Act I,
     Scene 3.

MANTOON: From the Italian mantone, this word signifies
a type of large cloak or mantle.

    ROMELIO:
    Look as you love your life, you have an eye
    Upon your mistress; I do henceforth bar her
    All visitants: I do hear there are bawds abroad,
    That bring cut-works, and mantoons, and convey
     letters
    To such young gentlewomen.
    --John Webster: The Devil's Law Case (ca. 1620);
     Act I, Scene 2.

MANTOPLICEE: An English RENDering of the French man-
teau plissé, a "pleated coat. "

    GOLDINGHAM: Has the Whetston Whore redeem'd
    her mantoplicee, and her silk-dy'd petticoat, with
    gold and silver lace?
    BELLAMOUR: No poor soul, she has had ill trad-
    ing of late.
    --Thomas Shadwell: The Miser (1671); Act I.

MAY-LORD, MAYLORD: It was usual at celebrations on May-day (the "May-games") to elect a Lord and a Lady of the May; these individuals then would preside over all the festivities: stage-plays, maypoles, bonfires, morris dances, chivalric shows, archery displays, etc. By usage over the years the word has come to be a contemptuous term for one in authority who is not well thought of by those under his power. Examples of the word can be found all through literature, in Thomas Nashe, George Wither, James Shirley, George Chapman, and in many others, including the following writers:

> RALPH:
> My name is Ralph, by due descent though not ignoble I,
> Yet far inferior to the stock of gracious grocery;
> And by the common counsel of my fellows in the Strand,
> With gilded staff and crossed scarf, the May-lord here I stand.
> --Francis Beaumont: The Knight of the Burning Pestle (ca. 1610); Act IV, Scene 5.

> FARMER: Here's vorty shillings; spare the child.
> CAPTAIN: I cannot.
> SOTO: Are you a man? will you cast away a May-lord?
> Shall all the wenches in the country curse you?
> --John Fletcher: Women Pleased (ca. 1620); Act IV, Scene 1.

> The shepherd-boys, who with the Muses dwell,
>   Met in the plain their May-lords new to choose,
> (For two they yearly choose) to order well
>   Their rural sports, and year that next ensues.
> --Phineas Fletcher: The Purple Island (1633); Canto I, stanza 2.

MEG, MEGG: A slang term for a coin, the English guinea (the half-guinea being, as Shadwell tells us, the ("smelt"). It was used principally from the close of the seventeenth century to the beginning of the nineteenth, the origin being unknown, as is the case with many slang and cant words.

> CAPT. HACKUM: Hark you, prithee noble squire, equip me with a couple of meggs, or two couple of smelts.

BELFOND SENIOR: Smelts! What shall we be-
speak another dish of fish for our dinner?
SHAMWELL: No, no, meggs are guineas, smelts
are half guineas: He would borrow a couple of
guineas.
BELFOND SENIOR: Meggs, smelts! Ha ha ha.
Very pretty by my troth. And so thou shalt, dear
Captain: There are two meggs! and I vow and
swear I am glad I have 'em to pleasure you, adad
I am.
--Thomas Shadwell: The Squire of Alsatia (1688);
    Act I, Scene 1.

MELOCOTON: A word of many spellings, including mallaga-
toon, melocotone, melicotony, malacaton, etc., referring to
the fruit resulting from the graft of a peach on a quince.
It comes through the Spanish melocoton, the Italian meloco-
togno, and the Latin mēlum cotōneum, from the Greek mēlon
kydōnion, "Cydonian apple," named for a town on the northern
coast of Crete (the word "quince" has principally the same
origin). It can be found in Francis Bacon, Randle Holme,
Arthur Dobbs (Countries Adjoining to Hudson's Bay, 1744),
and in the following:

LITTLEWIT: I envy no man, my delicates, Sir.
WIN-WIFE: Alas, you ha' the garden where they
grow still! A wife here with a strawberry-breath,
cherry-lips, apricot-cheeks, and a soft velvet head,
like a melicotton.
--Ben Jonson: Bartholomew Fair (1614); Act I,
    Scene 2.

ROMELIO:
Look as you love your life, you have an eye
Upon your mistress; I do henceforth bar her
All visitants: I do hear there are bawds abroad,
That bring cut-works, and mantoons, and convey
    letters
To such young gentlewomen, and there are others
That deal in corn-cutting, and fortune-telling--
Let none of these come at her on your life,
Nor Dewes-ace the wafer-woman, that prigs abroad
With muskmeloons, and malakatoones.
--John Webster: The Devil's Law-Case (ca. 1620);
    Act I, Scene 2.

MERD, MARD, MERDS: Feces, dung, excrement, ordure;

through the French merde, from the Latin synonym, merda.
It can be seen in Timothy Kendall's Flowers of Epigrammes
out of sundrie the most singular Authors (1577); in Burton's
Anatomy of Melancholy (1621), and in the following:

> SURLY: What else are all your terms,
> Whereon no one o' your writers 'grees with other?
> ...Of piss, and eggshells, women's terms, man's
>   blood,
> Hair o' the head, burnt clouts, chalk, merds, and
>   clay,
> Powder of bones, scalings of iron, glass,
> And worlds of other strange ingredients,
> Would burst a man to name?
> --Ben Jonson: The Alchemist (1610); Act II, Scene
>   3.

Also, MERDURINOUS: being made up of merd and
urine, as seen in John Taylor (1630), and in Jonson again:

> In the first jaws appear'd that ugly monster,
> Ycleped mud, which, when their oars did once stir,
> Belch'd forth an air, as hot, as at the muster
> Of all your night-tubs, when the carts do cluster,
> Who shall discharge first his merd-urinous load.
> --Ben Jonson: Epigram on the Famous Voyage
>   (1616); lines 61-65.

METHEGLIN: A word of many spellings, referring to a
spiced or medicated alcoholic liquor resembling mead, that
originated in Wales, usually made with honey. It comes
from the Welsh meddyglyn, from meddyg, "medicinal" (from
the Latin medicus), and llyn, "liquor." The word "methe"
also was an early name for mead. It can be located in
many writers, in Sir Thomas Elyot's The Castell of Health
(1533); John Coke's The Debate betwene the Heraldes of
Englande and Fraunce (1550); in Venner's Via Recta (1620),
and in the following:

> BROWNE: White-handed mistress, one sweet word
>   with thee.
> PRINCESS: Honey, and milk, and sugar; there is
>   three.
> BROWNE: Nay then, two treys, an if you grow so
>   nice,
> Metheglin, wort, and malmsey: well run, dice!
> There's half-a-dozen sweets.

--William Shakespeare: <u>Love's Labour's Lost</u> (ca. 1595); Act V, Scene 2.

MISTRESS PAGE: Why, Sir John, do you think, though we would have thrust virtue out of our hearts by the head and shoulders, and have given ourselves without scruple to hell, that ever the devil could have made you our delight?
FORD: What, a hodge-pudding? a bag of flax?
MISTRESS PAGE: A puff'd man?
FORD: Old, cold, wither'd, and of intolerable entrails? And one that is as slanderous as Satan?
PAGE: And as poor as Job?
FORD: And as wicked as his wife?
SIR HUGH EVANS: And given to fornications, and to taverns, and sack, and wine, and metheglins, and to drinkings, and swearings and starings, pribbles and prabbles?
--William Shakespeare: <u>The Merry Wives of Windsor</u> (1601); Act V, Scene 5.

RANDALL: Sounds, some metheglins here.
WIDOW: What does he call for?
JARVIS: Here are some eggs for you, sir.
RANDALL: Eggs, man! some metheglins, the wine of Wales.
--William Rowley: <u>A Match at Midnight</u> (1633); Act II, Scene 2.

So after the King's meat was taken away, we thither, but he could not stay; but left me there among two or three of the King's servants, where we dined with the meat that came from his table; which was most excellent, with most brave drink, cooled in Ice (which at this hot time was welcome); and I, drinking no wine, had Metheglin for the King's own drinking, which did please me mightily.
--Samuel Pepys' <u>Diary</u>: July 25th, 1666.

<u>MIDDLE EARTH</u>: The earth, as considered standing between heaven and hell, or as being the center of the universe; also, the real world, as opposed to the land of dreams. From middle-erd, "the world." It can be found in John Gower's <u>Confessio Amantis</u> (1390); in George Crabbe (1819) and Nathaniel Hawthorne (1860); and, more recently, as utilized by Prof. Tolkien in his <u>Lord of the Rings</u> trilogy.

SIR HUGH EVANS: Pray you, lock hand in hand;
   yourselves in order set;
And twenty glow-worms shall our lanterns be,
To guide our measure round about the tree.--
But stay; I smell a man of middle-earth.
SIR JOHN FALSTAFF: Heavens defend me from
   that Welsh fairy, lest he transform me to a piece
   of cheese!
   --William Shakespeare: The Merry Wives of Wind-
      sor (1601); Act V, Scene 5.

'That maid is born of middle earth,
   And may of man be won,
Though there have glided since her birth
   Five hundred years and one. "
   --Sir Walter Scott: The Bridal of Triermain
      (1813); Canto I, Stanza 9.

MILL-KEN: One who robs a residence; a house-breaker.
From the old terms mill, "to steal," and ken, "house,"
both of unknown origin. It can be found in Head's Canting
Academy (1673), and in the following:

'That the same capacity which qualifies a Mill-ken,
a Bridle-cull [highwayman], or a Buttock and File
[shoplifter], to arrive at any degree of eminence
in his profession, would likewise raise a man in
what the world esteem a more honourable calling,
I do not deny; nay, in many of your instances it
is evident, that more ingenuity, more art are
necessary to the lower, than the higher profi-
cients. "
   --Henry Fielding: Jonathan Wild (1743); Book I,
      chapter 5.

MIRLIGOES, MIRRLIGOES, MERRILY-GOES: An old Scottish term for dizziness, from the Scottish mirl, "to turn
around, to cause to become dizzy." It can be found in
Robert Fergusson (1773), and in the following:

'I'm sure my poor een see fifty colors wi' faint-
ness, and my head's sae dizzy wi' the mirligoes
that I canna stand my lane. "
   --Sir Walter Scott: Old Mortality (1816); chapter
      27.

MISGUGGLE, MISGOGGLE: To handle without care, and in

a rough, careless manner; to maul; also, to spoil. From
the old verb guggle, "to handle clumsily." Also, to mangle,
disfigure.

> "And in the mean while ye'll no hinder Gilliewhack-
> it to take the small-pox. There was not a doctor
> in Perth or Stirling would look near the poor lad,
> and I cannot blame them; for Donald had been
> misguggled by ane of these doctors about Paris,
> and he swore he would fling the first into the loch
> that he catched beyond the Pass."
> --Sir Walter Scott: Waverley (1814); chapter 18.

> "It may be different in foreign parts;" or, "They
> wha think differently on the great foundation of our
> covenanted reformation, overturning and mish-
> guggling the government and discipline of the kirk,
> and breaking down the carved work of our Zion,
> might be for sawing the craft wi' aits; but I say,
> pease, pease."
> --Sir Walter Scott: The Heart of Midlothian (1818);
>   chapter 8.

MOLL BLOOD: An old term for the gallows, from the
familiar diminutive form of the name Mary.

> "I must needs say," interposed Ratcliffe, "that it's
> d----d hard, when three words of your mouth would
> give the girl the chance to nick Moll Blood, that
> you make such scrupling about rapping to them.
> D--n me, if they would take me, if I would not
> rap to all Whatd'yecallum's--Hyssop's Fables, for
> her life--I am us'd to't, b--t me, for less mat-
> ters. Why, I have smacked calf-skin fifty times
> in England for a keg of brandy."
> --Sir Walter Scott: The Heart of Midlothian (1818);
>   chapter 20.

MORENA: A brunette, from the Spanish feminine form of
moreno, "brown."

> And so to Woolwich and there dined at Mr. Fal-
> coner's, of victuals we carried ourselfs--and one
> Mr. Dekins, the father of my Morena, of whom
> we have lately bought some hemp.
> --Samuel Pepys' Diary: January 27th, 1662.

MOSCARDINI, MOSCARDINO: A type of confection or sweet-meat flavored with musk; from the Latin word for musk, moschus.

> AMORPHUS: Give me my confects, my moscardini, and place those colours in my hat.
> --Ben Jonson: Cynthia's Revels (1600); Act V, Scene 4.

MOULDY-CHAPS, MOULDY-CHOPS: An old term of contempt, popular in the seventeenth century, from mouldy and chaps or chops, "jaws."

> DOLL TEARSHEET: Away, you cut-purse rascal! you filthy bung, away! by this wine, I'll thrust my knife in your mouldy chaps, an you play the saucy cuttle with me. Away, you bottle-ale rascal! you basket-hilt stale juggler, you!
> --William Shakespeare: King Henry The Fourth, Part II (1598); Act II, Scene 4.

> MERCHANT: Did not I tell you he would steal to you?
> SECOND CITIZEN: Sirrah,
> You mouldy-chaps! know your crib; I would wish you,
> And get from whence you came.
> --Philip Massinger: A Very Woman (1634); Act III, Scene 1.

MUG-HOUSE: A tavern or ale-house; says Dr. Johnson: "A low house of entertainment." It can be found in the letters of Horace Walpole; in William Hone's The Table-Book (1827), and in the following writers:

> He has the confidence to say, that there is a mug-house near Long-acre, where you may every evening hear an exact account of distresses of this kind. One complains that such a lady's finery is the occasion that his own wife and daughter appear so long in the same gown. Another, that all the furniture of her visiting apartment are no more her's, than the scenery of a play are the proper goods of the actress.
> --Sir Richard Steele: The Tatler, No. 180 (1710); paragraph 3.

Those who the succours of the fair despise,
May find that we have nails as well as eyes.
Thy female bards, O prince by fortune crost,
At least more courage than thy men can boast:
Our sex has dar'd the mug-house chiefs to meet,
And purchas'd fame in many a well-fought street.
--Thomas Tickell: An Epistle From a Lady in
    England to a Gentleman at Avignon (1717); lines
    67-72.

MUNDUNGUS, MUNDUNGO: Dung, offal, garbage, stinking
rubbish; hence, a vile-smelling kind of tobacco, of very
poor quality; shag tobacco.   Used from about 1640, it comes
from the Spanish mondongo, "tripe." Grose tells us: "Bad
or rank tobacco: from mondongo, a Spanish word signifying
tripes, or the uncleaned entrails of a beast, full of filth."
It can be located in John Taylor (1641); Brome (1652); in
Holme's Academy of the Armoury (1688); Aphra Behn's The
Widow Ranter (1690); in James Brome's Travels over Scotland, England, and Wales (1700); in George Gissing (1901),
and in the following:

> DRYBOB: Pox of these uncivil fellows, they won't
> let a man break a jest among 'em; and Madam, I
> am the son of a baboon, if stoppage of wit be not
> as great a pain to me as stoppage of urine.
> RAYMUND: Have not I seen you within these three
> months lolling out of Mundens [a coffee-house in
> Fleet Street] with a glass of windy-bottle-ale in one
> hand, and a pipe of mundungus in the other; and
> out of a brisk gay humour, drinking to passengers
> in the street.
> --Thomas Shadwell: The Humorists (1671); Act III.

> After h' had administer'd a dose
> Of snuff mundungus to his nose,
> And powder'd th' inside of his skull,
> Instead of th' outward jobbernol,
> He shook it with a scornful look.
> --Samuel Butler: Hudibras, Part Third (1678);
>   Canto II, lines 1005-1009.

> So saying, she sat down to her wheel, and seized
> while she spun her jet-black cutty pipe, from which
> she soon sent such clouds of vile mundungus vapor
> as must have cleared the premises of Lady Pene-
> lope, had she not been strong in purpose to share

the expected confession of the invalid.   As for
Miss Digges, she coughed, sneezed, retched, and
finally ran out of the cottage, declaring she could
not live in such a smoke, if it were to hear twenty
sick woman's last speeches; and that, besides, she
was sure to know all about it from Lady Penelope,
if it was ever so little worth telling over again.
--Sir Walter Scott: St. Ronan's Well (1823); chapter 32.

-N-

NAB: An old noun of unknown origin, possibly related to the
Swedish nabb, nobb, referring variously to (1) the head; (2)
a hat; (3) the head of a stick; and (4) an extravagant fop.
Examples of the first sense can be found in Harman's Caveat
for Vagabonds (1567); in Dekker (1608), and in the following:

> MOLL & TEARCAT:
> O I wud lib all the lightmans,
> O I wud lib all the darkmans
> By the salomon, under the ruffmans,
> By the salomon, in the hartmans,
> And scour the queer cramp ring,
> And couch till a palliard dock'd my dell,
> So my bousy nab might skew rom-bouse well.
> --Thomas Dekker & Thomas Middleton: The Roar-
>   ing Girl (1611); Act V, Scene 1.

> HIGGEN:
> I crown thy nab with a gage of benebowse [quart of
>   good drink],
> And stall thee by the salmon into the clowes [or-
>   dain thee by the beggars' oath].
> --John Fletcher: Beggars' Bush (1622); Act III,
>   Scene 4.

The second sense, that of a hat or cap (a large hat
was a "penthouse nab"), can be seen in Head's Canting Academy (1673), and in these:

> BELFOND SENIOR: Well, there's no making a
> whistle of a pig's tail; this puppy will never learn
> any breeding. Sirrah, behold me: here's rigging
> for you; here's a nab, you never saw such a one
> in your life.

CHEATLY: A rum nab: it is a beaver of five
pounds.
--Thomas Shadwell: The Squire of Alsatia (1688);
    Act II, Scene 1.

He had now got together a very considerable gang,
composed of undone gamesters, ruined bailiffs,
broken tradesmen, idle apprentices, and loose and
disorderly youth, who being born to no fortune,
nor bred to no trade or profession, were willing
to live luxuriously without labour. As these persons wore different principles, i. e. hats, frequent
dissentions grew among them. There were particularly two parties, viz. those who wore hats
fiercely cocked, and those who preferr'd the nab
or trencher hat, with the brim flapping over their
eyes; between which, jars and animosities almost
perpetually arose.
--Henry Fielding: Jonathan Wild (1743); Book II,
    chapter 6.

NABOBESS: An extremely wealthy woman, either by virtue
of marriage or inheritance; a female nabob. Through the
Spanish nabab and Portuguese nababo, from the Hindu naw-
wāb, "deputy governor of the Mogul Empire." It can be
found in the letters of Laurence Sterne and in the following:

MR. OLDWORTH: My worthy friend, brother let
me call you! I have robbed you of a pleasure; I
know you also had your eye upon my Maid of the
Oaks, for an exercise of your generosity.
GROVEBY: It is very true, I should have been as
well pleased as her lover to receive her only with
an under-petticoat, though not quite for the same
reason; but you may perceive how cursedly vexed
I am at the disappointment. Aye, I must alter the
disposition of my acres once more: I will have no
nabobs, nor nabobesses in my family.
--Gen. John Burgoyne: The Maid of the Oaks
    (1779); Act IV, Scene 1.

NAKER, NAKIR: An old kettle-drum. It comes through the
Old French nacre, the Latin nacaria, and the Greek anakara,
from the Persian synonym, naqāra. Examples of its use
can be seen in the poetry of Laurence Minot (1352); in
Chaucer's The Knight's Tale (1386); in Sir Degrevant (ca.
1440), and in Scott:

> Her description was here suddenly interrupted by
> the signal for assault, which was given by the
> blast of a shrill bugle, and at once answered by
> a flourish of the Norman trumpets from the battle-
> ments, which mingled with the deep and hollow
> clang of the nakers (a species of kettle-drum), re-
> torted in notes of defiance the challenge of the
> enemy.
> --Sir Walter Scott: Ivanhoe (1819); chapter 29.

NARE, NARES: A nostril (originally of a hawk), or nostrils.
From the Latin synonym, naris. Used principally from the
14th to the 17th centuries, it can be found in the Book of St.
Albans and in John de Trevisa (1398), as well as in the following:

> These be the cause of those thick frequent mists
> Arising in that place, through which, who goes,
> Must try th' un-used valour of a nose:
> And that ours did. For yet, no nare was tainted,
> Nor thumb, nor finger to the stop acquainted,
> But open and unarm'd encounter'd all.
> --Ben Jonson: Epigram on the Famous Voyage
>   (1616); lines 130-135.

> This feud, by Jesuits invented,
> By evil counsel is fomented;
> There is a Machiavellian plot
> (Tho' ev'ry nare olfact [nose smell] is not),
> And deep design in't to divide
> The well-affected that confide,
> By setting brother against brother,
> To claw and curry one another.
> --Samuel Butler: Hudibras, Part First (1663);
>   Canto I, lines 739-746.

NASH-GAB, NASH-GOB: An old Scottish term for trashy,
impertinent talk, or one who speaks it. Constructed from the
dialect form nash, "impertinence," and from the noun gab,
"talk," in contemporary use. It can be found in the writings of
many Scottish authors, especially in Scott:

> "See now, mither, what ye hae dune," whispered
> Cuddie; "there's the Philistines, as ye ca' them,
> are gaun to whirry awa' Mr. Henry, and a' wi'
> your nash-gab, deil be on't!"
> --Sir Walter Scott: Old Mortality (1816); chapter 7.

"I hae been a kind freend to them afore now, to
say naething o' ower-looking him last night, when
naming his name wad hae cost him his life--I'll be
hearing o' this in the council maybe frae Bailie
Grahame, and MacVittie, and some o' them. They
hae coost up my kindred to Rob to me already--
set up their nashgabs!"
    --Sir Walter Scott: Rob Roy (1817); chapter 26.

NAUGHTY PACK: A term of contempt for a woman of ques-
tionable virtue. From naughty and pack, "a person of low
character." It can be found in Palsgrave (1530); in Holland's
Livy (1600); in Jonathan Swift's Polite Conversation (1738),
and in the following:

> FLAVIA:
> You must not loiter lazily,
> And speak about the town, my friend, in taverns,
> In gaming-houses; nor sneak after dinner
> To public shows, to interludes, in riot,
> To some lewd painted baggage, trick'd up gaudily,
> Like one of us:--oh, fie upon them, giblets!
> I have been told they ride in coaches, flaunt it
> In braveries, so rich, that 'tis scarce possible
> To distinguish one of these vile naughty packs
> From true and arrant ladies; they'll inveigle
> Your substance and your body, --think on that.
> --John Ford: The Fancies, Chaste and Noble
>   (1635); Act III, Scene 2.

Other senses of this word include (1) a wicked or
evil man (in Coverdale, 1549, and in Arthur Golding's translations of John Calvin), and (2) a naughty child.

NAUNT: A variation of the word "aunt," from having the
"n" from myn aunt attached to the noun. "Nuncle" from
"uncle" is also existent, and can be seen in the Fletcher
quote. It was quite common, and can be found in Heywood
(1632); in William Shenstone's The Schoolmistress (1742), and
in the following:

> ALPHONSO: Go to the devil!--
> Was ever man tormented with a puppy thus?--
> Thou tell me news! thou be a guide!
> ALINDA: And, then, nuncle--
> ALPHONSO: Prithee, keep on thy way, good
>   naunt.

--John Fletcher: The Pilgrim (1621); Act IV,
   Scene 1.

WOODALL: Well, get thee gone, Squire Limber-
hamo, for the easiest fool I ever knew, next my
naunt of Fairies in the Alchemist. I have escap'd,
thanks to my mistresses Lingua Franca: I'll steal
to my chamber, shift my periwig, and cloaths;
and then, with the help of resty Gervase, concert
the business of the next campaign.
--John Dryden: The Kind Keeper (1678); Act I,
   Scene 1.

Julian could scarce forbear laughing: "I thought
you too much of a man, Lance, to fear a woman
marrying you whether you would or no. "
"It has been many an honest man's luck, for all
that, " said Lance; "and a woman in the very house
has so many deuced opportunities. And then there
would be two upon one; for naunt, though high
enough when any of your folks are concerned, hath
some look to the main chance; and it seems Mistress Deb is as rich as a Jew. "
--Sir Walter Scott: Peveril of the Peak (1823);
   chapter 26.

NEEDLEWOMAN: A woman who works with a needle or
sews; a seamstress. In later usage, a harlot. Found in
Jeremy Taylor (1667) and Thomas Carlyle (1849), as well as
in the following:

SEBASTIAN WENGRAVE: Prithee, look in; for all
the gentlemen are upon rising.
NEATFOOT: Yes, sir; a most methodical attendance shall be given.
SEBASTIAN WENGRAVE: And dost hear? if my
father call for me, say I am busy with a semp-
ster.
NEATFOOT: Yes, sir; he shall know it that you
are busied with a needle-woman.
--Thomas Dekker & Thomas Middleton: The Roaring Girl (1611); Act I, Scene 1.

He glanced at the gold cathedral-clock on the man-
telpiece, and proposed a stroll on the lawn before
dinner. Laetitia gathered up her embroidery work.
"As a rule, " he said, "authoresses are not

needle-women. "
　　"I shall resign the needle or the pen if it stamps
me an exception, " she replied.
　　--George Meredith: The Egoist (1879); chapter 14.

NETHERSTOCK: A stocking. Constructed from nether,
"pertaining to the legs, " and stock, "stocking. " It can be
located in Robert Greene (1592) and in Sala's Captain Dangerous (1863), as well as in these:

POINTZ: Welcome, Jack; where hast thou been?
SIR JOHN FALSTAFF: A plague of all cowards,
I say, and a vengeance too! marry, and amen!--
Give me a cup of sack, boy. --Ere I lead this life
long, I'll sew netherstocks, and mend them and
foot them too. A plague of all cowards!--Give
me a cup of sack, rogue. --Is there no virtue ex-
tant?
　　--William Shakespeare: King Henry The Fourth,
　　　Part I (1597); Act II, Scene 4.

EARL OF KENT: Hail to thee, noble master!
KING LEAR: Ha!
Makest thou this shame thy pastime?
EARL OF KENT: No, my lord.
FOOL: Ha, ha! he wears cruel garters. Horses
are tied by the heads, dogs and bears by the neck,
monkeys by the loins, and men by the legs: when
a man's over-lusty at legs, then he wears wooden
netherstocks.
　　--William Shakespeare: King Lear (ca. 1606); Act
　　II, Scene 4.

He had his smile with pretty Mistress Cicely, his
broad laugh with mine host, and his jest upon dash-
ing Master Goldthred, who, though indeed without
any such benevolent intention on his own part, was
the general butt of the evening. The pedlar and
he were closely engaged in a dispute upon the
preference due to the Spanish nether-stock over
the black Gascoigne hose, and mine host had just
winked to the guests around him, as who should
say, "You will have mirth presently, my masters, "
when the trampling of horses was heard in the
courtyard, and the hostler was loudly summoned,
with a few of the newest oaths then in vogue, to
add force to the invocation.

--Sir Walter Scott: <u>Kenilworth</u> (1821); chapter 19.

<u>(ST.) NICHOLAS' CLERKS</u>: An old term for highwaymen or footpads, from the name of the bishop of Myra, St. Nicholas (d. 326), the patron saint of schoolboys. This sense probably came from the notion connected with a previous usage of "St. Nicholas' clerks," in reference to "poor scholars." Also called St. Nicholas' clergymen. Used principally from the late 16th to early 19th centuries, it can be found in Robert Daborne's <u>A Christian turn'd Turke, a Tragedy</u> (1612), and in the following:

> CHAMBERLAIN: Good morrow, Master Gadshill.
> It holds current that I told you yesternight:--
> there's a franklin in the wild of Kent hath brought
> three hundred marks with him in gold: I heard
> him tell it to one of his company last night at
> supper; a kind of auditor, one that hath abundance
> of charge too, God knows what. They are up al-
> ready, and call for eggs and butter; they will away
> presently.
> GADSHILL: Sirrah, if they meet not with Saint
> Nicholas' clerks, I'll give thee this neck.
> CHAMBERLAIN: No, I'll none of it: I prithee,
> keep that for the hangman; for I know thou wor-
> ship'st Saint Nicholas as truly as a man of false-
> hood may.
> --William Shakespeare: <u>King Henry The Fourth,</u>
>   <u>Part I</u> (1597); Act II, Scene 1.

> BILBOE: He is not stol'n? No rogues among
> ourselves, I hope?
> TITERE TU: Neither.
> BILBOE: Or is he dead?
> TITERE TU: In law, I think he be. I was t'other
> night upon the randan, and who should I meet with
> but our old gang, some of St. Nicholas' clerks!
> --John Wilson: <u>The Cheats</u> (1662); Act I, Scene 1.

<u>NINNYHAMMER</u>: A fool or simpleton. From <u>ninny</u> (a con-traction from <u>innocent</u>), and a second unknown element, prob-ably used for <u>force</u> or impact. A popular word, it can be found (among others) in Thomas Nash (1592); in Samuel Row-lands' <u>Good Newes and Bad Newes</u> (1622); Dr. John Arbuth-not's <u>The History of John Bull</u> (1712), and in the following:

Never knock, you that strive to be ninny-hammers,

but with your feet spurn open the door and enter
into our school. You shall not need to buy books
--no, scorn to distinguish a B from a battledore.
Only look that your ears be long enough to reach
our rudiments and you are made for ever.
--Thomas Dekker: The Gull's Horn-Book (1609);
    proemium.

I have received many letters from persons of all
conditions in reference to my late discourse concerning the tucker. Some of them are filled with
reproaches and invectives. A lady, who sub-
scribes herself Teraminta, bids me, in a very
pert manner, mind my own affairs, and not pretend to meddle with their linen; for that they do
not dress for an old fellow, who cannot see them
without a pair of spectacles. Another, who calls
herself Bubnelia, vents her passion in scurrilous
terms; an old ninny-hammer, a dotard, a nincom-
poop, is the best language she can afford me.
--Joseph Addison: The Guardian No. 109 (1713);
    paragraph 1.

And here without staying for my reply, shall I be
called as many blockheads, numskulls, doddypoles,
dunderheads, ninnyhammers, goosecaps, joltheads,
nincompoops, sh-t-a-beds ... And I'll let them do
it, as Bridget said, as much as they please.
--Laurence Sterne: Tristram Shandy (1676); Book
    IX, chapter 25.

NOOP: The sharp point of the elbow. The origin is uncertain, but the word may be related to the Norwegian knöp,
"knuckle. " Principally a Scottish word.

    "That's according to the stuff they are made o',
    sir, " replied Ratcliffe--"But to make a lang tale
    short, I canna undertake the job. It gangs against
    my conscience. "
        "Your conscience, Rat? " said Sharpitlaw, with
    a sneer, which the reader will probably think very
    natural upon the occasion.
        "Ou ay, sir, " answered Ratcliffe calmly, "just
    my conscience; a'body has a conscience, though it
    may be ill wunnin at it. I think mine's as weel
    out o' the gate as maist folk's are; and yet it's
    just like the noop of my elbow, it whiles gets a

bit dirl [a tingling stroke] on a corner. "
--Sir Walter Scott: The Heart of Midlothian (1818);
     chapter 17.

NUB: An old cant term, meaning "to hang by the neck, to
execute on the gallows. " Used principally from the late
17th to middle 19th centuries, the origin, as is the case
with many cant words, is unknown. It can be found in
Head's Canting Academy (1673), and in Fielding:

> 'No, no, (says she) I am certain you will be found
> guilty Death. I knew what it would always come
> to. I told you it was impossible to carry on such
> a trade long; but you would not be advised, and
> now you see the consequence, now you repent when
> it is too late. All the comfort I shall have when
> you are nubbed, is that I gave you good advice. "
> --Henry Fielding: Jonathan Wild (1743); Book IV,
>   chapter 2.

NUBBING-CHEAT: The gallows. It comes from nub above,
and from cheat, another old cant term, meaning "thing, article. " Used principally from the late 17th to the 19th centuries, it can be found in Head's Canting Academy (1673);
in Fielding's Tom Jones (1745); in Ainsworth's Rookwood
(1834), and in Scott:

> 'I thank you, my good friends, " he said, looking
> back to the door, which they who had pushed him
> in were securing. "Point de ceremonie--no apology
> for tumbling, so we light in good company. Save
> ye--save ye, gentlemen all. What, à la mort,
> and nothing stirring to keep the spirits up, and
> make a night on't? the last we shall have, I take
> it; for a make to a million but we trine [hang] to
> the nubbing cheat to-morrow. "
> --Sir Walter Scott: Woodstock (1826); chapter 36.

NUPSON: A word of unknown origin, referring to a fool,
ninny, or absolute simpleton. Used by Jonson:

> BRAINWORM: I mean to appear no more afore
> him in this shape. I have another trick, to act,
> yet. O, that I were so happy, as to light on a
> nupson, now, of this Justice's novice.
> --Ben Jonson: Every Man in His Humour (1598);
>   Act IV, Scene 6.

PUG:
You are proud, sweet mistress! and withal,
A little ignorant, to entertain
The good that's proffer'd; and (by your beauty's
    leave)
Not all so wise, as some true politique wife
Would be: who having match'd with such a nupson
(I speak it with my master's peace) whose face
Hath left t'accuse him, now, for 't doth confess
    him,
What you can make him; will yet (out of scruple,
And a spic'd conscience) defraud the poor gentle-
    man,
At least delay him in the thing he longs for,
And makes it his whole study, how to compass,
Only a title.   Could but he write cuckold,
He had his ends.
    --Ben Jonson: The Devil Is an Ass (1616); Act II,
        Scene 2.

NUTCRACKER: One who cracks nuts; hence, a common
spectator in a theater; one who lounges in the "peanut gal-
lery." Popular with Jonson, found in The Poetaster (1601),
and in the following:

        A work not smelling of the lamp, to-night,
            But fitted for your Majesty's disport,
            And writ to the Meridian of your Court,
        We bring; and hope it may produce delight:
        The rather, being offered, as a rite,
            To scholars, that can judge, and fair report
            The sense they hear, above the vulgar sort
        Of nut-crackers, that only come for sight.
        --Ben Jonson: The Staple of News (1626); Pro-
            logue for the Court.

NUTHOOK: A long stick with a curved hook at one end,
used by nut-gatherers to pull down tree-branches; hence, a
constable or beadle, who "pulls down" criminals.   It can be
found in the poetry of John Cleaveland (1658), and in the
following:

        HOSTESS: No, thou arrant knave: I would to God
        that I might die, that I might have thee hang'd:
        thou hast drawn my shoulder out of joint.
        FIRST BEADLE: The constables have deliver'd
        her over to me; and she shall have whipping-cheer

enough, I warrant her: there hath been a man or
two lately kill'd about her.
DOLL TEARSHEET: Nut-hook, nut-hook, you lie.
Come on; I'll tell thee what, thou damn'd tripe-
visaged rascal, an the child I go with do miscarry,
thou wert better thou hadst struck thy mother,
thou paper-faced villain.
--William Shakespeare: King Henry The Fourth,
    Part II (1598); Act V, Scene 4.

NYM: Be advised, sir, and pass good humours:
I will say "marry trap" with you, if you run the
nuthook's humour on me; that is the very note of
it.
--William Shakespeare: The Merry Wives of Wind-
    sor (1601); Act I, Scene 1.

NYKIN: An old term of endearment, of unknown origin.
Used by Congreve:

> LAETITIA: I hope my dearest jewel is not going
> to leave me--are you Nykin?
> FONDLEWIFE: Wife--have you thoroughly con-
> sider'd how detestable, how heinous, and how cry-
> ing a sin, the sin of adultery is? For it is a
> very weighty sin; and although it may lie heavy
> upon thee, yet thy husband must also bear his
> part: for thy iniquity will fall upon his head.
> --William Congreve: The Old Batchelor (1693);
>   Act IV, Scene 1.

-O-

OBARNI, OBARNE: A Russian drink, mead obarni, "scalded
mead," known in the 17th century in England. It comes
from the Russian obvarnyi, "scalded," and can be found in
Hakluyt's Voyages and in the following:

> SATAN:
> Unless it be a vice of quality,
> Or fashion now, they take none from us. Carmen
> Are got into the yellow starch, and chimney-
>   sweepers
> To their tobacco, and strong waters, Hum,
> Meath and Obarni.
> --Ben Jonson: The Devil Is an Ass (1616); Act I,
>   Scene 1.

OBTRACT, OBTRECT: To speak of with malicious intent;
to slander; to detract from. From the Latin synonym
obtrectare, constructed from ob + tractare, "to drag."
Found in Trussell (1596), and in the following:

> USHER: What is my sister, centaur?
> COLONEL'S FRIEND: I say thy sister is a bron-
> strops [prostitute].
> USHER: A bronstrops?
> CHOUGH: Tutor, tutor, ere you go any further,
> tell me the English of that; what is a bronstrops,
> pray?
> COLONEL'S FRIEND: A bronstrops is in English
> a hippocrene.
> CHOUGH: A hippocrene; note it, Trim: I love to
> understand the English as I go.   (WRITES)
> TRIMTRAM: What's the English of hippocrene?
> CHOUGH: Why, bronstrops.
> USHER: Thou dost obtrect my flesh and blood.
> COLONEL'S FRIEND: Again I denounce, thy
> sister is a fructifier.
> --Thomas Middleton & William Rowley: A Fair
>   Quarrel (1617); Act IV, Scene 1.

OE: An island of small size. Connected with the Danish
öe, the Icelandic ey, and the Old English ieg, "islet."

> "I love my fathers' northern land,
>   Where the dark pine-trees grow,
> And the bold Baltic's echoing strand
>   Looks o'er each grassy oe."
> --Sir Walter Scott: Harold the Dauntless (1817);
>   Canto III, Stanza 10.

OIME, OIMEE: An old exclamation, roughly equivalent to
"Alas! Woe is me! Alack!" It comes from the Italian oimé,
ohime, from ohi, "alas!" and me, "me."

> DOGE: Farewell all social memory! all thoughts
> In common! and sweet bonds which link old friend-
>   ships,
> When the survivors of long years and actions,
> Which now belong to history, soothe the days
> Which yet remain by treasuring each other,
> And never meet, but each beholds the mirror
> Of half a century on his brother's brow,
> And sees a hundred beings, now in earth,

> Flit round them whispering of the days gone by,
> And seeming not all dead, as long as two
> Of the brave, joyous, reckless, glorious band,
> Which once were one and many, still retain
> A breath to sigh for them, a tongue to speak
> Of deeds that else were silent, save on marble--
> Oime! Oime!--and must I do this deed?
> --Lord Byron: Marino Faliero, Doge of Venice
>   (1820); Act III, Scene 2.

ONEYERS: A most unusual word, in that neither meaning nor etymology is known; it has been suggested, though, to refer to the associates of noble persons, as seen in the following:

> GADSHILL: I am join'd with no foot land-rakers, no long-staff sixpenny strikers, none of these mad mustachio purple-hued malt-worms; but with nobility and tranquillity, burgomasters and great oneyers, such as can hold in, such as will strike sooner than speak, and speak sooner than drink, and drink sooner than pray: and yet, zounds, I lie; for they pray continually to their saint, the commonwealth; or, rather, not pray to her, but prey on her,--for they ride up and down on her, and make her their boots.
> --William Shakespeare: King Henry The Fourth, Part I (1597); Act II, Scene 1.

ORPHARION: A large instrument of the cittern or lute family, with from six to nine pairs of wire strings, an elaborate outline, and played with a plectrum. It was essentially a cheap lute, less costly to build and repair, and was much in use in the 17th century. Its invention has traditionally been attributed to one John Rose, a Londoner living in Bridewell, around 1560. The name is from a construction of the proper names of two mythical Greek musicians, Orpheus and Arion.

> "Sound loud your trumpets then from London's
>   loftiest towers,
> To beat the stormy tempests back, and calm the
>   raging showers,
>   Set the cornet with the flute,
>   The orpharion to the lute,
> Tuning the tabor and the pipe to the sweet violins,
> And mock the thunder in the air with the loud
>   clarions. "

--Michael Drayton: Eclogue III (1593); stanza 23.

An Irish harp hath open air on both sides of the
strings: and it hath the concave or belly not along
the strings, but at the end of the strings. It
maketh a more resounding sound than a bandora,
orpharion, or cittern, which have likewise wire-
strings. I judge the cause to be, for that open
air on both sides helpeth, so that there be a concave; which is therefore best placed at the end.
--Francis Bacon: Sylva Sylvarum (1626); para-
    graph 146.

OVERSCUTCHED: A word of uncertain meaning: it may be
related to the verb scutch, "to whip, " and in that sense may
mean "over-beaten" or "beaten too much"; but in the Shakespeare quote, it probably refers to a prostitute; and in
Scott, it seems to be "worn from long service. "

SIR JOHN FALSTAFF: I do remember him at
Clement's-inn, like a man made after supper of
a cheese-paring: when a' was naked, he was, for
all the world, like a forkt radish, with a head
fantastically carved upon it with a knife; a' was
so forlorn, that his dimensions to any thick sight
were invisible: a' was the very genius of famine;
yet lecherous as a monkey, and the whores call'd
him mandrake: a' came ever in the rearward of
the fashion; and sung those tunes to the overscutcht
huswives that he heard the carmen whistle, and
sware they were his Fancies or his Good-nights.
--William Shakespeare: King Henry The Fourth,
    Part II (1598); Act III, Scene 2.

Again the summons I denied
In yon fair capital of Clyde:
My Harp--or let me rather choose
The good old classic form--my Muse,
(For Harp's an over-scutchèd phrase,
Worn out by bards of modern days)
My Muse, then--seldom will she wake,
Save by dim wood and silent lake.
--Sir Walter Scott: The Bridal of Triermain
    (1813); Canto III, Introduction, Stanza 5.

OXTER: An old Scottish word for the armpit; or, more
generally, the fleshy underside of the upper arm. Through

the Old English óxta, óhsta, from the Latin axilla, diminu-
tive of axula, same sense. Examples of its use can be lo-
cated in Dunbar's poetry in the sixteenth century; in Peter
Lowe's The Whole Course of Chirurgerie (1597); in Allan
Ramsay (1715); Jonathan Swift (1745); in Robert Williams
Buchanan's God and the Man (1881), and in the following:

> "It is but too true, " said Ravenswood, conscience-
> struck; "the penalties of extravagance extend far
> beyond the prodigal's own sufferings. "
> "However, " said the sexton, "this young man
> Edgar is like to avenge my wrangs on the haill of
> this kindred. "
> "Indeed?" said Ravenswood; "why should you
> suppose so?"
> "They say he is about to marry the daughter of
> Leddy Ashton; and let her ladyship get his head
> ance under her oxter, and see you if she winna
> gie his neck a thraw. "
> --Sir Walter Scott: The Bride of Lammermoor
> (1819); chapter 23.

> "If we keep together, we make but the ae line of
> it; if we gang separate, we make twae of them:
> the more likelihood to stave in upon some of these
> gentry of yours. And then, second, if they keep
> the track of us, it may come to a fecht for it yet,
> Davie; and then, I'll confess I would be blithe to
> have you at my oxter, and I think you would be
> none the worse of having me at yours. "
> --Robert Louis Stevenson: David Balfour (1892);
> chapter 11.

-P-

PACK: An old Scottish word of unknown origin, meaning "on
friendly terms" or "closely allied or linked together. " It
can be found in Janet Hamilton's Poems and Essays of a
Miscellaneous Character on Subjects of General Interest
(1863); Stevenson's David Balfour (1893), and in the following:

> "I met wi a cheel as I rade hame,
>   And thae queer stories said he;
> Sir, I saw this day a fairy queen
>   Fu pack wi a gypsie laddie. "

--"The Gypsy Laddie" in Child's English and Scottish Popular Ballads; Version E, stanza 12.

> Nae doubt but they were fain o' ither,
> An' unco pack an' thick thegither;
> Wi' social nose whyles snuff'd and snowkit;
> Whyles mice and moudieworts they howkit.
> --Robert Burns: The Twa Dogs (1786); lines 37-40.

PACKSTAFF: The wooden stick upon which peddlers or vagabonds would rest their "pack" or belongings while eating or stopping to rest. The quotes below illustrate its use in a popular old saying, "as plain as a packstaff" (cf. similar construct, "in the twinkling of a bedstaff"). Also found in Thomas Becon's David's Harp (1542); in Robert Greene (1591); Joseph Hall's Satires: Virgidemiarum (1597); Henry Brooke's The Fool of Quality (1772); and, as a term of reproach, in John Marston's The Scourge of Villainie (1598).

> DRYFAT: I tell thee, there's no averment against our book-cases. 'Tis the law called make-peace: it makes them even when they are at odds; it shows 'em a flat case as plain as a pack-staff, that is, knocks 'em down without circumstance.
> --Thomas Middleton: The Family of Love (1602);
>   Act V, Scene 3.

> AMPHITRYON: What gross absurdities are these!
> SOSIA: O Lord, O Lord, what absurdities! as plain as any packstaff.
> --John Dryden: Amphitryon (1690); Act III, Scene 1.

PADDOCK: An old word meaning (1) a frog; (2) a toad; (3) hence, a term of reproach applied to a person. "A great frog or toad," says Johnson. It comes from the Anglo-Saxon pad, "frog, toad," the late Old English pade, similar to the Old Norse padda.

Sense (1) can be located in John Wycliffe (1388); Palsgrave (1530); Topsell (1608); Allan Ramsay (1724); Hugh Miller (1854), and in Dryden:

> The water snake, whom fish and paddocks fed,
> With staring scales lies poison'd in his bed:
> To birds their native heav'ns contagious prove;

PADDOCK (cont.)   204

>From clouds they fall, and leave their souls above.
--John Dryden: Translation of Virgil's Georgics
(1697); Book IV, lines 812-815.

Sense (2) appears again in Palsgrave (1530), and in these:

Where I was wont to seeke the honey Bee,
Working her formall rowmes in Wexen frame:
The grieslie Todestoole growne there mought I see
And loathed Paddocks lording on the same.
--Edmund Spenser: The Shepheardes Calender
(1579); December, lines 67-70.

HAMLET: 'Twere good you let him know;
For who, that's but a queen, fair, sober, wise,
Would from a paddock, from a bat, a gib,
Such dear concernings hide? who would do so?
--William Shakespeare: Hamlet (1600); Act III,
Scene 4.

ELDER LOVELESS:
>From thee, false dice, jades, cowards, and plaguy
summers,
Good Lord, deliver me! (EXIT)
LADY: But hark you, servant, hark ye!--Is he
gone?
Call him again.
ABIGAIL YOUNGLOVE: Hang him, paddock!
LADY: Art thou here still? fly, fly, and call my
servant;
Fly, or ne'er see me more.
--Francis Beaumont & John Fletcher: The Scorn-
ful Lady (ca. 1610); Act IV, Scene 1.

But his fate lay before him; on he went,
And through the gilded doors, now open wide,
He passed, and found the flowery hangings rent,
And past his feet did hissing serpents glide,
While from the hall wherein the mourners died
A grey wolf glared, and o'er his head the bat
Hung, and the paddock on the hearth-stone sat.
--William Morris: The Earthly Paradise (1870);
The Man Who Never Laughed Again, stanza 115.

Sense (3) is found in these:

FIRST WITCH: When shall we three meet again
In thunder, lightning, or in rain?
SECOND WITCH: When the hurlyburly's done,
When the battle's lost and won.
THIRD WITCH: That will be ere the set of sun.
FIRST WITCH: Where the place?
SECOND WITCH: Upon the heath.
THIRD WITCH: There to meet with Macbeth.
FIRST WITCH: I come, Graymalkin!
SECOND WITCH: Paddock calls:--anon!
--William Shakespeare: Macbeth (1606); Act I,
    Scene 1.

When the corp was examined the leid draps hadna
played buff upon the warlock's body; sorrow a leid
drap was to be fund; but there was grandfaither's
siller tester in the puddock's heart of him.
--Robert Louis Stevenson: David Balfour (1893);
    chapter 15.

PALERMO: An old wine that originated in Palermo in northern Sicily.

        GRANICHUS: O for a bowl of fat canary,
        Rich Palermo, sparkling sherry,
        Some nectar else, from Juno's dairy,
        O these draughts would make us merry.
        --John Lyly: Campaspe (ca. 1580); Act I, Scene
            2.

        ASTUTIO:
        Well, have more wit hereafter: for this time,
        You are ransomed.
        JACOMO: Off with their irons.
        RODERIGO: Do, do:
        If you are ours again, you know your price.
        ANTONIO: Pray you dispatch us: I shall ne'er
            believe
        I am a free man, till I set my foot
        In Sicily again, and drink Palermo,
        And in Palermo too.
        --Philip Massinger: The Maid of Honour (1632);
            Act III, Scene 1.

PALFRENIER: A groom in charge of the horses at a stable,
mansion, or inn; an ostler. It comes through the French
palefrenier and the Late Latin paraveredus, from the Greek

para, "beside," and veredus, "horse"; palfrey is a related
word.   Examples of its use can be found in William Caxton
(1489); and, more recently, in Thackeray's Paris Sketch-
Book (1840), Sala's Captain Dangerous (1863), and in the
following:

> "You will hear the advanced enfans perdus, as the
> French call them, and so they are indeed, namely,
> children of the fall, singing unclean and fulsome
> ballads of sin and harlotrie.   And then will come
> on the middle-ward, when you will hear the canti-
> cles and psalms sung by the Reforming nobles,
> and the gentry, and honest and pious clergy, by
> whom they are accompanied.   And last of all, you
> will find in the rear a legion of godless lackeys,
> and palfreniers, and horse-boys, talking of nothing
> but dicing, drinking, and drabbing. "
> --Sir Walter Scott: The Monastery (1820); chapter
>   35.

PANCAKE-BELL: A bell rung about eleven in the morning
on Shrove Tuesday to call the people to confession before
Lent, thus associated with the making of breakfast pancakes.
It is still extant in certain areas of England.   Found in John
Taylor (1620), and in Dekker:

> EYRE: This day, my fellow prentices of London
> come to dine with me too, they shall have fine
> cheer, gentlemanlike cheer.   I promised the mad
> Cappadocians, when we all served at the Conduit
> together, that if ever I came to be mayor of Lon-
> don, I would feast them all, and I'll do't, I'll
> do't, by the life of Pharaoh; by this beard, Sim
> Eyre will be no flincher.   Besides, I have pro-
> cured that upon every Shrove-Tuesday, at the
> sound of the pancake bell, my fine dapper Assyrian
> lads shall clap up their shop windows, and away.
> This is the day, and this day they shall do't, they
> shall do't.
> --Thomas Dekker: The Shoemaker's Holiday
>   (1599); Act V, Scene 1.

PARTAN: A Scottish term for a crab.   It comes from the
Gaelic partan, and the Irish partón, but further etymology is
uncertain.   It can be seen in Sir Robert Sibbald (1710); in
Samuel Rutherford Crockett's The Raiders (1894), and in
Scott:

"Eighteen-pence!!!" (in a loud tone of astonish-
ment, which inclined into a sort of rueful whine,
when the dealer turned as if to walk away)--"Ye'll
no be for the fish then?"--(then louder, as she
saw him moving off)--'I'll gie ye them--and--and
--and a half-a-dozen o' partans to make the sauce,
for three shillings and a dram."
--Sir Walter Scott: The Antiquary (1816); chapter
    11.

The word also means a sour, ill-tempered person:
in J. M. Barrie's Sentimental Tommy (1896), and, again,
in Crockett (1899).

PASH: The head; of unknown origin (possibly echoic from
sharp blows applied to the skull). Also, says Johnson, "a
kiss." It can be found in William Cleland's poetry (1697);
in Allan Ramsay (1719), and in John Struthers' poem Dych-
mont (1836), as well as in Shakespeare:

LEONTES:
Thou want'st a rough pash, and the shoots that I
    have,
To be full like me:--yet they saw we are
Almost as like as eggs; women say so,
That will say any thing.
--William Shakespeare: The Winter's Tale (1610);
    Act I, Scene 2.

PAVONE: A peacock. Through the Italian pavone from the
Latin synonym, pavo.

And at the upper end of that faire rowme,
There was an Altar built of pretious stone,
Of passing valew, and of great renowme,
On which there stood an Image all alone,
Of massy gold, which with his owne light shone;
And wings it had with sundry colours dight,
More sundry colours, then the proud Pavone
Beares in his boasted fan, or Iris bright,
When her discolourd bow she spreds through heaven
    bright.
--Edmund Spenser: The Faerie Queene, Book III
    (1590); Canto XI, stanza 47.

PEAK-GOOSE, PEA-GOOSE: A silly booby or simpleton; a
blockhead or numbskull. From the old word peak, same

sense, of unknown origin, with goose as suffix. Used in Roger Ascham's The Scholemaster (1568); Gabriel Harvey's Pierces Supererogation; or, a new Prayse of the Old Asse (1593); John Crowne's The Married Beau (1694), and in these:

> RHODERIQUE: Your Lordship has the right garb of an excellent courtier, respects a clown, supple-jointed, courtesies a very peagoose; tis stiff-ham'd audacity that carries it; get once within their distance, and you are in their bosoms instantly.
> --George Chapman: Monsieur D'Olive (1606); Act III, Scene 1.

> LA-WRIT: My name is Cock-a'-two; use me respectively,
> I will be cock of three else.
> DINANT: What's all this?
> You say, you did abuse a lady.
> LA-WRIT: You lie.
> DINANT: And that you wrong'd her honour.
> LA-WRIT: That's two lies.
> Speak suddenly, for I am full of business.
> DINANT: What art thou, or what canst thou be, thou peagoose,
> That dar'st give me the lie thus? thou mak'st me wonder.
> --John Fletcher & Philip Massinger: The Little French Lawyer (ca. 1620); Act II, Scene 3.

> GETA: Thou talk'st as if
> Thou wert lousing thyself; but yet I will make danger;
> If I prove one of the Worthies, so: however,
> I'll have the fear of the gods before my eyes,
> And do no hurt, I warrant you.
> NIGER: Come, march on,
> And humour him for our mirth.
> FIRST GUARD: 'Tis a fine peak-goose.
> NIGER: But one that fools to the emperor, and, in that,
> A wise man, and a soldier.
> FIRST GUARD: True morality!
> --John Fletcher: The Prophetess (1622); Act IV, Scene 2.

PELLOCK, PELLACH, PELLACK: An old word for the

porpoise; of unknown origin. It can be found in Sir John
Ballenden (1541); Sir Robert Sibbald (1710); Samuel Rutherford Crockett (1894), and in the following:

> "Saint Mary! father Simon, and do you, who are
> so good and prudent that you have been called the
> Wise Glover of Perth, let your daughter attend
> the ministry of one who--the saints preserve us!--
> may be in league with the foul Fiend himself?
> Why, was it not a priest who raised the devil in
> the Meal Vennel, when Hodge Jackson's house was
> blown down in the great wind?--did not the devil
> appear in the midst of the Tay, dressed in a
> priest's scapular, gamboling like a pellach amongst
> the waves, the morning when our stately bridge
> was swept away?"
> --Sir Walter Scott: The Fair Maid of Perth (1828);
> chapter 3.

PENBARD, PENBARDD: The head or principal bard of a
group. From the Welsh penbardd, constructed from pen,
"head," and bardd, "bard." It can be located in Lytton's
Harold, the Last of the Saxon Kings (1848), and in the following:

> Every Penbardd and Pencerdd was allowed to take
> in disciples for a certain space of time, but not
> above one at a time. A disciple was not qualified
> to make another. Each was to be with his teacher
> during Lent, unless prevented by sickness or im-
> prisonment, under pain of losing his degree.
> --Antiquities section in the Annual Register for the
> Year 1779; Section II, page 144.

PENNY-FATHER: A miserly skinflint; one who "fathers"
his "pennies"; hoarder. Found in Chaloner (1549); in Motteux's translation of Rabelais (1694), and in these:

> To nothing fitter can I thee compare,
> Than to the son of some rich penny-father,
> Who having now brought on his end with care,
> Leaves to his son all he had heap'd together;
> This new rich novice, lavish of his chest,
> To one man gives, doth on another spend,
> Then here he riots, yet amongst the rest,
> Haps to lend some to one true honest friend.
> --Michael Drayton: Ideas (1594); stanza 10.

PHILIP: But then their saving penny proverb
  comes,
And that is this, "They that will to the wine,
By'r Lady mistress, shall lay their penny to mine. "
This was one of this penny-father's bastards,
For, on my life, he was never begot
Without the consent of some great proverb-monger.
--Henry Porter: The Two Angry Women of Abing-
  ton (1599); Act II, Scene 1.

At last I met, at half turn, one whom I had spent
mine eyes so long for, an hoary money-master,
that had been off and on some six-and-fifty years
damned in his counting-house, for his only recrea-
tion was but to hop about the Burse before twelve,
to hear what news from the Bank, and how many
merchants were banqrout [bankrupt] the last change
of the moon. This rammish penny-father I
rounded [whispered] in the left ear, winded in my
intent, the place and hour; which no sooner he
sucked in, but smiled upon me in French, and
replied, --
  O mounsieur Diabla,
  I'll be chief guest at your tabla!
--Thomas Middleton: The Black Book (1604).

But who do I lose myself in seeking thee, when
thou art found of few but illiterate hinds, rude
boors, and hoary penny-fathers, that keep thee in
perpetual durance, in vaults under false boards,
subtle-contrived walls, and in horrible dark dun-
geons bury thee most unchristian-like, without
amen, or the least noise of a priest or clerk, and
make thee rise again at their pleasures many a
thousand time before doomsday; and yet will not
all this move thee once to forsake them, and keep
company with a scholar that truly knows how to
use thee?
--Thomas Middleton: "The Ant's Tale when he
  was a Scholar, " in Father Hubburd's Tales
  (1604).

PENSTER: A term for a writer of petty literature; a liter-
ary hack. Found since the 17th century.

He threw back his head like a swimmer tossing
spray from his locks.

"You have read the paper?" he asked.
"You have horsewhipped the writer?" she re-
joined.
"Oh! the poor penster!"
"Nay, we can't pretend to pity him!"
"Could we condescend to offer him satisfaction?"
"Would he dare to demand it?"
--George Meredith: The Adventures of Harry
Richmond (1871); chapter 21.

PETER-SEE-ME, PETER-SA-MEENE: An old type of rich
and delicate Spanish wine, popular in the 17th century. The
name is a corruption of the name of a famous Spanish grape,
the Pedro Ximenes, named for its introducer. Says Ford
in 1846 in Gatherings from Spain: "The Pedro Ximenez, or
delicious sweet-tasted grape which is so celebrated, came
originally from Madeira, and was planted on the Rhine,
whence about two centuries ago one Peter Simon brought it
to Malaga." Examples of its use can be found in Richard
Brathwait's Law of Drinking (1617); in John Taylor (1623),
and in the following:

SANCHO:
Welcome, poet, to our ging [company]!
  Make rhymes, we'll give thee reason;
Canary bees thy brains shall sting,
  Mull-sack did ne'er speak treason;
Peter-see-me shall wash thy noul [head]
  And malaga glasses fox thee;
If, poet, thou toss not bowl for bowl,
  Thou shalt not kiss a doxy.
--Thomas Middleton & William Rowley: The
Spanish Gipsy (ca. 1623); Act III, Scene I.

VECCHIO:
By old Claret I enlarge thee,
By Canary thus I charge thee,
By Britain Matthewglin [British metheglin], and
  Peter,
Appear, and answer me in metre!
                    Why, when?
                    Why, Gill!
                    Why, when?
--John Fletcher: The Chances (1627); Act V,
Scene 3.

MATHEO: Here's ordnance able to sack a city.

> LODOVICO: Come, repeat, read this inventory.
> FIRST VINTNER: Imprimis, a pottle of Greek
> wine, a pottle of Peter-sameene, a pottle of
> Charnico, and a pottle of Leatica.
> --Thomas Dekker: The Honest Whore, Part II
>   (1630); Act IV, Scene 3.

> CLEM: You are welcome, gentleman. What wine
> will you drink? Claret, metheglin, or muscadine?
> Cider, or perry, to make you merry? Aragoosa,
> or peter-see-me? Canary, or charnico? But, by
> your nose, sir, you should love a cup of malmsey:
> you shall have a cup of the best in Cornwall.
> GOODLACK: Here's a brave drawer, will quarrel
> with his wine.
> --Thomas Heywood: The Fair Maid of the West,
>   Part I (1631); Act III, Scene 4.

PIG-SCONCE: A pig-headed person; a dull, stupid blockhead; a boor. Constructed from pig and sconce, "head or
skull," which comes from the Dutch schans, "fortress,"
originally, "wicker-basket." Used principally from the 17th
to 19th centuries, it can be found in George Meredith's The
Egoist (1879), and in Massinger:

> GOLDWIRE:
> We come not to fright you, but to make you merry:
> A light lavolta.
> SHAVE'EM: I am tired; no more.
> This was your device?
> DING'EM: Wholly his own? he is
> No pig-sconce, mistress.
> SECRET: He has an excellent headpiece.
> GOLDWIRE: Fie! no, not I; your jeering gallants
>   say
> We citizens have no wit.
> DING'EM: He dies that says so;
> This was a masterpiece.
> --Philip Massinger: The City Madam (1632); Act
>   III, Scene 1.

PILLOW-CUP: A nightcap; a drink given around before re-
tiring at night.

> At the same moment the landlord again appeared,
> and, with more of the usual manners of a publican
> than he had hitherto exhibited, commanded his

waiter, Geoffrey, to hand round to the company a
sleeping-drink, or pillow-cup, of distilled water,
mingled with spieces, which was indeed as good as
Philipson himself had ever tasted.
> --Sir Walter Scott: Anne of Geierstein (1829);
>   chapter 19.

PINCH-GUT: One who forces himself or others to abstain
from food; a "pinch-belly." It can be located in Thomas
Flatman (1682), and in the following:

> FIRST BOY: She was a tirewoman at first in the
> suburbs of Milan; but falling into an ebb of fortune,
> and hearing the quaint and various fancies of our
> country damosellas, she took upon her this adven-
> ture to improve her annual pension; which she has
> by the dexterity of her wit and incomparable curi-
> osity of art highly enlarged, and by this unexpected
> means--for it happened, to give an addition to her
> future happiness, that one Sir Gregory Shapeless,
> a mundungo monopolist, a paltry-penurious-pecking
> pinchgut, who had smoked himself into a mercenary
> title of knightship, set his affection upon her soon
> after her arrival here; whom thou may imagine,
> Nick, to be no sooner wooed than won.
> --Anonymous: Lady Alimony (1659); Act II, Scene
>   2.

PISHERY-PASHERY: Disparaging, trifling talk; gossip of no
value. The word results from a reduplication of pish, a
natural exclamation of disgust.

> EYRE: Peace, Firk; peace, my fine Firk! Stand
> by with your pishery-pashery, away! I am a man
> of the best presence; I'll speak to them, an they
> were Popes.
> --Thomas Dekker: The Shoemaker's Holiday (1599);
>   Act I, Scene 1.

> EYRE: Be ruled, sweet Rose: th'art ripe for a
> man. Marry not with a boy that has no more hair
> on his face than thou hast on thy cheeks. A
> courtier, wash, go by, stand not upon pishery-
> pashery: those silken fellows are but painted
> images, outsides, outsides, Rose; their inner lin-
> ings are torn.
> --Thomas Dekker: The Shoemaker's Holiday (1599);
>   Act III, Scene 5.

PISSING-WHILE: An old word, principally used from the 16th through the 19th centuries, referring to a short period of time; an instant. The allusion is blatantly obvious. It can be found in Nashe and Palsgrave, and in the following authors:

> ROISTER: Alas! thou hittest me still.
> Hold!
> MERRYGREEK: Save yourself, sir!
> ROISTER: Help! out alas! I am slain.
> MERRYGREEK: Truce, hold your hands! truce,
> for a pissing while or twain.
> --Nicholas Udall: Ralph Roister Doister (ca.
>   1550); Act IV, Scene 8.

> DOCTOR RAT:
> A man were better twenty times be a bandog and
>   bark,
> Than here among such a sort be parish priest or
>   clerk.
> Where he shall never be at rest one pissing while
>   a day,
> But he must trudge about the town this way, and
>   that way,
> Here to a drab, there to a thief, his shoes to tear
>   and rent,
> And that which is worst of all, at every knave's
>   commandment.
> --William Stevenson: Gammer Gurton's Needle
>   (1553); Act IV, Scene 1.

> LAUNCE: He thrusts me himself into the company of three or four gentlemanlike dogs, under the duke's table: he had not been there (bless the mark!) a pissing while, but all the chamber smelt him. "Out with the dog," says one; "What cur is that?" says another; "Whip him out," says the third; "Hang him up," says the duke.
> --William Shakespeare: The Two Gentlemen of
>   Verona (ca. 1594); Act IV, Scene 4.

Also used by Ben Jonson in The Magnetic Lady (1632).

PIZE, PIES, PYES: An old curse or imprecation, used in various ways; the origin is not known, but it may perhaps be a variation of "pox" or "pest," which were also commonly used. Examples can be found in Thomas Duffet's The

Mock Tempest (1674); Tobias Smollett's The Adventures of
Ferdinand Count Fathom (1753); Samuel Foote's The Knights
(1754); Richardson's Sir Charles Grandison (1754); Scott's
Journal, November 2nd (1826), and in these:

> ROGERO: Ha, Vollupo!
> BALTHEZAR: No; but a better.
> ROGERO: Pox on't.
> BALTHEZAR: Pies on't!
> What luck is this? But, sir, you part not so;
> Whate'er you be, I'll have a bout with you.
> ROGERO: Content; this is joy mixed with spite,
> To miss a lord, and meet a prince in fight.
> --Anonymous: Jeronimo, Part I (1604); Act III,
>   Scene 2.

> TAILBY: Pize on't, I pawned a good beaver hat
> to master Frip last night, Jack: I feel the want of
> it now.
> --Thomas Middleton: Your Five Gallants (ca.
>   1606); Act IV, Scene 2.

> ANDREW: He was as like our Master Shape as
>   could be;
> But that he had a patch upon his cheek
> And a black beard, I should have sworn 'twere he:
> It was somebody in his clothes, I'm sure.
> MEANWELL: Some cunning cheater, upon my life,
>   won
> His cloak and suit too!
> ANDREW: There it is for certain,
> Pyes take him! doth he play for cloaks still?
>   Surely
> He hath a fly only to win good clothes.
> --William Cartwright: The Ordinary (ca. 1634);
>   Act II, scene 4.

> OLD BELLAIR: You need not look so glum, sir.
> A wife is no curse when she brings the blessing
> of a good estate with her. But an idle town flirt,
> with a painted face, a rotten reputation, and a
> crazy fortune, adod, is the devil and all; and such
> a one I hear you are in league with.
> YOUNG BELLAIR: I cannot help detraction, sir.
> OLD BELLAIR: Out, a pize o' their breeches,
> there are keeping fools enough for such flaunting
> baggages, and they are e'en too good for 'em.

--Sir George Etherege: The Man of Mode (1676);
Act II, Scene 1.

BELFOND SENIOR: Ay, I vow, pretty rogues!
No pride in them in the world; but so courteous
and familiar, as I am an honest man they'll do
whatever one would have them presently. Ah
sweet rogues; while in the country, a pies take
them, there's such a stir with pish, fie, nay Mr.
Timothy, what do you do?
--Thomas Shadwell: The Squire of Alsatia (1688);
Act I, Scene 1.

ANGELICA: I assure you, I know very considerable beaus, that set a good face upon fifty, fifty!
I have seen fifty in a side box by candle-light,
out-blossom five and twenty.
SIR SAMPSON: Outsides, outsides; a pize take
'em, mere outsides: hang your side-box beaus; no,
I'm none of those, none of your forc'd trees, that
pretend to blossom in the fall; and bud when they
should bring forth fruit: I am of a long liv'd race,
and inherit vigour, none of my ancestors marry'd
'till fifty, yet they begot sons and daughters 'till
fourscore: I am of your patriarchs, I, a branch
of one of your Antideluvian families, fellows, that
the flood could not wash away.
--William Congreve: Love for Love (1695); Act
V, Scene 2.

PLISKY, PLISKIE: An old Scottish word of unknown origin,
meaning (1) a prank or trick, or (2) an awkward situation.
The first sense can be found in Scott's The Antiquary (1816)
and St. Ronan's Well (1823); in Peter MacNeill's Blawearie;
or, Mining Life in the Lothians Forty Years Ago (1887), and
in Burns:

This while she's been in crankous mood,
Her lost Militia fir'd her bluid;
(Deil na they never mair do guid,
                    Play'd her that pliskie!)
An' now she's like to rin red-wud
                    About her Whisky.
--Robert Burns: The Author's Earnest Cry and
Prayer (1786); stanza 16.

Sense (2) appears in the following:

"Ech! ech!" exclaimed Joseph. "Weel done, Miss
Cathy! weel done, Miss Cathy! Howsiver, t'
maister sall just tum'le o'er them brocken pots;
un' then we's hear summut; we's hear how it's
to be. Gooid-for-naught madling! ye desarve
pining fro' this to Churstmas, flinging t' precious
gifts o' God under fooit i' yer flaysome rages!
But, I'm mista'en if ye show yer sperrit lang.
Will Hathecliff bide sich bonny ways, think ye?
I nobbut wish he may catch ye i' that plisky. I
nobbut wish he may."
    --Emily Brontë: Wuthering Heights (1847); chapter
    13.

POLL-HILL: A humorous name for a bump on the head:
a "hill" formed on the "poll." Poll comes through the Middle English polle from the Dutch polle and the Low German
polle, same sense.

'Tis strange how like a very dunce,
Man--with his bumps upon his sconce,
Has lived so long, and yet no knowledge he
Has had, till lately, of Phrenology--
A science that by simple dint of
Head-combing he should find a hint of,
When scratching o'er those little poll-hills,
The faculties throw up like mole-hills.
    --Thomas Hood: Craniology (1845); stanza 1.

POMEWATER: An old name for a kind of large apple, very
sweet and juicy. It comes through the Old French pome and
Late Latin poma, "apple," from the original Latin ponum,
"fruit," which later came to mean "apple" also. Examples
of its use can be found in Lydgate (1430); in Richard Ligon's
History of Barbadoes (1657); in Leigh Hunt (1832), and in
these:

SIR NATHANIEL: Very reverend sport, truly; and
done in the testimony of a good conscience.
HOLOFERNES: The deer was, as you know,
sanguis,--in blood; ripe as a pomewater, who now
hangeth like a jewel in the ear of coelo,--the sky,
the welkin, the heaven; and anon falleth like a
crab on the face of terra,--the soil, the land, the
earth.
    --William Shakespeare: Love's Labour's Lost (ca.
    1595); Act IV, Scene 2.

BOTH: Buy any apples, feene apples of Tamasco,
feene Tamasco peepins: peeps feene, buy Tamas-
co peepins.
AGRIPYNE: Damasco apples? good my Lord
  Montrose,
Call yonder fellows.
MONTROSE: Sirrah coster-monger.
SHADOW: Who calls: peeps of Tamasco, feene
peeps: Ay, fat 'tis de sweetest apple in de world,
'tis better den de Pome water, or apple John.
--Thomas Dekker: Old Fortunatus (1600); Act IV,
  Scene 2.

POMPILLION: An old term of reproach or contempt given
to a man. It probably comes from pompion, a kind of
pumpkin, which was also used as a contemptuous name for
a (big) man. Through the Latin pepo from the Greek pepōn,
"large melon. "

BARTELLO:
You see this youth; will you not cry him quittance?
Body 'me, I would pine, but I would pepper him:
I'll come anon. (ASIDE TO ISABELLA) --He, hang
  him, poor pompillion!
How like a wench bepiss'd he looks!
--John Fletcher: Women Pleased (ca. 1620); Act
  III, Scene 4.

POOP: To cheat or deceive; to fool; to take advantage of.
The origin is uncertain; it may be related to the Dutch poep,
"a clown. " It can be found in Thomas Nashe (1596); Thomas
May (1650); in John Dryden's The Wild Gallant, Act IV
(1663), and in these:

HODGE: Nay, nay, there was a fouler fault, my
  Gammer ga' me the dodge:
Seest not how cham [I am] rent and torn, my
  heels, my knees, and my breech?
Chad thought, as ich sat by the fire, help here
  and there a stitch;
But there ich was pouped indeed.
--William Stevenson: Gammer Gurton's Needle
  (1553); Act II, Scene 1.

BOULT: But shall I search the market?
BAWD: What else, man? The stuff we have, a
strong wind will blow it to pieces, but they are so

pitifully sodden.
PANDAR: Thou sayest true: they're too unwhole-
some, o' conscience. The poor Transylvanian is
dead, that lay with the little baggage.
BOULT: Ay, she quickly poopt him; she made
him roast-meat for worms.
--William Shakespeare: Pericles (ca. 1606); Act
    IV, Scene 2.

PORKER, "PIGSTICKER": An old kind of sword. The
porker probably got its name from a corruption of poker,
but the origin of pigsticker is disputed. Found principally
in the late 17th and early 18th centuries.

CHEATLY: The prigster lugg'd out in defense of
his natural; the Captain whipt his porker out, and
away rubb'd prigster and call'd the watch.
--Thomas Shadwell: The Squire of Alsatia (1688);
    Act I, Scene 1.

POTAGERE: An herb-garden; small kitchen-garden. It
comes from the French potager, in jardin potager, "kitchen-
garden." Evelyn used it, in his last major work, Acetaria;
or a Discourse of Sallets (1699), and in the following:

I was this day very ill of a pain in my limbs,
which continued most of this week, and was in-
creased by a visit I made to my old acquaintance,
the Earl of Norwich, at his house in Epping Forest,
where are many good pictures put into the wainscot
of the rooms, which Mr. Baker, his Lordship's
predecessor there, brought out of Spain; especially
the History of Joseph, a picture of the pious and
learned Picus Mirandula, and an incomparable one
of old Breugel. The gardens were well under-
stood, I mean the potager. I returned late in the
evening, ferrying over the water at Greenwich.
--John Evelyn's Diary: September 2nd, 1669.

POTARGO: A variation of botargo (q.v.).

CROCALE: By this hand, we'll starve ye.
MASTER: 'Tis a noble courtesy:
I had as lief ye should famish me as founder me;
To be jaded to death is only fit for a hackney.
Here be certain tarts of tar about me,
And parcels of potargo in my jerkin:

As long as these last--
JULETTA: Which will not last ever.
TIBALT: Then we'll eat one another like good
    fellows;
A shoulder of his for a haunch of mine.
--John Fletcher & Philip Massinger: The Sea-
    Voyage (1622); Act IV, Scene 3.

CHARLES: What loads are these?
ANDREW: Meat, meat, sir, for the kitchen;
And stinking fowls the tenants have sent in, --
They'll ne'er be found out at a general eating:
And there's fat venison, sir.
CHARLES: What's that?
ANDREW: Why, deer;
Those that men fatten for their private pleasures,
And let their tenants starve upon the commons.
CHARLES: I've read of deer, but yet I ne'er eat
    any.
ANDREW: There's a fishmonger's boy with cavi-
    are, sir,
Anchovies, and potargo, to make you drink.
CHARLES: Sure, these are modern, very modern
    meats,
For I understand 'em not.
--John Fletcher: The Elder Brother (ca. 1625);
    Act III, Scene 3.

POZ, POS, POZZ: An abbreviated expression meaning
"Positive, certain, " or, as adverb, "Positively, certainly. "
Found in Thomas Surr (1801) and in these:

"SIR,
"I Cou'd n't get the things you sent for all about
Town--I thôt to ha come down myself, and then
I'd ha' brôut 'um; but I han't don't, and I believe
I can't do't, that's Pozz. "
--Jonathan Swift: The Tatler No. 230 (1710); para-
    graph 5.

ABIGAIL: Sure never any lady had such servants
as mine has! Well, if I get this thousand pound,
I hope to have some of my own. Let me see,
I'll have a pretty tight girl--just such as I was
ten years ago, (I'm afraid I may say twenty,) she
shall dress me and flatter me--for I will be flatter'd, that's pos!

--Joseph Addison: The Drummer, or the Haunted
House (1715); Act III, Scene 1.

"As for the girl, you can have her, Tom Trippet,
if you take a fancy to her; and as for the Corporal,
he may be handed over to my successor in Cutts's:
--for I will have a regiment to myself, that's poz;
and to take with me such a swindling, pimping,
thieving, brandy-faced rascal as this Brock will
never do. Egad! he's a disgrace to the service.
As it is, I've often a mind to have the superannu-
ated vagabond drummed out of the corps. "
--William Makepeace Thackeray: Catherine: A
Story (1839); chapter 2.

PRATTLE-BASKET, PRATTLE-BOX: An old name for a
person who talks too much; a prattler. The formation is
the same as with "chatterbox. " It can be seen in Nicholas
Breton (1602); Joseph Glanvill (1671); John Locke (1696); in
Robert Paltock's The Life and Adventures of Peter Wilkins,
a Cornish Man (1751), and in Shadwell:

BERNARDO: What, love another besides you!
You take me for a monster, sure: I'd have you
know I'm none of those that are all love, and no
conscience.
ROSANIA: Good Sir, do not beat my aunt, I be-
seech you.
BERNARDO: Sweet Prattle-basket be quiet; peace
little one, or I shall grow passionate.
--Thomas Shadwell: The Amorous Bigot (1690);
Act II.

PRICKADO: A pierce, stab, or thrust with a sword. It is
a humorous phrase formed from the analogy of passado,
which is the name for the forward thrust in fencing.

PISTON: After we had got the chain in mummery,
And lost our box in counter cambio,
My master wore the chain about his neck;
Then Ferdinando met us on the way,
And revil'd my master, saying he stole the chain.
With that they drew, and there Ferdinando had the
prickado.
--Thomas Kyd: Soliman and Perseda (1592); Act
II, Scene 2.

PRICK-ME-DAINTY, PRICK-MY-DAINTY: A fussy, fastidi-
ous, finical dandy, who dresses exquisitely. It comes from
the old word prick, "success, excellence."

> SEPTIMUS PASSUS:
> But syr amonge all
> That sate in that hall
> There was a pricke me deintie
> Sate lyke a saintye
> And began to paintye
> As thoughe she woulde fainty.
> --John Skelton: The Tunnyng of Elynour Rumming
>   (1529); lines 580-585.

> TRUEPENNY: Marry, then, prick-me-dainty!
> come, toast me a fig.
> --Nicholas Udall: Ralph Roister Doister (ca.
>   1550); Act II, Scene 3.

The word is also used as an adjective: in James
Hogg (1820), and in Scott:

> But Luckie Dods rejected the information thus
> tendered with contemptuous scorn. "Nane of your
> deil's play-books for me," said she; "it's an ill
> world since sic prick-my-dainty doings came in
> fashion. It's a poor tongue that canna tell its ain
> name, and I'll hae nane of your scarts [scratches]
> upon pasteboard."
> --Sir Walter Scott: St. Ronan's Well (1823); chap-
>   ter 12.

PRORUMP: To burst or pour forth. From the Latin pro-
rumpere, constructed of pro, "before," and rumpere, "burst
asunder."

> HORACE: It's come up, thanks to Apollo, and
> Aesculapius: Yet, there's another; you were best
> take a pill more?
> CRISPINUS: O, no: ô--ô--ô--ô.
> HORACE: Force yourself then, a little with your
> finger.
> CRISPINUS: O--ô--prorumped.
> TIBULLUS: Prorumped? What a noise it made!
> as if his spirit would have prorumpt with it.
> --Ben Jonson: The Poetaster (1601); Act V, Scene
>   3.

PUCKFIST, PUCKFOIST: An old word meaning (1) the puff-
ball fungus; (2) hence, used as a term of reproach for a
"puffed" or bragging swaggerer; (3) a miser or skinflint.
It comes from the old word for the fungus, fist, of uncertain derivation, with the name of the fairy sprite Puck used
as a prefix.

    The first sense can be found in Jonson's The Poetast-
er (1601), and in John Ford; the second, in James Shirley
and John Taylor, and in these:

> MACILENTE: Torment and death! break head and
>   brain at once,
> To be deliver'd of your fighting issue.
> Who can endure to see blind Fortune dote thus?
> To be enamour'd on this dusty turf?
> This clod? a whoreson puck-fist?
> --Ben Jonson: Every Man Out of His Humour
>   (1599); Act I, Scene 2.

> RUTILIO:
> To any honest well-deserving fellow,
> An 'twere but to a merry cobbler, I could sit still
>   now,
> I love the game so well; but that this puckfist,
> This universal rutter--Fare ye well, sir;
> And if you have any good prayers, put 'em for-
>   ward,
> There may be yet a remedy.
> --John Fletcher & Philip Massinger: The Custom
>   of the Country (ca. 1620); Act I, Scene 2.

> ANDRUGIO: What pride
> Of pamper'd blood has mounted up this puck-foist?
> --Thomas Middleton: More Dissemblers Besides
>   Women (1623); Act IV, Scene 2.

> "Thou art drunk, thou villain!" said Varney to him.
>   "Doubtless, noble sir," replied the unabashed
> Michael, "we have been drinking all even to the
> glories of the day, and to my noble Lord of Lei-
> cester, and his valiant master of the horse. --
> Drunk! odds blades and poniards, he that would
> refuse to swallow a dozen healths on such an
> evening, is a base besognio, and a puckfoist, and
> shall swallow six inches of my dagger!"
> --Sir Walter Scott: Kenilworth (1821); chapter 18.

Sense (3) can be found in Richard Middleton's Epi-grammes and Satyres (1608), and in the following:

> LAZARO: And a grazier may
> (For those are pinching puckfoists, and suspicious)
> Suffer a mist before his eyes sometimes too,
> And think he sees his horse eat half-a-bushel;
> When the truth is, rubbing his gums with salt
> Till all the skin come off, he shall but mumble
> Like an old woman that were chewing brawn,
> And drop 'em out again.
> --John Fletcher: Love's Pilgrimage (1616); Act I,
>   Scene 1.

> PECK: They have ever oats in their cloke-bags,
>   to affront us.
> FLY: And therefore 'tis an office meritorious,
> To tithe such soundly.
> PIERCE: And a grazier's may--
> FERRET: O, they are pinching puckfists!
> TRUNDLE: And suspicious.
> --Ben Jonson: The New Inn (1628); Act III, Scene
>   1.

PUFFKIN: A small puff; hence, a giddy woman; "cork-heeled," according to Dekker.

> FULGOSO:
> Pish, man! the best, though call 'em ladies,
>   madams,
> Fairs, fines, and honies, are but flesh and blood,
> And now and then too, when the fit's come on 'em,
> Will prove themselves but flirts, and tirliry-
>   [trifling] pufkins.
> --John Ford: The Lady's Trial (1638); Act III,
>   Scene 1.

PUGGY: An old colloquial term of endearment for women and children; the origin is not known. Principally used in the 17th and early 18th centuries, it can be found in Thomas D'Urfey's Pills to Purge Melancholy (1719), and in Beaumont:

> MERRYTHOUGHT:
> Begone, begone, my juggy, my puggy,
> Begone, my love, my dear!
>   The weather is warm,
>   'Twill do thee no harm;

Thou canst not be lodged here.
--Francis Beaumont: The Knight of the Burning
    Pestle (ca. 1610); Act III, Scene 5.

PUKY: Sickly; ill; about to puke. The origin is not certain, but it is related to the German spucken, "to spit."

> 'I tell you kindly that we (who, you will acknowl-
> edge, must count for something here) do not sanc-
> tion any change that revolutionizes our domestic
> relations," said Wilfrid; while Mrs. Chump heaved
> and rolled on the swell of the big words like an
> overladen boat. "You have only to understand so
> much, and this--that if we resist it, as we do,
> you, by continuing to contemplate it, are provoking
> a contest which will probably injure neither you
> nor me, but will be death to him in his present
> condition."
>   Mrs. Chump was heard to mumble that she
> alone knew the secret of restoring him to health,
> and that he was rendered peaky and puky only by
> people supposing him so.
>   --George Meredith: Sandra Belloni (1864); chapter
>   33.

PUNK, PUNG: An old term referring to a prostitute or
whore; a harlot. Used since the late 16th century, it is of
unknown origin. Says Nares: "A coarse term, which is
deservedly growing obsolete," and Grose tells us: "A
soldier's trull." Examples of its use can be found in many
works:

> PISTOL:
> This punk is one of Cupid's carriers:--
> Clap on more sails; pursue; up with your fights;
> Give fire; she is my prize, or ocean whelm them
>   all!
> --William Shakespeare: The Merry Wives of Wind-
>   sor (1601); Act II, Scene 2.

> HEROD: Then, my Pythagoras, shall thou and I
> make a transmigration of souls. Thou shalt marry
> my daughter, or my wife shall be thy gracious
> mistress. Seventeen punks shall be thy proportion.
> --John Marston: The Fawn (1604); Act I, Scene 2.

> DUKE: What, are you married?

MARIANA: No, my lord.
DUKE: Are you a maid?
MARIANA: No, my lord.
DUKE: A widow, then?
MARIANA: Neither, my lord.
DUKE: Why, you are nothing, then:--neither
maid, widow, nor wife?
LUCIO: My lord, she may be a punk; for many
of them are neither maid, widow, nor wife.
DUKE: Silence that fellow: I would he had some
   cause
To prattle for himself.
--William Shakespeare: Measure For Measure
    (1604); Act V, Scene 1.

DUKE: Upon mine honour, thou shalt marry her.
Thy slanders I forgive; and therewithal
Remit thy other forfeits. --Take him to prison;
And see our pleasure herein executed.
LUCIO: Marrying a punk, my lord, is pressing
to death, whipping, and hanging.
DUKE: Slandering a prince deserves it.
--William Shakespeare: Measure For Measure
    (1604); Act V, Scene 1.

SALEWOOD: And is she but your underput, Master
Lethe?
LETHE: No more, of my credit; and a gentlewoman of a great house, noble parentage, unmatch-
able education, my plain pung. I may grace her
with the name of a courtesan, a backslider, a
prostitution, or such a toy; but when all comes to
all, 'tis but a plain pung.
--Thomas Middleton: Michaelmas Term (ca. 1605);
    Act III, Scene 1.

COCLEDEMOY: Hang toasts, you are an ass!
Much o' your worship's brain lies in your calves.
Bread o' God, boy, I was at supper last night with
a new-wean'd bulchin--bread o' God!--drunk, hor-
ribly drunk! There was a wench, one Frank
Frailty, a punk, an honest polecat, of a clean in-
step, sound leg, smooth thigh, and the nimble
devil in her buttock.
--John Marston: The Dutch Courtesan (ca. 1605);
    Act II, Scene 1.

FACE: This is a travelled punk-master, and does
    know
All the delays: a notable hot rascal,
And looks, already, rampant.
--Ben Jonson: The Alchemist (1610); Act IV,
    Scene 3.

PUNKATEERO: A humorous formation from punk, referring
to a pimp or pander; a whore-master.

CURVETTO [after being drenched with water]:
Umph, drown'd! Noah's flood! duck'd over head
    and ears!
O sconce, and O sconce! an old soaker, O!
I sweat now till I drop: What, villains, O!
Punks, punkateroes, nags, hags! I will ban:
I've catch'd my bane.
--Thomas Middleton: Blurt, Master-Constable
    (1602); Act IV, Scene 1.

PURDY: And old word of unknown origin, meaning: ill-
tempered, haughty, surly, or proud. "Puffed up. "

WOODCOCK: You are a son of a whore, dear
heart, to tell me I lie.
NINNY: You are a son of a whore as well as my
self, to tell me so, and you go to that.
WOODCOCK: I, I, you may say your pleasure;
but have a care, bully-rook, for if you give me
the least affront, I'll break your pate, take that
from me.
NINNY: I'll take it from no man: If you do, I'll
break yours agen man, for all you are so brief:
'Slife, one shan't speak to you one of these days,
you are grown so purdy.
--Thomas Shadwell: The Sullen Lovers (1668);
    Act V.

BELLAMOUR: Do you see Sir how abominably
drunk he is?
GOLDINGHAM: He is a little in beer, he is; he
is disguis'd, that's the truth on't.
TIMOTHY: There Mrs. Thea, I have done it,
faith you shall pledge me by word of mouth; de'
see, nay fack I am sound, you may drink after
me, de' conceive me?
BELLAMOUR: You see Sir he is too drunk to be

married to night.
GOLDINGHAM: Come come, he's the fitter for't,
for being drunk, if he be sober, he may repent
him, and ask a portion: stay here, I will fetch a
parson immediately. (EXIT).
BELLAMOUR: This is worse and worse. Madam,
did you hear him?
THEODORA: Yes, to my grief, I must into my
chamber, and be very sick. (SHE OFFERS TO
GO).
TIMOTHY: Nay, if you stir I am a rogue, a very
rogue, de' see? we'll be very merry, Diseases
and Troubles, &c.
BELLAMOUR: Who taught you this insolence?
unhand her.
TIMOTHY: Why you saucy fellow you, what's to
do with you? Ha, you are so purdy.
--Thomas Shadwell: The Miser (1671); Act IV,
    Scene 1.

-Q-

QUAB: Originally, a sea slug or burbot; hence, any amor-
phous, shapeless object. It comes through the Middle Dutch
quabbe from the Low German quabbe, "fat piece of flesh, "
and the Old Low German quappa, and can be located in William Tooke's A View of the Russian Empire during the Reign
of Catharine II and to the Close of the present Century
(1799), and in the following:

CORAX:
Lights and attendance! I will show your highness
A trifle of mine own brain. If you can,
Imagine you were now in the university.
You'll take it well enough: a scholar's fancy,
A quab; 'tis nothing else, a very quab.
--John Ford: The Lover's Melancholy (1628); Act
    III, Scene 3.

QUACKING-CHEAT: An old cant term for a duck, in use
from the late 16th to middle 19th centuries. It is constructed of quacking and cheat, "thing, article. " Thus, a
"quacking-thing. " It can be found in Robert Smythe Hichens'
The Londoners (1898), and in these earlier writers:

When the darkmans have been wet,

    Thou the crackmans [hedge] down didst beat
For glimmer, whilst a quacking cheat
    Or Tib o'th'buttery [a goose] was our meat.
--Thomas Dekker: English Villainies Discovered
    by Lantern and Candlelight (1608); chapter 24.

ALL: Doxy, Moll? what's that?
MOLL: His wench.
TRAPDOOR: My doxy? I have, by the salomon
[by the mass], a doxy that carries a kinchin mort
[infant girl] in her slate at her back, besides my
dell and my dainty wild dell [virgin], with all whom
I'll tumble this next darkmans [night] in the strom-
mel [straw], and drink ben bouse [good drink],
and eat a fat gruntling cheat [a pig], a cackling
cheat [a chicken], and a quacking cheat.
--Thomas Middleton & Thomas Dekker: The Roar-
    ing Girl (1611); Act V, Scene 1.

QUACKSALVER: A charlatan; a phony doctor; a quack.
Says Grose: "A mountebank, a seller of salves." It comes
from the early modern Dutch quacksalver (modern Dutch
kwakzalver), constructed from quacken, "to cry, to quack,"
and salf, zalf, "ointment, salve, medicine." Thus, a quacksalver is a person who cries out or quacks the reliability of
his salves which he has for sale. Used principally in the
17th century, it can be found in many writings, including
Stephen Gosson's The Schoole of Abuse, containing a plesaunt
invective against Poetes, Pipers, Players, Jesters, and such
like Caterpillars of a Commonwealth (1579); D'Urfey's Pills
to Purge Melancholy (1719); Algernon Swinburne's Study of
Ben Jonson (1889), and the following:

    PEREGRINE: They are quacksalvers;
    Fellows, that live by venting oils and drugs.
    --Ben Jonson: Volpone; or, the Fox (1606); Act
        II, Scene 1.

    From thence you should blow yourself into the
    tobacco ordinary, where you are likewise to spend
    your judgment like a quacksalver upon that mysti-
    cal wonder to be able to discourse whether your
    cane or your pudding be sweetest, and which pipe
    has the best bore and which burns black, which
    breaks in the burning, etc.
    --Thomas Dekker: The Gull's Horn-Book (1609);
        chapter 8.

QUAICH, QUAIGH: An old Scottish word for a type of shallow drinking-cup, made of wood, and having two handles and a silver rim. Often the cup was made entirely of silver. It comes through the Gaelic cuach, "cup," and the Old Irish cúach, from the Latin caucus and Greek kauka, same sense. Examples of its use can be located in Allan Ramsay (1711); in Alexander Pennecuik's Geographical Historical Description of the Shire of Tweeddale (1715); in Smollett's Humphrey Clinker (1771); Queen Victoria's More Leaves from the Journal of a Life in the Highlands (1884), and in the following:

> The quaighs were deep, the liquor strong,
> And on the tale the yeoman-throng
> Had made a comment sage and long,
>   But Marmion gave a sign:
> And, with their lord, the squires retire;
> The rest, around the hostel fire,
>   Their drowsy limbs recline.
> --Sir Walter Scott: Marmion (1808); Canto III,
>   Stanza 26.

QUAIL: A mistress or harlot; prostitute. From the notion that the quail is an amorous bird. The origin of quail itself is probably echoic, coming through the Middle English quaile, the Old French quaille, and the medieval Latin cuacula. It can be found in Motteux's translation of Rabelais (1694), and in the following:

> THERSITES: Here's Agamemnon,--an honest fellow, enough, and one that loves quails: but he has not so much brain as ear-wax.
> --William Shakespeare: Troilus and Cressida (ca. 1600); Act V, Scene 1.

> URSULA: An you be right Bartholomew birds, now show yourselves so: we are undone for want of fowl in the Fair, here. Here will be Zekiel Edgworth, and three or four gallants with him at night, and I have neither plover nor quail for them: persuade this between you two, to become a bird o'the game, while I work the velvet woman within, as you call her.
> --Ben Jonson: Bartholomew Fair (1614); Act IV, Scene 3.

QUARREL: A square or diamond-shaped piece of glass used

in the construction of lattice-windows, so named from the
quarrel, a square-headed missile used in ancient crossbows.
It comes through the Old French quarel, quarrel (modern
French carreau), the Provencal cairel, the Italian quadrello,
the Spanish cuadrillo, and the medieval Latin quadrellus,
diminutives ultimately from the Latin quadrus, "a square."
Examples of its use can be found in Andrew Borde (1542);
in George Puttenham's The Arte of English Poesie, Book II
(1589); in Robert Boyle (1669); Charles Lockyer's Trade in
India (1711), and in the following:

> CHOUGH: My name is Chough, a Cornish gentle-
> man; my man's mine own country man too, i'
> faith: I warrant you took us for some of the small
> islanders.
> JANE: I did indeed, between the Scotch and Irish.
> CHOUGH: Red-shanks? I thought so, by my
>   truth: no, truly,
> We are right Cornish diamonds.
> TRIMTRAM: Yes, we cut
> Out quarrels and break glasses where we go.
> --Thomas Middleton & William Rowley: A Fair
>   Quarrel (1617); Act II, Scene 2.

> GALOSHIO: I earn'd
> Four crowns a-month most dearly, gentlemen:
> And one he must have, when the fit's upon him;
> He would break else some forty pounds in case-
>   ments,
> And in five hundred years undo the kingdom;
> I have cast it up to a quarrel.
> --John Fletcher: The Nice Valour (ca. 1624); Act
>   III, Scene 1.

> 'If thou hast adjusted my wimple amiss, my Flem-
> ing, or if Catharine hath made a wry stitch in her
> broidery when she was thinking of something else
> than her work, or if Roland Graeme hath missed
> a wild duck on the wing, and broke a quarrel-pane
> of glass in the turret window, as chanced to him
> a week since, now is the time to think on your
> sins and to repent of them. "
> --Sir Walter Scott: The Abbot (1820); chapter 34.

QUAT, QUOT: A word of unknown origin, referring to a
pimple; hence, a term of reproach for a young, inexperi-
enced upstart. It can be seen in William Langham's Garden

of Health (1579), and in the following:

> IAGO:
> I have rubb'd this young quat almost to the sense,
> And he grows angry. Now, whether he kill Cassio,
> Or Cassio him, or each do kill the other,
> Every way makes my gain.
> --William Shakespeare: Othello (1604); Act V,
>   Scene 1.

> Whosoever desires to be a man of good reckoning
> in the City and like your French lord to have as
> many tables furnished as lackeys (who, when they
> keep least, keep none): whether he be a young
> quat of the first year's revenue; or some austere
> and sullen-faced steward ... my counsel is that
> he take his continual diet at a tavern, which out
> of question is the only rendezvous of boon com-
> pany, and the drawers the most nimble, the most
> bold and most sudden proclaimers of your largest
> bounty.
> --Thomas Dekker: The Gull's Horn-Book (1609);
>   chapter 7.

> JULIO: And what's your counsel?
> ARIOSTO: Why, I would have you leave your
>   whoring.
> JULIO: He comes hotly upon me at first: whor-
>   ing?
> ARIOSTO: O young quat, incontinence is plagued
> In all the creatures of the world.
> JULIO: When did you ever hear, that a cockspar-
>   row
> Had the French pox?
> ARIOSTO: When did you ever know any of them
>   fat, but in the nest?
> --John Webster: The Devil's Law-Case (ca. 1620);
>   Act II, Scene 1.

QUELLIO: An ornamental Spanish ruff, worn at the collar.
It comes from the Spanish cuello, same sense, from the
Latin word for neck, collum. Used by James Shirley (1633),
and the following writers:

> LUKE: Then, as I said,
> The reverend hood cast off, your borrow'd hair,
> Powder'd and curl'd, was by your dresser's art

Form'd like a coronet, hang'd with diamonds,
And the richest orient pearl; your carcanets
That did adorn your neck, of equal value:
Your Hungerford bands, and Spanish quellio ruffs;
Great lords and ladies feasted to survey
Embroider'd petticoats; and sickness feign'd
That your night-rails of forty pounds a piece
Might be seen with envy of the visitants.
--Philip Massinger: The City Madam (1632); Act
    IV, Scene 4.

GUZMAN:
Imagine first our rich mockado doublet,
With our cut cloth-of-gold sleeves, and our quellio,
Our diamond-button'd callamanco hose,
Our plume of ostrich, with the embroider'd scarf,
The duchess Infantasgo roll'd our arm in.
--John Ford: The Lady's Trial (1638); Act II,
    Scene 1.

QUEST-HOUSE: The chief watch-house of a parish, where
the inquests were held; thus a shortened form of "inquest-
house." This word can be found in Dekker & Webster's
Northward Ho (1607); Francis Quarles' Emblems (1635), and
in the following:

> WATER-CAMLET: She has a book, which I may
>   truly nominate
> Her Black Book, for she remembers in it,
> In short items, all my misdemeanours;
> as, item, such a day I was got foxed [drunk] with
> foolish metheglin, in the company of certain Welsh
> chapmen: item, such a day, being at the Artillery
> Garden, one of my neighbours, in courtesy to
> salute me with his musket, set a-fire my fustian
> and ape's breeches: such a day I lost fifty pound
> in hugger-mugger at dice, at the Quest-house.
> --Thomas Middleton: Anything for a Quiet Life
>   (ca. 1617); Act I, Scene 1.

> ...and so home to dinner, and after dinner car-
> ried my wife to the Temple, and thence she to a
> play, and I to St. Andrew's church, in Holburne,
> at the 'Quest House, where the company meets to
> the burial of my cozen Joyce; and here I staid
> with a very great rabble of four or five hundred
> people of mean condition, and I staid in the room

with the kindred till ready to go to church, where
there is to be a sermon of Dr. Stillingfleete, and
thence they carried him to St. Sepulchre's.
--Samuel Pepys' Diary: January 24th, 1668.

QUESTRIST: One who seeks or goes in quest of another.
Ultimately it comes from the Latin quaerere, "to seek,
ask. "

> DUKE OF CORNWALL: How now! where's the
>   king?
> OSWALD: My Lord of Gloster hath convey'd him
>   hence:
> Some five or six and thirty of his knights,
> Hot questrists after him, met him at gate;
> Who, with some other of the lords dependants,
> Are gone with him towards Dover; where they
>   boast
> To have well-armed friends.
> --William Shakespeare: King Lear (ca. 1606);
>   Act III, Scene 7.

QUIBIBLE: An old word of unknown origin and meaning, but
probably referring to some type of whistle or musical pipe.
Found in James Shirley (1642), and in the following:

> Your braynes are ydell
> It is time for you to brydell
> And pype in a quibyble
> For it is impossible
> For you to bring about
> Our kyng for to drive out
> Of this his realme royall
> And lande imperiall.
> --John Skelton: Duke of Albany and the Scottes
>   (1529); lines 387-394.

QUIBLIN: A sorry pun or tricky phrase; "tricks"; a quibble.
Probably from the Latin quibus, from qui, "who, which. "

> SECURITY:
> And hark you gossip, when you have her here,
> Have your boat ready, ship her to your ship
> With utmost haste, lest master Bramble stay you,
> To o're reach that head that outreacheth all heads?
> Tis a trick rampant; tis a very quiblyn;
> I hope this harvest, to pitch cart with lawyers;

Their heads will be so forked; this sly touch
Will get apes to invent a number such.
--George Chapman, Ben Jonson & John Marston:
    Eastward Ho (1604); Act III, Scene 2.

FACE: Who's that?
DOL: Your master:
The master of the house.
SUBTLE: How, Dol!
FACE: She lies.
This is some trick.   Come, leave your quiblins,
    Dorothy.
--Ben Jonson: The Alchemist (1610); Act IV,
    Scene 7.

LITTLEWIT: When a quirk or a quiblin does
'scape thee, and thou dost not watch and apprehend
it, and bring it afore the constable of conceit,
(there now, I speak quib too,) let them carry thee
out o' the archdeacon's court into his kitchen, and
make a Jack of thee, instead of a John.
--Ben Jonson: Bartholomew Fair (1614); Act I,
    Scene 1.

TURFE: You stood my friend,
I thank your justice-worship; pray you be
Present anon at tendering of the money,
And zee me have a discharge; vor I have no craft
In your law quiblins.
--Ben Jonson: A Tale of a Tub (1633); Act IV,
    Scene 1.

QUOP: To throb or to beat regularly; to palpitate.   The
origin is uncertain, but the word may be related to the German quappen, "to flop," or to quappeln, "to quiver, fidget."
Examples of its use can be found in Chaucer (1374), John
Cleaveland (1658), George Gissing (1889), and in the following:

        SAINTLY: Oh, my eyes grow dim! my heart
        quops, and my back aketh! here I will lay me
        down, and rest me.
        --John Dryden: The Kind Keeper (1678); Act III,
            Scene 2.

QUOTHA: An old exclamation, formed from "Quoth he,"
and meaning variously, Indeed! Forsooth! In truth! I'faith!

It can be found throughout English literature, and was used
by Heywood (1600), John Dryden (1680), and by the following
writers:

> "Sound!" cries out the infected cobbler. "Alas,
> sir, I see now that some diseases have power to
> make dunces of doctors themselves. 'Sound, '
> quotha! Why, sir, I am sick at heart. I am
> struck with the plague; I have such a plague-sore
> upon me your doctor's cap is not able to cover it,
> 'tis so broad. "
> --Thomas Dekker: The Raven's Almanac: A
>   Medicine to Cure the Plague of a Woman's
>   Tongue, Experimented on a Cobbler's Wife
>   (1609).

> MRS. HARDCASTLE: Tony Lumpkin has a good
> fortune. My son is not to live by his learning.
> I don't think a boy wants much learning to spend
> fifteen hundred a year.
> HARDCASTLE: Learning, quotha! a mere com-
> position of tricks and mischief.
> --Oliver Goldsmith: She Stoops to Conquer (1773);
>   Act I, Scene 1.

> "Attributes, quotha? Here's poor flesh and blood,
> Like thine and mine and every man's, a prey
> To hell-fire! Has thou lost thy wits for once?"
> --Robert Browning: Ferishtah's Fancies: Mihrab
>   Shah (1884); lines 99-101.

-R-

RAGABASH: A word of many spellings, including raggabash,
ragabosh, rag-a-buss, etc., referring to an idle loafer or
useless person; lazy bum. Hence, in a collective sense,
many idle loafers; the mob or rabble. It comes from the
word rag, "fragment, " through the Middle English ragge,
from the Old Norse rogg, "piece of fur. " Examples of its
use can be seen in John Healey's Discovery of a New World,
Teuterbelly, New Land, and Forliana (1609); James Hutton
(1781); George Sala's Twice Round the Clock (1859), and in
the following:

> The raggabash of the Sultan's following had slunk
> away ashamed.
> --Hall Caine: The Scapegoat (1891); chapter 25.

RAGGED ROBIN: A popular name for the double garden
variety of the red campion flower, Lychnis floscuculi; hence,
a ragged person, dishevelled individual. The sense of the
flower was used in John Clare's The Village Minstrel (1821)
and John Ruskin's Fors Clavigera (1875); the personalized
sense can be located in Tennyson (1859), and in Scott:

> '"Tis true, I took thee up when thou wert but a
> ragged Robin, made a keeper of thee, and so
> forth. What of that? Sailors think no longer of
> the wind than when it forwards them on the voyage:
> thy betters turn with the tide, why should not such
> a poor knave as thou?"
> --Sir Walter Scott: Woodstock (1826); chapter 2.

RAMGUNSHOCH: An old Scottish adjective, meaning "rough,
rugged, cross-tempered, tough." Its origin is unknown.
It can be found in James Kelly's Scottish Proverbs (1721),
and in Burns:

> Sae craftilie she took me ben,
>   And bade me make nae clatter;
> "For our ramgunshoch glum gudeman
>   Is out and ower the water:"
> Whae'er shall say I wanted grace,
>   When I did kiss and dawte her,
> Let him be planted in my place,
>   Syne say I was the fautor [trespasser].
> --Robert Burns: Had I the Wyte (1795); stanza 2.

RAMPALLION: An old term of abuse or contempt for a
scoundrel or crafty rogue; a jade. The origin is uncertain,
but it may be related to ramp, meaning "to creep or crawl
close to the ground"; but the origin of this word is not
known. Examples of its use can be located in Nashe's
Strange Newes (1593); in R. Davenport (1639), and in these:

> ORLEANS: And what say the rabble? am not I
> the subject of their talk?
> LAVERDINE: Troth, my lord, the common mouth
> speaks foul words.
> ORLEANS: Of me, for turning away my wife, do
> they not?
> LAVERDINE: Faith, the men do a little murmur
> at it, and say, 'tis an ill precedent in so great a
> man; marry, the women, they rail outright.
> ORLEANS: Out upon them, rampallions! I'll keep

myself safe enough out of their fingers.
--Francis Beaumont, John Fletcher & Philip
   Massinger: The Honest Man's Fortune (1613);
   Act II, Scene 2.

"Weel, and if ye be an honest woman" (here he
peeped under her muffler), "as an honest woman
ye seem likely to be--though, let me tell you;
they are a kind of cattle not so rife in the streets
of this city as I would desire them--I was almost
strangled with my own band by twa rampallians,
wha wanted yestreen, nae farther gane, to harle
me into a change-house. "
--Sir Walter Scott: The Fortunes of Nigel (1822);
   chapter 26.

The word was also used with reference to a woman;
see Samuel Rowlands' Greene's Ghost (1602), and the following:

HOSTESS: Good people, bring a rescue or two. --
Thou wo't, wo't thou? Thou wo't, wo't ta? do,
do, thou rogue! do, thou hemp-seed!
SIR JOHN FALSTAFF: Away, you scullion! you
rampallian! you fustilarian! I'll tickle your catas-
trophe.
--William Shakespeare: King Henry The Fourth,
   Part II (1598); Act II, Scene 1.

RAW-HEAD: see Bloody-bones.

RAYON: A ray of light; from the French rayon, from rai,
same sense. It can be found in Alexander Hume's Day
Estival (1609); Rev. Robert Corbet Singleton's translation of
Virgil (1859), and in Spenser:

On high hills top I saw a stately frame,
An hundred cubits high by just assize,
With hundreth pillours fronting faire the same,
All wrought with Diamond after Dorick wize:
   Nor brick, nor marble was the wall in view,
But shining Christall, which from top to base
Out of her womb a thousand rayons threw,
On hundred steps of Afrike golds enchase.
--Edmund Spenser: The Visions of Bellay (1591);
   stanza 2.

REECHY: Dr. Johnson tells us about this word: "Smoky;
sooty; tanned." Also, squalid; filthy; rancid. It comes
from reech, an old form of reek, of Germanic origin. It
can be found in John Russell's Boke of Nurture (1444);
Thomas Blount's Boscobel (1660), and in the following:

> BORACHIO: Seest thou not, I say, what a de-
> form'd thief this fashion is? how giddily 'a turns
> about all the hot bloods between fourteen and five-
> and-thirty? sometimes fashioning them like Phar-
> aoh's soldiers in the reechy painting, sometime
> like god Bel's priests in the old church-window,
> sometime like the shaven Hercules in the smircht
> worm-eaten tapestry, where his codpiece seems
> as massy as his club?
> --William Shakespeare: Much Ado About Nothing
>   (1599); Act III, Scene 3.

> JUNIUS BRUTUS:
> All tongues speak of him, and the bleared sights
> Are spectacled to see him: your prattling nurse
> Into a rapture lets her baby cry
> While she chats him: the kitchen malkin pins
> Her richest lockram 'bout her reechy neck,
> Clamb'ring the walls to eye him.
> --William Shakespeare: Coriolanus (1608); Act II,
>   Scene 1.

The adverb form, reechily, can be found in Dabridg-
court Belcher's translation of Hans Beerport, his Risible
Comedy of See me and See me not (1618).

REMBLE: An old verb meaning "to move, to rouse, to
stir," of unknown origin.

> D' ya moind the waäste, my lass? naw, naw,
>   that was not born then;
> Theer wur a boggle in it, I often 'eärd 'um mysén;
> Moäst loike a butter-bump, fur I 'eärd 'um about
>   an' about,
> But I stubb'd 'um oop wi' the lot, an' raäved an'
>   rembled 'um out.
> --Alfred, Lord Tennyson: Northern Farmer, Old
>   Style (1864); stanza 8.

REW: A street or town; taken directly from the French
word for street, rue. A very old word, found in Wyntoun

(1425); in Sir John Ballenden's translation of <u>Livy</u> (1533),
and in the following:

> Then was the slaughter so wicked,
> That all the rews ran of blood.
> --John Barbour: <u>The Bruce</u> (1375); Book XV,
>   lines 70-71.

RIGOL, RIGOLL: A circle or ring; a groove. It comes
from the French <u>rigole</u>, "gutter, furrow, channel of water."
Used by Shakespeare:

> About the mourning and congealed face
> Of that black blood a watery rigol goes,
> Which seems to weep upon the tainted place:
> And ever since, as pitying Lucrece' woes,
> Corrupted blood some watery token shows.
> --William Shakespeare: <u>The Rape of Lucrece</u>
>   (1594); lines 1744-1748.

Also found in the second part of <u>King Henry the
Fourth</u> (1598).

RIPPON: A town near Harrogate in Yorkshire, England,
where spurs of good quality were made; hence, applied to
the spurs themselves. Examples of this word can be located
in Thomas Fuller's <u>History of the Worthies of England</u> (1661);
Jonathan Swift's <u>A Discourse Concerning the Mechanical
Operation of the Spirit</u> (1704); Washington Irving's <u>Abbotsford</u>
(1835); F. W. Fairholt's <u>Costume in England; A History of
Dress to the close of the 18th Century</u> (1850), and in the
following:

> PENNYBOY JUN.: What do you stay for, sirrah?
> SPURRIER: To my box, sir.
> PENNYBOY JUN.: Your box! why, there's an
> angel; if my spurs be not right Rippon--
> --Ben Jonson: <u>The Staple of News</u> (1626); Act I,
>   Scene 3.

> ELDER PALLATINE: I have offended, knight!
> Whip me with wire, headed with rowels of
> Sharp Ripon spurs: I'll endure any thing
> Rather than thee.
> --Sir William Davenant: <u>The Wits</u> (1636); Act V,
>   Scene 2.

RIVO: An old cry used at celebrations and drinking-bouts, probably from Spanish sources: it may be from arriba, "Up!" or from rio, referring to the liquid. Found in the anonymous play Look About You (1600), and in these:

> ITHAMORE: Hey, Rivo Castiliano! a man's a man.
> BELLAMIRA: Now to the Jew.
> ITHAMORE: Ha! to the Jew; and send me money he were best.
> --Christopher Marlowe: The Jew of Malta (1587); Act IV, Scene 6.

> QUADRATUS:
> Sing, sing, or stay--we'll quaff or anything:
> Rivo, Saint Mark, let's talk as loose as air,
> Unwind youth's colours, display ourselves
> So that yon envy-starved cur may yelp
> And spend his chaps at our phantastickness.
> --John Marston: What You Will (1607); Act II, Scene 1.

> VITELLI: There's gold: be thou free too,
> And master of my shop, and all the wares
> We brought from Venice.
> GAZET: Rivo, then!
> --Philip Massinger: The Renegado (1624); Act II, Scene 6.

ROB-POT: A drinker who really drinks a lot, who "robs the pot"; a "merry toper." It can be located in Henry Porter's The Two Angry Women of Abingdon (1599); in Thomas Dekker's The Wonderfull Yeare (1603), recounting the plague in London; and in the following collaboration:

> SPUNGIUS: Bacchus, the god of brew'd wine and sugar, grand patron of rob-pots, upsy-freesy tipplers, and super-naculum takers; this Bacchus, who is head warden of Vintners'-hall, ale-conner, mayor of all victualling-houses, the sole liquid benefactor to bawdy houses; lanceprezade to red noses, and invincible adelantado over the armado of pimpled, deep-scarleted, rubified, and carbuncled faces--
> HIRCIUS: What of all this?
> SPUNGIUS: This boon Bacchanalian skinker, did I make legs to.

> --Philip Massinger & Thomas Dekker: The Virgin-
> Martyr (ca. 1622); Act II, Scene 1.

ROKY, ROAKY: Foggy; misty; obscured; rainy; smoky; driz-
zly. It comes from the old word roke, "mist, smoke," of
uncertain (probably Scandinavian, says N.E.D.) origin. It
can be found in the poetry of Picken (1813); in H. Rider
Haggard (1888), and in Tennyson:

> "Yet weep not thou, lest, if thy mate return,
> He find thy favor changed and love thee not"--
> Then pressing day by day thro' Lyonesse
> Last in a roky hollow, belling, heard
> The hounds of Mark, and felt the goodly hounds
> Yelp at his heart, but, turning, past and gain'd
> Tintagil, half in sea and high on land,
> A crown of towers.
> --Alfred, Lord Tennyson: The Last Tournament
> (1859); lines 498-505.

ROUNCE ROBBLE HOBBLE: The imitation by Stanyhurst
in his Aeneis (1582) representing the sound of thunder:

> A clapping fyerbolt (such as oft, with rowne robel
> hobble, Jove toe the ground clattreth.)

Later, the word was used in allusion or derision to
this passage by other writers:

> DILDO: Faith, our masters are like a case of
> rapiers sheathed in one scabbard of folly.
> CATZO: Right Dutch blades. But was't not rare
> sport at the sea-battle, whilst rounce-robble-hobble
> roar'd from the ship sides, to view our masters
> pluck their plumes and drop their feathers for fear
> of being men of mark.
> --John Marston: Antonio and Mellida (ca. 1600);
>   Act II, Scene 1.

> HIRCIUS: The first thing I do, I'll take her over
>   the lips.
> SPUNGIUS: And I the hips,--we may strike any-
>   where.
> HARPAX: Yes, anywhere.
> HIRCIUS: Then I know where I'll hit her.
> HARPAX: Prosper, and be mine own; stand by, I
>   must not

To see this done, great business calls me hence:
He's made can make her curse his violence.
(EXIT).
SPUNGIUS: Fear it not, sir; her ribs shall be
basted.
HIRCIUS: I'll come upon her with rounce, robble-
hobble, and thwick-thwack thirlery bouncing.
--Philip Massinger & Thomas Dekker: The Virgin-
Martyr (ca. 1622); Act IV, Scene 2.

RUDAS: An old Scottish term for an old hag; a scold. Of
unknown origin. It can be found in Allan Ramsay's The
Gentle Shepherd (1725), and in Scott:

> "And you--you that are now yourself trodden down
> in the very kennel, are you not sorry for what
> you have done? Do you not repent having occa-
> sioned the poor widow-woman's death?"
> "What for should I repent?" said Peter. "The
> law was on my side--a decreet of the bailies, fol-
> lowed by poinding and an act of warding, a suspen-
> sion intended, and the letters found orderly pro-
> ceeded. I followed the auld rudas through twa
> courts; she cost me mair money than her lugs
> were worth. "
> --Sir Walter Scott: Redgauntlet (1824); chapter 20.

The adjective, meaning "haggard, coarse, like a
hag, " was used by Scott in Rob Roy (1817), and in the following:

> "Troth, hinny, " answered the Nereid, "if they let
> naebody but papists come there, it'll no be muckle
> o' a show in this country, for the auld harlot, as
> honest Mr. Blattergowl ca's her, has few that
> drink o' her cup o' enchantments in this corner o'
> our chosen lands. --But what can ail them to bury
> the auld carlin (a rudas wife she was) in the night
> time?--I dare say our gudemither will ken. "
> --Sir Walter Scott: The Antiquary (1816); chapter
> 26.

RUFFMANS: A hedge or bushes; a little wood or copse.
This is old cant, probably from rough and the -mans suffix,
roughly meaning "rough thing, rough time, " similar in construction to crackmans, darkmans, lightmans, etc. Used
principally from the early 17th to middle 19th centuries, it

can be located in Harman's Caveat for Vagabonds (1567),
and in the following:

> TRAPDOOR: Ben mort, shall you and I heave a
> bough, mill a ken, or nip a bung, and then we'll
> couch a hogshead under the ruffmans, and there
> you shall wap with me, and I'll niggle with you.
> --Thomas Dekker & Thomas Middleton: The Roar-
>   ing Girl (1611); Act V, Scene 1.

> HIGGEN: I crown thy nab with a gage of bene-
>   bowse,
> And stall thee by the salmon into the clowes;
> To maund on the pad, and strike all the cheats,
> To mill from the ruffmans commission and slates.
> --John Fletcher: Beggars' Bush (1622); Act III,
>   Scene 3.

RUMBO: An old kind of strong rum-punch, made from rum,
water, and sugar, and popular in the late 18th and early
19th centuries. It can be found in Sir Walter Scott's The
Pirate (1821); Sir Arthur Conan Doyle's Micah Clarke (1889),
and in the following:

> That everything might be answerable to the magnifi-
> cence of this delicate feast, he had provided vast
> quantities of strong beer, flip, rumbo, and burnt
> brandy, with plenty of Barbadoes water, for the
> ladies; and hired all the fiddles within six miles,
> who, with the addition of a drum, bagpipe, and
> Welch harp, regaled the guests with a most melo-
> dious concert.
> --Tobias Smollett: Peregrine Pickle (1751); chap-
>   ter 9.

> ROVER: Has the lady ever seen me?
> JOHN: Pshaw! none of your jokes, man! you
> know, that her ladyship, no more than myself, has
> set eyes upon you since you was the bigness of a
> rumbo canakin.
> --John O'Keeffe: Wild Oats (1798); Act II, Scene
>   3.

> "Will you have a can of flip, or a jorum of hot
> rumbo, or will you splice the main-brace (showing
> a spirit-flask)? Will you have a quid, or a pipe,
> or a cigar?--a pinch of snuff at least, to clear

your brains and sharpen your apprehension?"
--Sir Walter Scott: Redgauntlet (1824); chapter 13.

-S-

SACKBUT: The sackbut was an old musical instrument,
used from the Middle Ages through the 18th century, that
was an early form of the trombone, or bass trumpet. In-
troduced into England in the 15th century, it was originally
of boxwood, and had a slide for the altering of the pitch.
In the Book of Daniel, the sackbut is mentioned; but this is
an error in translation of the Aramaic sabbĕkha, which was
an instrument of the lyre variety. It comes through the
French saquebute and the Old Northern French saqueboute,
"a hooked lance used for pulling riders off their horses,"
and also from the Spanish sacabuche, "draw-tube." The
word also is found with many different spellings: sagbut,
shakbott, sacbutt, shagbush, etc. Illustrations of its use
can be located in Stephen Hawes' The Passetyme of Pleasure
(1506); Sir Thomas Elyot's The Castell of Health (1533);
Holinshed's Chronicles (1587); John Playford's A Brief Introduction to the Skill of Music (1674), and in the following:

SECOND MESSENGER: Why, hark you!
The trumpets, sackbuts, psalteries, and fifes,
Tabors, and cymbals, and the shouting Romans,
Make the sun dance. Hark you!
--William Shakespeare: Coriolanus (1608); Act V,
    Scene 4.

Intent they meditate the future lay,
And watch impatient for the dawn of day.
The morn rose clear, and shrill were heard the
    flute,
The cornet, sackbut, dulcimer, and lute;
To Babylon's gay streets the throng resort,
Swarm through the gates, and fill the festive court.
--Robert Southey: The Triumph of Woman (1797);
    lines 105-110.

Well versed was he in Hebrew books,
Talmud and Targum, and the lore
Of Kabala; and ever-more
There was a mystery in his looks;
His eyes seemed gazing far away,
As if in vision or in trance

He heard the solemn sackbut play,
And saw the Jewish maidens dance.
--Henry Wadsworth Longfellow: Tales of a Way-
    side Inn (1863); Prelude, lines 207-214.

SAGA: A witch or hag; an enchantress. It comes directly from the Latin synonym, sāga.

Arbaces had tarried only till the cessation of the
tempest allowed him, under cover of night, to
seek the Saga of Vesuvius.
--Edward George Bulwer-Lytton: The Last Days
    of Pompeii (1834); Book III, chapter 10.

SALTIMBANCO: A word of many spellings, referring to a quack medicine-man, or a mountebank. It comes through the Italian from saltare, "to leap," in, "on," and banco, "bench"; thus, one who leaps up on a bench to shout to the people about the quality of what he is selling. In French, it is saltimbanque. It can be found in Charles Cotton and Sir Thomas Browne, and more recently in George Sala's My Diary in America in the Midst of War (1865), as well as in the following:

Quoth Hudibras, I now perceive
You are no conj'rer, by your leave:
That paltry story is untrue,
And forged to cheat such gulls as you.
    Not true? quoth he; Howe'er you vapour,
I can what I affirm make appear;
Whachum shall justify 't t' your face,
And prove he was upon the place:
He play'd the Saltinbancho's part,
Transform'd t'a Frenchman by my art;
He stole your cloak, and pick'd your pocket,
Choused and caldesed ye like a blockhead;
And what you lost I can produce,
If you deny it, here i'th' house.
--Samuel Butler: Hudibras, Part Second (1664);
    Canto III, lines 999-1112.

SAVAGESS: A savage of the female sex. Through the Middle English sauvage and Old French savaige, from the Latin silva, "forest." Hence, a forest person.

"When the singing-woman came down from her
throne, Jack Morris must introduce my Virginian

to her. I saw him blush up to the eyes, and make
her, upon my word, a very fine bow, such as I
had no idea was practised in wigwams. 'There is
a certain jenny squaw about her, and that's why
the savage likes her,' George said--a joke certainly not as brilliant as a firework. After which
it seemed to me that the savage and the savagess
retired together. "
--William Makepeace Thackeray: The Virginians
    (1859); chapter 40.

SCHINKEL: A raw ham, or gammon of raw bacon. From
the Dutch schinkel, same sense, and schink. In German
the word for "ham" is schinken.

> COLLEN: Dread Emperour and Emperess for to
>   day,
> I your appointed Cook until tomorrow,
> Have by the Marshal sent my just excuse,
> And hope your highness is therewith content,
> Our Carter here for whom I now do speak,
> Says that his axletree broke by the way,
> That is his answer, and for you shall not famish,
> He and his fellow bowrs of the next dorp,
> Have brought a schinkel of good raw bacon,
> And that's a common meat with us, unsod,
> Desiring you, you would not scorn the fare;
> 'Twil make a cup of wine taste nippitate.
> --George Chapman: Alphonsus, Emperor of Ger-
>   many (1634); Act III.

SCHLAFROCK: An old kind of European dressing-gown. It
comes from the German schlafen, "to sleep, " and rock,
"coat. " It can be found in Thackeray's Vanity Fair (1848),
and in the following:

> Took leave of friends and acquaintances. One
> nasty little professor in a dirty schlafrock took the
> pipe out of his mouth and kissed me on the lips.
> I had a great mind to shake him by the ears.
> --Henry Wadsworth Longfellow: Journal in Swit-
>   zerland, August 26th, 1836.

SCOTOSCOPE: A portable type of camera obscura, which
enables the user to see things in the dark. From the Greek
scotos, "darkness, " and scopein, "to see. "

Up; and before I went to the office comes my
Taylor with a coat I have made to wear within
doors, purposely to come no lower then my knees;
for by my wearing a gown within doors comes all
my tenderness about my legs.   There comes also
Mr. Reeve with a Microscope and Scotoscope; for
the first I did give him 5£ 10s, a great price;
but a most curious bauble it is, and he says as
good, nay, the best he knows in England, and he
makes the best in the world.   The other he gives
me, and is of value; and a curious curiosity it is
to [see] objects in a dark room with.   Mightily
pleased with this, I to the office, where all morning.
--Samuel Pepys' Diary: August 13th, 1664.

SCROYLE, SCROILE: A wretched person; a rascally scoundrel. The origin is unknown; it can be located in many
works: in John Taylor (1622); I. Williams (1794), and in
the following:

BASTARD:
By heaven, these scroyles of Angiers flout you,
    kings,
And stand securely on their battlements,
As in a theatre, whence they gape and point
At your industrious scenes and acts of death.
--William Shakespeare: King John (ca. 1595);
    Act II, Scene 1.

TUCCA: No more, we conceive thee. Which of
these is thy wedlock, Menelaus? thy Helen? thy
Lucrece? that we may do her honour; mad boy?
CRISPINUS: She i'the little fine dressing, sir, is
my mistress.
ALBIUS: For fault of a better, sir.
TUCCA: A better, profane rascal? I cry thee
mercy (my good scroile) was't thou.
ALBIUS: No harm, Captain.
--Ben Jonson: The Poetaster (1601); Act IV, Scene
    3.

"Hang him, foul scroyle, let him pass, " said the
mercer; "if he be such a one, there were small
worship to be won upon him. "
--Sir Walter Scott: Kenilworth (1821); chapter 19.

<u>SEGARA</u>: A cigar; from the Spanish, related to <u>cigarro</u>.

> The fire now flashed from a pair of Andalusian
> eyes, as black as charcoal and not less inflam-
> mable, and taking the segara from his mouth, with
> which he had vainly hoped to have regaled his nos-
> trils in a sharp winter's evening by the way,
> raised such a thundering troop of angels, saints,
> and martyrs, from St. Michael downwards, not
> forgetting his own namesake Saint Nicolas de
> Tolentino by the way, that if curses could have
> made the mule to go, the dispute would have been
> soon ended, but not a saint could make her stir
> any other ways than upwards and downwards at a
> stand.
> --Richard Cumberland: <u>The Observer</u> No. 88
>   (1785); paragraph 1.

<u>SEY, SAY</u>: An old Scottish word of unknown origin, refer-
ring to the spare-rib or sirloin; the choice beef cut.   It
can be seen in Allan Ramsay, in Henry Stephens' <u>The Book</u>
<u>of the Farm</u> (1844), and in Scott:

> "He's a shabby body the laird o' Monkbarns," said
> Mrs. Heukbane; "he'll make as muckle about buy-
> ing a forequarter o' lamb in August as about a
> back sey o' beef."
> --Sir Walter Scott: <u>The Antiquary</u> (1816); chapter
>   15.

> "I hae gotten but five herring instead o' sax, and
> this disna look like a gude saxpennys, and I dare-
> say this bit morsel o' beef is an unce lighter than
> ony that's been dealt round; and it's a bit o' the
> tenony hough, mair by token that yours, Maggie,
> is out o' the back-sey."
> --Sir Walter Scott: <u>The Bride of Lammermoor</u>
>   (1818); chapter 34.

<u>SHAND, SHAN</u>: An old cant term referring to a counterfeit
or "base" coin.   The origin is not known, but it may be related to the adjective <u>shan</u>, "paltry."

> "I doubt Glossin will prove but <u>shand</u> after a',
> mistress," said Jabos, as he passed through the
> little lobby beside the bar; "but this is a gude
> half-crown ony way."

--Sir Walter Scott: Guy Mannering (1815); chapter
32.

SHANGAN, SHANGIN: A wooden stick that is split at one
end in order that it may be attached to an animal's tail,
especially a dog's. It comes through the Gaelic seangan,
but further etymology is uncertain; it may be related to
seang, "narrow." Examples of its use can be found in David
Davidson's Thoughts on the Seasons (1789), and in Burns:

Curst Common-sense, that imp o' hell,
    Cam in wi' Maggie Lauder;
But Oliphant aft made her yell,
    An' Russel sair misca'd her;
This day M'Kinlay takes the flail,
    An' he's the boy will blaud her!
He'll clap a shangan on her tail,
    An' set the bairns to daud her
                    Wi' dirt this day.
--Robert Burns: The Ordination (1787); stanza 2.

SHARD: An old word referring to a lump of cow-dung. It
comes from sharn, "cattle dung," from the Old English
scearn, the Old Frisian skern, Old Norse skarn, from the
Original Teutonic skarnom, from skar, "to separate." It
can be located in George Pettie's A Petite Pallace of Pettie
his Pleasure (1576), and in the following:

DOMITIUS ENOBARBUS: His love to Antony. But
as for Caesar,
Kneel down, kneel down, and wonder.
AGRIPPA: Both he loves.
DOMITIUS ENOBARBUS: They are his shards,
and he their beetle.
--William Shakespeare: Antony and Cleopatra
    (1607); Act III, Scene 2.

But if they think at all, 't is sure no high'r
Than matter, put in motion, may aspire:
Souls that can scarce ferment their mass of clay:
So drossy, so divisible are they,
As would but serve pure bodies for allay:
Such souls as shards produce, such beetle things
As only buzz to heav'n with ev'ning wings;
Strike in the dark, of fending but by chance,
Such are the blindfold blows of ignorance.
--John Dryden: The Hind and the Panther (1687);
    Part I, lines 316-324.

There is also recorded the form <u>sharded</u>, "living in
dung, " with reference to the beetle again, in the following:

> BELARIUS:
> And you may then revolve what tales I have told
>   you
> Of courts, of princes, of the tricks in war:
> This service is not service, so being done,
> But being so allow'd: to apprehend thus,
> Draws us a profit from all things we see;
> And often, to our comfort, shall we find
> The sharded beetle in a safer hold
> Than is the full-wing'd eagle.
> --William Shakespeare: <u>Cymbeline</u> (1610); Act III,
>   Scene 3.

<u>SHAT</u>: An old term of endearment used when addressing an
Irish person; from the Irish <u>séad</u>, "jewel. " This sense can
be found in Beaumont and Fletcher's <u>The Coxcomb</u> (1616).
Also, this was an old slang word for a gossip or babbler.
The origin is not known.

> If a virgin blushes, we no longer cry "she blues. "
> He that drinks till he stares is no more "tow-
> row, " but "honest. " "A youngster in a scrape, "
> is a word out of date; and what bright man says,
> "I was joabed by the Dean?" "Bamboozling" is
> exploded; "a shat" is "a tatler;" and if the mus-
> cular motion of a man's face be violent, no mortal
> says, "he raises a horse, " but "he is a merry
> fellow. "
> --Sir Richard Steele: <u>The Tatler</u> No. 71 (1709);
>   paragraph 11.

<u>SHEAT</u>: An old word of uncertain meaning, possibly "neat"
or "tidy. " The origin, needless to say, is equally uncertain, but it may be related to the Anglo-Saxon <u>scēot</u>, "fris-
ky. "

> BURDEN: Who is the master and chief of this
>   crew?
> MILES: <u>Ecce asinum mundi, figura rotundi;</u>
> Neat sheat and fine, as brisk as a cup of wine.
> BURDEN: What are you?
> RAPHE: I am, father doctor, as a man would
> say, the bellwether of this company: these are
> my lords, and I the prince of Wales.

> --Robert Greene: Friar Bacon and Friar Bungay
> (1591); Act II, Scene 4.

SHEEP'S HEAD: A numbskull or empty-head; fool; simple-
ton. The origin is not known, but it may be related to the
German schafskopf and the Dutch schaapskop, same sense.
It also can mean a garrulous person, as Grose tells us:
"Like a sheep's head, all jaw; saying of a talkative man or
woman. " Found in John Gee's The Foot out of the Snare;
or, Detection of Practices and Impostures of Priests and
Jesuits (1624), and in these:

> GOSTANZO:
> What, no more complement? kiss her, you sheep's-
> head,
> Why, when? Go, go, Sir, call your sister hither.
> Lady, you'll pardon our gross bringing up?
> We dwell far off from court, you may perceive:
> The sight of such a blazing star as you,
> Dazzles my rude son's wits.
> --George Chapman: All Fools (1599); Act II,
> Scene 1.

> "You must know, " said Mrs. Flint, at breakfast,
> "that I am assured that Jemmy is very like the
> Count de Provence, the king of France's own
> brother. Now Jemmy is sitting for his picture to
> Martin; and I thought it would be right to get the
> friseur, whom you saw last night, he is just ar-
> rived from Paris, to dress his hair like the Count
> de Provence, that Mr. Martin might make the re-
> semblance more complete. Jemmy has been un-
> der his hands since seven o'clock. --Oh, here he
> comes! "--"Is it not charmang? " exclaimed Miss
> Juliana. "I wish Miss Punaise saw you, " added
> the happy mother. My pupil, lost in the labyrinth
> of cross curls, seemed to look about for himself.
> "What a powdered sheep's head have we got here? "
> cried Captain Winterbottom.
> --The Mirror No. 98 (1780); paragraph 13.

SIMAGRE: An affected look or grimace; a leer; a sly look.
It comes directly from the French simagrée, but further
history is unknown. Used by Dryden:

> PLEASANCE: By these languishing eyes, and
> those simagres of yours, we are given to

understand, Sir, you have a mistress in this company: Come, make a free discovery which of 'em
your poetry is to charm; and put the other out of
pain.
TRICKSY: No doubt 'twas meant to Mrs. Brainsick.
MRS. BRAINSICK: We wives are despicable
creatures: we know it, madam, when a mistress
is in presence.
--John Dryden: The Kind Keeper (1678); Act III,
    Scene 1.

Now in the crystal stream he looks, to try
His simagres, and rolls his glaring eye.
His cruelty and thirst of blood are lost,
And ships securely sail along the coast.
--John Dryden: Translation of Ovid's Metamor-
    phoses (1693); Book XIII: "The Fable of Acis,
    Polyphemus, and Galatea"; lines 30-33.

SKYRGALIARD: A wild youth; a frivolous, drinking, gambling, carousing individual. The first element is unknown;
the second is from galliard, "a spirited rogue," through the
Old French and Spanish, but of unknown origin. It can be
seen in Horace Smith's The Tor Hill (1826), and, much
earlier, in Skelton:

        Kynge Jamy, Jemmy, Jocky my joye
        Summond our king, why did ye so
        To you, nothing it did accord
        To summon our king, your soveraigne lorde
        A kyng a summer, it was great wonder
        Know ye not suger, and salt asonder
        Your summer to saucye, to malepert
        Your harrold in armes, not yet halfe expert
        Ye thought ye did, yet valiauntlye
        Nor worth thre skippes of a pye
        Syr skyr galyard, ye were so skit
        Your wil, than ran before your wyt.
        --John Skelton: Against the Scottes (1529); lines
            91-102.

        By your duke of Albany
        We set nat a prane
        By such a dronken drane
        We set nat a myght
        By such a cowarde knyght

Suche a proude palyarde
Suche a skyrgaliarde.
--John Skelton: Duke of Albany and the Scottes
(1529); lines 162-168.

SLANGWHANGER: An abusive and noisy person, one who
"whangs slang." Slang is old cant of uncertain origin; whang
is echoic. It can be found in Thomas Chandler Haliburton's
The Clockmaker; or, the Sayings and Doings of Samuel Slick
of Slickville (1836), and in Irving:

>There is still preserved in this country some re-
>mains of that gothic spirit of knight-errantry,
>which so much annoyed the faithful in the middle
>ages of the hegira. As, notwithstanding their
>martial disposition, they are a people much given
>to commerce and agriculture, and must, neces-
>sarily, at certain seasons be engaged in these em-
>ployments, they have accomodated themselves by
>appointing knights, or constant warriors, incessant
>brawlers, similar to those who, in former ages,
>swore eternal enmity to the followers of our divine
>prophet.--These knights, denominated editors or
>SLANG-WHANGERS, are appointed in every town,
>village, and district, to carry on both foreign and
>internal warfare, and may be said to keep up a
>constant firing "in words." Oh, my friend, could
>you but witness the enormities sometimes com-
>mitted by these tremendous slang-whangers, your
>very turban would rise with horror and astonish-
>ment.
>--Washington Irving: Salmagundi (1807); Volume I,
>No. 7.

SLOBBER-CHOPS: A person who sprays lustily while engaged in eating; a slobbering feeder. Also, a variety of
pear. It can be seen in Dr. Josiah Gilbert Holland's The
Bay Path: a Colonial Tale (1857), and in the following:

>TRINCALO: Vice-roys! keep good tongues in your
>heads
>I advise you, and proceed to your business, for I
>have
>Other affairs to dispatch of more importance be-
>twixt
>Queen Slobber-Chops and my self.
>--Sir William Davenant & John Dryden: The
>Tempest (1667); Act III, Scene 1.

SLUBBERDEGULLION: A word used since the 17th century,
referring to a person who slobbers saliva; a driveller; a
slobbering kisser; also, a worthless slob. Dr. Johnson
tells us: "A paltry, dirty, sorry wretch," and Grose says:
"A dirty nasty fellow." Slubber is of unknown origin, but
is probably Low German or Dutch, with reference to mud.
Degullion is probably a meaningless whimsical ending. It
can be found in John Taylor (1630); in Ford's Thistledown
(1891), and in these:

> RUTILIO: How now! what livery's this? do you
>   call this a wedding?
> This is more like a funeral.
> CHARINO: It is one.
> And my poor daughter going to her grave, --
> To his most loath'd embraces that gapes for her. --
> Make the earl's bed ready. --Is the marriage done,
>   sir?
> RUTILIO: Yes, they are knit. But must this
>   slubberdegullion
> Have her maidenhead now?
> CHARINO: There's no avoiding it.
> --John Fletcher & Philip Massinger: The Custom
>   of the Country (ca. 1620); Act I, Scene 2.

> Quoth she, Although thou has deserved,
> Base slubberdegullion, to be served
> As thou didst vow to deal with me,
> If thou had'st got the victory;
> Yet I shall rather act a part
> That suits my fame, than thy desert.
> --Samuel Butler: Hudibras, Part First (1663);
>   Canto III, lines 885-890.

SMELL-SMOCK: A dirty old man; a licentious chaser of
women; says Cotgrave: "A cunning solicitor of a wench."
From smell and smock, "a woman's undergarment; chemise."
It can be found in John Bale (1550); James Pilkington's Ex-
position Upon Abdias (1562); Thomas Heywood's A Maidenhead
Well Lost (1634); Head's Canting Academy (1673), and in
Middleton:

> GUDGEON: Faith, friend Lipsalve, I perceive you
> would fain play with my love. A pure creature
> 'tis, for whom I have sought every angle of my
> brain; but either she scorns courtiers, as most of
> them do, because they are given to boast of their

> doings, or else she's exceedingly strait-laced:
> therefore to prevent this smell-smock, I'll to my
> friend doctor Glister, a man exquisite in th'art
> magic, who hath told me of many rare experi-
> ments available in this case.
> --Thomas Middleton: The Family of Love (1602);
>   Act II, Scene 3.

> DONDOLO: O monstrous, horrible, terrible, in-
> tolerable! are you not big enough to air a shirt?
> were it a smock now, you liquorish page, you'd
> be hanged ere you'd part from't. If thou dost not
> prove as arrant a smell-smock as any the town
> affords in a term-time, I'll lose my judgment in
> wenching.
> --Thomas Middleton: More Dissemblers Besides
>   Women (1623); Act I, Scene 4.

SNAFFLING-LAY: The profession of highwayman; "highway-
manship." Used from about 1750 to about 1830, it comes
from snaffle, "to steal," and lay, roughly "thing," both cant
words of unknown origin.

> Blear-Eyed Moll then came up to Mr. Booth with
> a smile, or rather grin on her countenance, and
> asked him for a dram of gin; and when Booth as-
> sured her that he had not a penny of money, she
> replied, --"D--n your eyes, I thought by your look
> you had been a clever fellow, and upon the snaf-
> fling lay at least: but d--n your body and eyes, I
> find you are some sneaking budge rascal."
> --Henry Fielding: Amelia (1751); Book I, chapter
>   3.

'SNAILS: A mild oath or asseveration, abbreviated from
"By God's nails." Used since the late 16th century, it can
be located in Sir John Hayward's Life of Henry IV (1599),
and in the following:

> CUNNINGHAM: Oh, master Pompey! how is't,
> man?
> POMPEY: 'Snails, I'm almost starved with love,
> and cold, and one thing or other. Has not my
> lady sent for me yet?
> CUNNINGHAM: Not that I hear: sure, some un-
> friendly messenger is employed betwixt you.
> --Francis Beaumont & John Fletcher: Wit at
>   Several Weapons (1616); Act V, Scene 1.

PHYSICIAN: Your intended bride is a whore;
that's freely, sir.
CHOUGH: Yes, faith, a whore's free enough, and
she hath a conscience: is she a whore? foot, I
warrant she has the pox then.
PHYSICIAN: Worse, the plague; 'tis more incur-
able.
CHOUGH: A plaguy whore? a pox on her, I'll none
of her!
PHYSICIAN: Mine accusation shall have firm evidence;
I will produce an unavoided witness,
A bastard of her bearing.
CHOUGH: A bastard? 'snails, there's great sus-
picion she's a whore then! I'll wrestle a fall with
her father for putting this trick upon me, as I am
a gentleman.
--Thomas Middleton & William Rowley: A Fair
    Quarrel (1617); Act V, Scene 1.

"There may be fair play betwixt us, sure," thought
Wayland, "where there is but one man on each
side, and yonder fellow sits on his horse more
like a monkey than a cavalier. Pshaw! if it
comes to the worst, it will be easy unhorsing him.
Nay, 'snails! I think his horse will take the matter in his own hand, for he has the bridle betwixt
his teeth. "
--Sir Walter Scott: Kenilworth (1821); chapter 24.

"A fair sight we are; and had I but a rebeck or a
guitar at my back, and a jackanapes on my
shoulder, we should seem as joyous a brace of
strollers as ever touched string at a castle gate. --
'Snails!" he ejaculated internally, "were any
neighbor to meet me with this little harlotry's
basket at my back, her dog under my arm, and
herself hanging on my cloak, what would they think
but that I had turned mumper in good earnest?"
--Sir Walter Scott: The Fair Maid of Perth (1828);
    chapter 12.

SNEAKSBY: A low, sneaking person; a rascal. Grose tells
us: "A mean-spirited fellow, a sneaking cur." The origin
is not known, but the descent is through Middle English and
Anglo-Saxon. Found in Claudius Hollyband's The Treasure
of the French Tong (1580), and in Dryden:

> MERCURY: Hold your peace, Dame Partlet, and
> leave your cackling: my master charg'd me to
> stand sentry without doors.
> BROMIA: My master! I dare swear thou bely'st
> him, my master's more a gentleman than to lay
> such an unreasonable command upon a poor dis-
> tressed marri'd couple, and after such an absence
> too. No, there's no comparison between my
> master and thee, thou sneaksby.
> --John Dryden: Amphitryon (1690); Act II, Scene
>   2.

SNIPPER-SNAPPER: A young know-it-all; an insignificant
person who believes himself to be significant. The origin
is whimsical, similar to whippersnapper. It can be located
in these writers:

> HORSE-COURSER: O, yonder is his snipper-
>   snapper. --
> Do you hear? you hey-pass, where's your master?
> MEPHISTOPHILIS: Why, sir, what would you?
>   You cannot speak with him.
> HORSE-COURSER: But I will speak with him.
> MEPHISTOPHILIS: Why, he's fast asleep. Come
>   some other time.
> HORSE-COURSER: I'll speak with him now, or
> I'll break his glass windows about his ears.
> --Christopher Marlowe: Doctor Faustus (1588);
>   Scene 11.

> SPADONE: Thou art a prick-ear'd foist, a cittern-
> headed gew-gaw, a knack, a snipper-snapper.
> Twit me with the decrements of my pendants!
> though I am made a gelding, and, like a tame
> buck, have lost my dowsets,--more a monster
> than a cuckold with his horns seen,--yet I scorn
> to be jeered by any checker-approved barbarian of
> ye all. Make me a man! I defy thee.
> --John Ford: The Fancies, Chaste and Noble
>   (1635); Act I, Scene 2.

SPADROON: A very light cutting-and-thrusting sword. It
comes through the French espadon, which was a good-sized
two-handed sword used in the 15th, 16th, and 17th centuries;
from the Spanish espada.

"This is about the time when, as Will says, the

household affairs will call my daughter hence; I
will therefore challenge you, young gentleman, to
stretch your limbs in a little exercise with me,
either at single rapier, or rapier and poniard,
backsword, spadroon, or your national weapons of
broadsword and target; for all or any of which I
think we shall find implements in the hall. "
--Sir Walter Scott: Woodstock (1826); chapter 23.

SPEAKLESS: Unable to be spoken; indescribable; beyond the
power of description; unspeakable.   Basically, speak is descended from the Latin spargere, "to sprinkle," from the
Indo-European base.   Thus, "speak" means "to sprinkle
words. "

SCUDMORE: Happy's that wretch, in my opinion,
That never own'd scarce jewels or bright sums:
He can lose nothing but his constant wants;
But speakless is his plague, that once had store,
And from superfluous state falls to be poor.
--Nathan Field: A Woman Is a Weathercock (1612);
     Act III, Scene 2.

SPOON-MEAT: Soft, liquid food; soup or broth.   Dr. Johnson says: "Liquid food; nourishment taken with a spoon. "

COURTEZAN: Your man and you are marvellous
merry, sir.   Will you go with me?   We'll mend
our dinner here.
DROMIO OF SYRACUSE: Master, if you do, expect spoon-meat; so bespeak a long spoon.
ANTIPHOLUS OF SYRACUSE: Why, Dromio?
DROMIO OF SYRACUSE: Marry, he must have a
long spoon that must eat with the devil.
--William Shakespeare: The Comedy of Errors
     (ca. 1590); Act IV, Scene 3.

ALMACHILDES: I do expect now to be made away
'Twixt this and Tuesday night: if I live Wednesday,
Say I have been careful, and shunn'd spoon-meat.
--Thomas Middleton: The Witch (ca. 1604); Act
     IV, Scene 1.

STAGGY: A colt; a Scottish diminutive form of stag.   It
can be located in Galloway (1792); in Sir Alexander Boswell's
Songs, chiefly in the Scottish Dialect (1803), and in Burns:

> A guid New-Year I wish thee, Maggie!
> Hae, there's a ripp to thy auld baggie:
> Tho' thou's howe-backit, now, an' knaggie,
>   I've seen the day,
> Thou could hae gane like ony staggie
>   Out-owre the lay.
>   --Robert Burns: The Auld Farmer's New-Year
>   Morning Salutation to His Auld Mare, Maggie
>   (1786); stanza 1.

START, STERT: An old Dutch word of contempt for an Englishman. The origin is not certain, but perhaps it is related to the Dutch staart, "tail," with reference to the old legend that all the English possessed tails. Used by Dryden:

> HARMAN SENIOR: Hang 'em, base English sterts,
> let 'em e'en take their part of their own old
> proverb, save a thief from the gallows: they
> wou'd needs protect us rebels, and see what comes
> to themselves.
> --John Dryden: Amboyna (1672); Act I, Scene 1.

> HARMAN: 'Tis done as I wou'd wish it:
> Now, brethren, at my proper cost and charges,
> Three days you are my guests; in which good time
> We will divide their greatest wealth by lots,
> While wantonly we rifle for the rest:
>   Then in full romers, and with joyful hearts
>   We'll drink confusion to all English starts.
> --John Dryden: Amboyna (1672); Act V, Scene 1.

STEAK RAID: An old Scottish custom, in which any group of robbers who drove stolen cattle over a man's land gave that man a part of the spoil. It comes through the Gaelic staoig rathaid, "collop road." Examples of its use can be seen in Lachlan Shaw's History of the Province of Moray (1775), and in Scott:

> "After all, Fergus," said Flora, "and with every
> allowance, I am surprised you can countenance
> that man."
> "I countenance him? This kind sister of mine
> would persuade you, Captain Waverley, that I take
> what the people of old used to call "a steakraid,"
> that is, a "collop of the foray," or, in plainer
> words, a portion of the robber's booty, paid by

him to the Laird, or Chief, through whose grounds
he drove his prey. "
--Sir Walter Scott: Waverley (1814); chapter 23.

STEARING: An unknown type of bird.

> Saw some men of war Birds and Egg Birds and in
> the Morning saw more Egg Birds and Tropic Birds.
> The Man of War and Tropic Birds are pretty well
> known but the Egg Bird (as it is call'd in the
> Dolphins Journals) require some description to
> know it by that name. It is a small slender Bird
> of the Gull kind and all white, and not much un-
> like the small white Gulls we have in England,
> only not so big; there are also Birds in Newfound-
> land call'd Stearings that are of the same shape
> and Bigness only they are of a Greyish Colour.
> --Capt. James Cook: Journal of the Voyage of the
>   Endeavour, March 23rd, 1769.

STEPONY, STEPNEY: A word of many spellings, referring
to old raisin wine, made with sugar and lemon.   Grose tells
us: "A decoction of raisins of the sun and lemons in con-
duit water, sweetened with sugar and bottled up. "   The
origin is not known; Blount, in his Glossographia (1656),
says that it was named for a parish in eastern London
called Stepney, because it was known to have been drunk "in
some places of London in the summer time. " Examples of
the word can be found in Hannah Woolley (1672); in Poor
Robin's Intelligencer (1676), and in the following:

> SIR FREDERICK: Jenny, come hither; I'll make
> thee amends, as well as thy mistress, for the in-
> jury I did thee th'other night: Here is a husband
> for thee too: Mr. Palmer, where are you?
> PALMER: Alas, Sir Frederick, I am not able to
> maintain her.
> SIR FREDERICK: She shall maintain you, Sir.
> Do not you understand the mystery of stiponie,
> Jenny?
> MAID: I know how to make Democcuana, Sir.
> SIR FREDERICK: Thou art richly endow'd, i'faith:
> Here, here, Palmer; no shall I, shall I; this or
> that, which you deserve better.
> --Sir George Etherege: The Comical Revenge
>   (1664); Act V, Scene 4.

STITTY-STITTY: An old term of contempt for one who stammers; the origin is probably echoic.

> BLOCK:
> Come to the butter bar, stitty-stitty stammerer;
>   come, honest
> Constable, hey! the watch of our town; we'll drink,
>   try-lill, i'faith.
> --Anonymous: Look About You (1600); Scene 9.

STONE-BOW: A catapult or cross-bow that was able to shoot stones as well as arrows and bolts.

> FABIAN: O, peace! now he's deeply in: look how imagination blows him.
> MALVOLIO: Having been three months married to her, sitting in my state, --
> SIR TOBY BELCH: O, for a stone-bow, to hit him in the eye!
> --William Shakespeare: Twelfth Night (1601); Act II, Scene 5.

> FIRST WOODMAN: He shall shoot in a stone-bow for me. I never loved his beyond-sea-ship since he forsook the say, for paying ten shillings.
> --Francis Beaumont & John Fletcher: Philaster (1611); Act IV, Scene 2.

> MARDONIUS:
> There's not a rib in's body, o' my conscience,
> That has not been thrice broken with dry beating;
> And now his sides look like two wicker targets,
> Every way bended:
> Children will shortly take him for a wall,
> And set their stone-bows in his forehead.   He
> Is of so base a sense, I cannot in
> A week imagine what should be done to him.
> --Francis Beaumont & John Fletcher: A King and No King (1611); Act V, Scene 1.

STRUNT: An old Scottish term for any type of very strong alcoholic beverage; of unknown origin. Used by Burns:

> Wi' merry sangs, and friendly cracks,
>   I wat they did na weary;
> And unco tales, an' funnie jokes,
>   Their sports were cheap and cheary;

Till butter'd So'ns wi' fragrant lunt,
   Set a' their gabs a-steerin;
Syne, wi' a social glass o' strunt,
   They parted aff careerin
Fu' blythe that night.
--Robert Burns: <u>Halloween</u> (1785); stanza 28.

O, ken ye what Meg o' the Mill lo'es dearly?
An' ken ye what Meg o' the Mill lo'es dearly?
A dram o' guid strunt in a morning early,
And that's what Meg o' the Mill lo'es dearly!
--Robert Burns: <u>Meg O' the Mill</u> (1788); stanza 2.

<u>STUNKARD</u>: Old Scottish, meaning roughly "sullen, pout-ing, obstinate." The origin is not known. It can be located in Allan Ramsay (1737), and in Scott:

> "Las-a-day! it's a sore thing to see a stunkard
> cow kick down the pail when it's reaming fou.
> But, after all, it's an ill bird that defiles its ain
> nest. I must cover up the scandal as well as I
> can. "
> --Sir Walter Scott: <u>Redgauntlet</u> (1824); chapter 2.

<u>SUPPLE-JACK</u>: A kind of cane or walking-stick, made from the stem of the supple-jack, a tropical and subtropical plant with greenish-white flowers and purplish fruit. From <u>sup-ple</u>, with reference to the stick's pliability, and <u>jack</u>, an old word often found in the names of plants. Examples of the word's use can be located in John Wolcot (1785); in Scott's <u>Rob Roy</u> (1817), and in the following:

> In my way to the cock-pit ... I was met by the
> same midshipman who had used me so barbarously
> in the tender. He, seeing me free from my
> chains, asked, with an insolent air, who had re-
> leased me? To this question I foolishly answered,
> with a countenance that too plainly declared the
> state of my thoughts, 'Whoever did it, I am per-
> suaded did not consult you in the affair. " I had
> no sooner uttered these words, than he cried,
> 'D--n you, you saucy son of a bitch, I'll teach
> you to talk so to your officer. " So saying, he
> bestowed on me several severe stripes with a
> supple-jack he had in his hand; and, going to the
> commanding officer, made such a report of me,
> that I was immediately put in irons by the

master-at-arms, and a sentinel placed over me.
--Tobias Smollett: <u>Roderick Random</u> (1748); chapter 24.

"You have an eye at my stick. It was a legacy
to me, by word of mouth, from a seaman of a
ship I sailed in, who thought I had done him a
service; and he died after all. He fell overboard
drunk. He perished of the villain stuff. One of
his messmates handed me the stick in Cape Town,
sworn to deliver it. A good knot to grasp; and
it's flexible, and strong; stick or rattan, which-
ever you please; it gives point or caresses the
shoulder; there's no break in it, whack as you
may. They call it a Demerara supple-jack. I'll
leave it to you. "
--George Meredith: <u>One of Our Conquerors</u> (1890);
chapter 31.

SWARF: An old Scottish word, meaning, "to swoon, faint,
languish. " It probably comes from the Old Norse svarfa,
"to disturb, to upset, " and has many spellings, including
swerf, swaif, swarve, etc. Examples of its use can be
found in Douglas' Aeneis (1513); in Sir William Mure (1614);
in Scott's The Antiquary (1816); in the poems of Robert
Nicoll (1837), and in Burns:

'O how deil, Tam, can that be true?
    The chase gaed frae the north, man:
I saw mysel, they did pursue
    The horsemen back to Forth, man;
And at Dumblane, in my ain sight,
They took the brig wi' a' their might,
And straught to Stirling wing'd their flight;
But, cursed lot! the gates were shut,
And monie a huntit, poor red-coat,
    For fear amaist did swarf, man. "
--Robert Burns: On the Battle of Sheriff-Muir
(1790); stanza 4.

SYRINX: An old Greek musical instrument, the Pandean
pipes or Panpipes, made of a series of reeds attached to
each other, and played by blowing across them, as with an
harmonica. The word comes through the Latin from the
Greek word for "tube. " Examples of its use can be located
in Thomas Mitchell's The Frogs of Aristophanes (1839), and
in the following:

Honey from out the gnarled hive I'll bring,
And apples, wan with sweetness, gather thee, --
Cresses that grow where no man may them see,
And sorrel untorn by the dew-claw'd stag:
Pipes will I fashion of the syrinx flag,
That thou mayst always know whither I roam,
When it shall please thee in our quiet home
To listen and think of love.
--John Keats: Endymion (1817); Book IV, lines
    682-689.

-T-

TAGLIONI: An overcoat worn in the early 19th century,
named after the Taglioni family of ballet dancers, which included Marie Taglioni (1804-1884), the greatest ballerina of
the Romantic era. She made her debut in Vienna in 1822,
and scored her most memorable success with La Sylphide
at the Paris Opéra a decade later. Examples of the use of
the overcoat can be found in Barham's Ingoldsby Legends
(1845) and in Thackeray:

Eglantine's usual morning costume was a blue
satin neckcloth embroidered with butterflies and
ornamented with a brandy-ball brooch, a light
shawl waistcoat, and a rhubarb-coloured coat of
the sort which, I believe, are called Taglionis,
and which have no waist-buttons, and make a
pretence, as it were, to have no waists, but are
in reality adopted by the fat in order to give them
a waist.
--William Makepeace Thackeray: The Ravenswing
    (1837); chapter 3.

TALLOW-FACE: A face resembling tallow, pale and faintly
yellow; hence, a term of contempt for someone with such a
face. Tallow comes through the Middle English and Middle
Low German, and is related to the Anglo-Saxon telgan, "to
color, " a curious origin, because the word as it is used
here actually implies a lack of color. It can be located in
Sir Thomas Herbert's A Relation of some Yeares Travels
into Africa, and the greater Asia (1638), and in these:

CAPULET:
Out, you green-sickness carrion! out, you bag-
    gage!

You tallow-face!
--William Shakespeare: Romeo and Juliet (ca.
    1594); Act III, Scene 5.

Whom have we yonder with a pipe at's head?
He lookes as if he were true Indian bred.
O, 'tis Fumoso with the tallow face,
He that of late hath got a speciall grace,
And that's to be the best Tobacconist
That ever held a pipe within his fist.
--R. C.: The Times' Whistle (1616); Satire V,
    lines 2235-2240.

TALMA: A long black cape for men, but sometimes for
women, worn in the 19th century, coming to be used as
traditional garb for tragedy. It is named for the famous
French actor François Joseph Talma (1763-1826), who was
an advocate of historical costumes for the stage. The word
is used by Hawthorne:

> In truth, allowing for the difference of costume,
> and if a lion's skin could have been substituted
> for his modern talma, and a rustic pipe for his
> stick, Donatello might have figured perfectly as
> the marble Faun, miraculously softened into flesh
> and blood.
> --Nathaniel Hawthorne: The Marble Faun (1860);
>   chapter 1.

TASS: A small cup or goblet, especially one of silver, used
mainly in Scotland; hence, that which is drunk out of one, a
draught of liquor or ale. The diminutive form tassie is also
used. It comes through the Old French tasse, the medieval
Latin tassa, Spanish taza, Italian tazza, probably from the
Arabic tass, "basin, bowl," and the Persian tast, "drinking-
cup." It can be seen in William Caxton (1483); in Gavin
Douglas's Aeneis (1513); Urquhart's translation of Rabelais
(1653); Allan Ramsay's The Gentle Shepherd (1725); Scott's
Rob Roy (1817); Samuel Rutherford Crockett's Kit Kennedy
(1899), and in the following:

> "You see that scandal flourishes at the borders of
> the wilderness, and in the New World as well as
> the Old."
>   "I have suffered from it myself, my dear,"
> said Madam Bernstein demurely. "Fill thy glass,
> child! A little tass of cherry-brandy! 'Twill do

thee all the good in the world. "
--William Makepeace Thackeray: The Virginians
(1859); chapter 54.

Tassie is used by Burns:

Go fetch to me a pint o' wine,
    An' fill it in a silver tassie;
That I may drink before I go,
    A service to my bonie lassie.
--Robert Burns: My Bonie Mary (1788); stanza 1.

TEEDLE: An old Scottish word, probably echoic in origin,
meaning "to hum. " Used by Scott:

Turning from thence, my steps naturally directed
themselves to my own humble apartment, where
my little Highland landlady, as dapper and as tight
as ever (for old women wear a hundred times better than the hard-wrought seniors of the masculine
sex), stood at the door, "teedling" to herself a
Highland song as she shook a table-napkin over the
fore-stair, and then proceeded to fold it up neatly
for future service.
--Sir Walter Scott: The Chronicles of the Canon-
gate (1827); chapter 5.

THIN-GUT: A person in possession of a gaunt or slender
body; one who looks as though he is starving. It can be
found in Samuel Rowlands' Diogenes Lanthorne (1607); Massinger's Believe as You List (1631), and in the following:

PILCHER: But ere he'll go, I think, indeed, he
and I together shall press the constable.
DANDYPRAT: No matter; squeeze him, and leave
no more liquor in him than in a dried neat's tongue.
Sirrah thin-gut, what's thy name?
--Thomas Middleton: Blurt, Master-Constable
(1602); Act I, Scene 2.

FURNACE: What's this? marry this; when I am
    three-parts roasted,
And the fourth part parboil'd, to prepare her vi-
    ands,
She keeps her chamber, dines with a panada,
Or water-gruel, my sweat never thought on.
ORDER: But your art is seen in the dining-room.

FURNACE: By whom?
By such as pretend love to her; but come
To feed upon her. Yet, of all the harpies
That do devour her, I am out of charity
With none so much as the thin-gutted squire,
That's stolen into commission.
ORDER: Justice Greedy?
FURNACE: The same, the same: meat's cast
   away upon him,
It never thrives; he holds this paradox,
Who eats not well, can ne'er do justice well.
His stomach's as insatiate as the grave,
Or strumpets' ravenous appetites.
   --Philip Massinger: A New Way to Pay Old Debts
      (ca. 1626); Act I, Scene 2.

TICKLE-FOOTED: Of uncertain mind; able to go either way;
inconstant; unable to decide.

ELDER LOVELESS:
Lady, I would not undertake you, were you
Again a haggard, for the best cast of
Sore ladies i' the kingdom: you were ever
Tickle-footed, and would not truss round.
   --Francis Beaumont & John Fletcher: The Scorn-
      ful Lady (1610); Act V, Scene 4.

TIDDY: A word of unknown origin, referring to the four of
trumps in the game of gleek (q.v.). In The Compleat Gamester (1680) we read: "The turned up Card is the Dealers;
and if it be Tiddy turn'd up is four apiece from each to the
Dealer. The Ace is called Tib, the Knave Tom, the four
of Trumps Tiddy." It can also be seen in Holme's Academy
of the Armoury (1688), and in Scott:

"We vied the ruff, and revied, as your lordship
may suppose, till the stake was equal to half my
yearly exhibition--fifty as fair canary birds as
e'er chirped in the bottom of a green silk purse.
Well, my lord, I gained the cards, and lo you!
it pleases his lordship to say that we played without tiddy; and as the rest stood by and backed
him, and especially the sharking Frenchman, why,
I was obliged to lose more than I shall gain all
the season. "
   --Sir Walter Scott: The Fortunes of Nigel (1822);
      chapter 16.

TILLY-VALLY, TILLY-FALLY: An old exclamation ex-
presing impatience or annoyance of a delay, or of contempt,
as 'Ridiculous! Nonsense!" The origin is not known. Dr.
Johnson tells us: "A word used formerly when any thing
said was rejected as trifling or impertinent." Used principally from the early 16th to the late 19th centuries, it can
be located in John Skelton (1529); in Roper's Life of Sir
Thomas More (ca. 1630), and in these:

> SIR JOHN FALSTAFF: Dost thou hear, hostess?--
> HOSTESS: Pray ye, pacify yourself, Sir John:
> there comes no swaggerers here.
> SIR JOHN FALSTAFF: Dost thou hear? it is mine
> ancient.
> HOSTESS: Tilly-fally, Sir John, ne'er tell me:
> your ancient swaggerer comes not in my doors.
> --William Shakespeare: King Henry The Fourth,
>   Part II (1598); Act II, Scene 4.

> SIR TOBY BELCH: My lady's a Cataian, we are
> politicians, Malvolio's a Peg-a-Ramsey, and
> 'Three merry men be we." Am not I consan-
> guineous? am I not of her blood? Tilly-vally,
> lady! 'There dwelt a man in Babylon, lady,
> lady!"
> CLOWN: Beshrew me, the knight's in admirable
> fooling.
> --William Shakespeare: Twelfth Night (1601); Act
>   II, Scene 3.

> 'You are welcome to my symposion, Mr. Lovel.
> And now let me introduce you to my Clogdogdo's,
> as Tom Otter calls them--my unlucky and good-
> for-nothing womankind--malae bestiae, Mr. Lovel."
>   'I shall be disappointed, sir, if I do not find
> the ladies very undeserving of your satire."
>   'Tilley-valley, Mr. Lovel,--which, by the way,
> one commentator derives from tittivillitium, and
> another from talley-ho--but tilley-valley, I say--a
> truce with your politeness. You will find them but
> samples of womankind."
> --Sir Walter Scott: The Antiquary (1816); chapter
>   6.

TIRRIVEE: An old Scottish word of many spellings, referring to an outbreak or outburst of rage or passion; the origin is unknown. It can be found in James Hogg's The

Queen's Wake, a Legendary Poem (1813), and in Scott:

> "The heads are ower the Scotch yate, as they ca'
> it.   It's a great pity of Evan Dhu, who was a
> very weel-meaning, good-natured man, to be a
> Hielandman; and indeed so was the Laird o' Glenna
> quoich too, for that matter, when he wasna in ane
> o' his tirrivies. "
> --Sir Walter Scott: Waverley (1814); chapter 69.

TOAD-EATER: A sycophant, a flatterer, a parasite; simi-
larly, a "toady, " a fawner.   Grose tells us about the origin:
"A poor female relation, an humble companion or reduced
gentlewoman, in a great family, the standing butt, on whom
all kinds of practical jokes are played off, and all ill humours vented.   This appellation is derived from a mountebank's servant, on whom all experiments used to be made
in public by the doctor, his master; among which was the
eating of toads, formerly supposed poisonous.   Swallowing
toads is here figuratively meant for swallowing or putting up
with insults, as disagreeable to a person of feeling, as
toads to the stomach. "   It can be located in the letters of
Horace Walpole (1742); in Washington Irving's Salmagundi
(1808), and in the following:

> He wished for himself what he felt to be good, and
> was not conscious of wishing harm to any one
> else; unless, perhaps, it were just now a little
> harm to the inconvenient and impertinent Gwendo-
> len.   But the easiest-humored amateur of luxury
> and music, the toad-eater the least liable to
> nausea, must be expected to have his susceptibil-
> ities.
> --George Eliot: Daniel Deronda (1876); chapter
>   25.

As Grose has told us, another meaning of toad-
eater is in reference to a female dependent or attendant.
This use can be located in Henry Fielding (1744); Francis
Coventry's Pompey the Little (1751); Eleanor Sleath's Bristol
Heiress (1808); in Thomas DeQuincey (1853), and in Walpole:

> You will perceive by my date that I am got into a
> new scene; and that I am retired hither like an
> old summer dowager; only that I have no toad-eater
> to take the air with me in the back part of my
> lozenge coach, and to be scolded.

--Horace Walpole to Horace Mann, August 21st, 1746.

TOD: An old name for the fox. The origin is uncertain, but it may be related to the old word tod, "bushy patch," possibly with reference to the fox's tail. The word can be located in Reginald of Durham's Libellus de admirandis Beati Cuthberti (1170); in Sir David Lindsay (1535); Sir John Ballenden (1536); Allan Ramsay (1721); in Edward Peacock's Ralf Skirlaugh, the Lincolnshire Squire (1871), and in the following:

TUCK:
When to one goat, they reach that prickly weed,
Which maketh all the rest forbear to feed;
Or strew tods'-hairs, or with their tails do sweep
The dewy grass, to d'off the simpler sheep.
--Ben Jonson: The Sad Shepherd (1637); Act I, Scene 4.

"I could hae wished it had been the deil himself-- be good to and preserve us!--rather than Christie o' the Clinthill," said the matron of the mansion, "for the word runs rife in the country, that he is ane of the maist masterfu' thieves ever lap on horse."
"Hout-tout, Dame Elspeth," said Tibb, "fear ye naething frae Christie; tods keep their ain holes clean. You kirk-folk make sic a fasherie about men shifting a wee bit for their living!"
--Sir Walter Scott: The Monastery (1820); chapter 4.

"Were those who entertained an opinion so strange not wise enough to know that it requires twenty pairs of hands to make a thing so trifling as a pin, twenty couple of dogs to kill an animal so insignificant as a fox--?"
"Hout, man!" said a stout countryman, "I have a grew bitch at hame will worry the best tod in Pomoragrains before ye could say dumpling."
--Sir Walter Scott: The Betrothed (1825); Introduction.

Hence, tod is also used figuratively, with reference to a foxy or crafty person. This use can be found in Dunbar (1520); James Kelly's Scottish Proverbs (1721), and in the following:

Daddy Auld, Daddy Auld, there's a tod in the fauld,
  A tod meikle waur than the Clerk;
Tho' ye can do little skaith, ye'll be in at the
      death,
  And gif ye canna bite, ye may bark.
--Robert Burns: The Kirk's Alarm (1789); stanza
    8.

...here he suddenly leaned down and whispered in
my ear: "Take care of the old tod; he means
mischief. Come aboard till I can get a word with
ye."
--Robert Louis Stevenson: Kidnapped (1886); chap-
    ter 6.

TOTTY: An old word meaning "shaky, dizzy, confused in
thought, tipsy." Grose defines totty-headed as "giddy, hair-
brained." The origin is probably the same as that of totter,
from the Old Norse. Examples of its use can be found in
Lydgate (1420); Thomas More (1522), and in these:

Aleyn up-rist, and thoughte, "er that it dawe,
I wol go crepen in by my felawe;"
And fond the cradel with his hand anon,
"By god," thoghte he, "al wrang I have misgon;
Myn heed is toty of my swink to-night,
That maketh me that I go nat aright."
--Geoffrey Chaucer: The Reeve's Tale in The
    Canterbury Tales (1386); lines 329-334.

Then came October full of merry glee:
  For, yet his noule was totty of the must,
  Which he was treading in the wine-fats see,
  And of the joyous oyle, whose gentle gust
  Made him so frollick and so full of lust.
--Edmund Spenser: The Faerie Queene, Book VII
    (1605); Canto VII, stanza 39.

"The priest," said Clement, "is not half so con-
fident of the Jew's conversion since he received
that buffet on the ear."
  "Go to, knave, what pratest thou of conver-
sions?--what, is there no respect?--all masters
and no men?--I tell thee, fellow, I was somewhat
totty when I received the good knight's blow, or I
had kept my ground under it. But an thou gibest
more of it, thou shalt learn I can give as well as
take."

--Sir Walter Scott: Ivanhoe (1819); chapter 32.

"Can I be of avail?" asked Alleyne. "Say the word
and the thing is done, if two hands may do it. "
   'Nay, nay, your head I can see is still totty,
and i'faith little head would you have, had your
bassinet not stood your friend. "
--Sir Arthur Conan Doyle: The White Company
      (1890); chapter 17.

TRANCHEFER: An old kind of sword; from the French
tranche, "to cut, to slice" and fer, "iron. " It can be found
in John Bourchier, Lord Berners' The Hystory of the moost
noble and valyaunt knyght Arthur of lytell Brytayne (1530),
and in Scott:

   "There is also, " said Agelastes, who saw that he
   would gain his point by addressing himself to the
   curiosity of the strangers, "the huge animal, wearing on its back an invulnerable vestment, having
   on its nose a horn, and sometimes two, the folds
   of whose hide are of the most immense thickness,
   and which never knight was able to wound. "
      'We will go, Robert--will we not?" reiterated
   the Countess.
      "Ay, " replied the Count, "and teach these
   Easterns how to judge of a knight's sword, by a
   single blow of my trusty Tranchefer. "
   --Sir Walter Scott: Count Robert of Paris (1831);
        chapter 13.

TRETIS: A very old word, meaning "handsome, graceful,
well-proportioned. " It comes through the Old French tretis,
"slender, " from the Latin tractus, "drawn-out, slender, "
from trahere, "to draw. " It is found in William Caxton
(1490), and in the following:

   That other bowe was of a plante
   Withoute wem, I dar warante,
   Ful even, and by proporcioun
   Tretys and long, of good fasoun.
   --Geoffrey Chaucer: The Romaunt of the Rose
        (1366); lines 929-932.

   Her visage was fair and tretis,
   Her body gentle and pure fetys,
              And semblych of stature.
   --Sir Ferumbras (ca. 1380); lines 5883-5884.

Ful semely hir wimpel pinched was;
Hir nose tretys; hir eyen greye as glas;
Hir mouth ful smal, and ther-to softe and reed;
But sikerly she hadde a fair forheed.
--Geoffrey Chaucer: Prologue to The Canterbury
Tales (1386); lines 151-154.

TRILLIBUBS: A word of many spellings, referring to the
entrails of animals, and thus coming to mean anything small
or trifling. The origin is unknown. Examples of its use
can be located in William Horman (1519); Andrew Borde's
Dyetary of Health (1542); Thomas Dekker's The Shoemaker's
Holiday (1600); Ben Jonson's Bartholomew Fair (1614); in
Richard Brome (1632), and in the following:

SIMONIDES: I am for drinking; your wet weapon
there.
LYSANDER: That wet one hast cost many a prin-
cox life;
And I will send it through you with a powder!
SIMONIDES: Let [it] come, with a pox! I care
not, so't be drink.
I hope my guts will hold, and that's e'en all
A gentleman can look for of such trillibubs.
--Thomas Middleton & William Rowley: The Old
Law (1599); Act III, Scene 2.

FAIRFIELD:
But I forgive thee, and forget thy tricks
And trillabubs, and will swear to love thee heartily;
Wenches must have their ways.
--James Shirley: Hyde Park (1637); Act III, Scene
2.

TUFT-HUNTER: A fawning parasite who attached himself to
the young rich men at Oxford and Cambridge universities,
the "tuft" being the gold tassel worn by these young men.
Says Grose: "An university parasite, one who courts the
acquaintance of nobility, whose caps are adorned with a gold
tuft. "

I remember to have heard a cousin of mine, who
was formerly at Cambridge, often mentioning a
sect of philosophers, distinguished by the rest of
the collegians under the appellation of Tuft-Hunt-
ers. These were not disciples of the Stoics or
Epicureans, or the advocates for the old or new

philosophy, but the followers, literally speaking,
of the fellow-commoners, noblemen, and other
rich students, whom, it seems, the courtesy of
the university has honoured with a cap adorned
with a gold tassel.   These gold threads have almost as much influence in the university, as a
red or blue riband at court; and always draw after
the wearer a train of humble companions, who will
be at his call to breakfast, dine, or sup with him
whenever he pleases, will go with him any where,
drink with him, wench with him, borrow his money,
or let him pay their reckoning.   They are, I am
told, a sort of disease of the place, which a man
of fortune is sure to catch as soon as he arrives
there.
--George Colman & Bonnel Thornton: The Con-
    noisseur No. 97 (1755); paragraph 1.

Stinginess is snobbish.   Ostentation is snobbish.
Too great profusion is snobbish.   Tuft-hunting is
snobbish.   But I owne there are people more snobbish than all those whose defects are above mentioned: viz. , those individuals who can, and don't
give dinners at all.
--William Makepeace Thackeray: The Book of
    Snobs (1848); chapter 19.

How eager he was to get a card to this party or
that! how attentive to the givers of such entertain-
ments!   Some friends of his accused him of being
a tuft-hunter and flatterer of the aristocracy, on
account of his politeness to certain people; the
truth was, he wanted to go wherever Miss Ethel
was; and the ball was blank to him which she did
not attend.
--William Makepeace Thackeray: The Newcomes
    (1855); chapter 45.

TWIRE: An old verb meaning "to pry; to peer; to look at
secretly; to peep at. "   The origin is not known, but the word
is similar to the Middle High German zwieren, "to peer. "
It can be located in William Motherwell (1832), and in the
following:

I tell the day, to please him thou art bright,
And dost him grace when clouds do blot the heaven:
So flatter I the swart-complexion'd night,

When sparkling stars twire not thou gild'st the
   even.
--William Shakespeare: Sonnet 28 (1600); lines 9-
   12.

BALURDO: In good sadness I would have sworn I
had seen Mellida even now; for I saw a thing stir
under a hedge and I peep'd and I spied a thing;
and I peer'd and I tweer'd underneath, and truly a
right wise man might have been deceived, for it
was--
PIERO: What, in the name of heaven?
BALURDO: A dun cow.
--John Marston: Antonio and Mellida (ca. 1600);
   Act IV, Scene 1.

But note the cross star that always dogged my fortunes: I had not long rested there, but I saw the
tweering constable of Finsbury, with his bench of
brown-bill men, making towards me, meaning indeed to stop some prison-hole with me, as your
soldiers, when the wars have done with them, are
good for nothing else but to stop holes withal.
--Thomas Middleton: "The Ant's Tale when he was
   a Soldier" in Father Hubburd's Tales (1604).

Suppose twixt noon and night, the Sun his half way
   wrought
(The shadows to be large, by his descending
   brought)
Who with a fervent eye looks through the twyring
   glades,
And his dispersed rays commixeth with the shades,
Exhaling the milch dew, which there had tarried
   long,
And on the ranker grass till noon-sted hung.
--Michael Drayton: Polyolbion (1612); Song XIII,
   lines 167-172.

SOTO:
Go to! I'll lay the best part of two pots now
Thou art in love, and I can guess with whom too;
I saw the wench that twir'd and twinkled at thee,
The other day; the wench that's new come hither,
The young smug wench.
--John Fletcher: Women Pleased (ca. 1620); Act
   IV, Scene 1.

MAUDLIN:
He should present them with more pleasant things,
Things natural, and what all women covet
To see: the common parent of us all!
Which maids will twire at, 'tween their fingers,
    thus!
With which his sire began him! He's get another!
And so beget posterity upon her!
--Ben Jonson: The Sad Shepherd (1637); Act II,
    Scene 3.

TOM: What? A sad thing to walk? Why, Madame
Phillis, do you wish yourself lame?
PHILLIS: No, Mr. Tom, but I wish I were generally carried in a coach or chair, and of a fortune neither to stand nor go, but to totter, or
slide, to be short-sighted, or stare, to fleer in
the face, to look distant, to observe, to overlook,
yet all become me; and, if I was rich, I could
twire and loll as well as the best of them. Oh
Tom! Tom! Is it not a pity that you should be
so great a coxcomb and I so great a coquette and
yet be such poor devils as we are?
--Sir Richard Steele: The Conscious Lovers (1721);
    Act I, Scene 1.

The noun form from twire, meaning "a leer," can be
located in Aphra Behn's The Feigned Courtesans (1679) and
The False Count (1682); Thomas D'Urfey's Pills to Purge
Melancholy (1719), and in Etherege:

YOUNG BELLAIR: Most people prefer Hyde Park
to this place.
HARRIET: It has a better reputation, I confess;
but I abominate the dull diversions there--the for-
mal bows, the affected smiles, the silly by-words
and amorous tweers in passing.
--Sir George Etherege: The Man of Mode (1676);
    Act III, Scene 3.

-U-

UDS: An old trivial minced oath, popular in the 16th and
17th centuries, meaning "God's" or "God save," and used
with various curious and unusual nouns in equally various
phrases. Some of those of interest are: "Uds blood" in

Dekker & Webster's Northward Ho (1607); "Udz niggs" in the poetry of Henry Bold (1664); "Udds Bobblekens" in Thomas Flatman (1681); "Udsbows" in Thomas D'Urfey (1684); "Udsdeath" in Sir John Vanbrugh (1702); "Udsfoot" in Sidney (1586) and Day (1608); "Udslife" in Vanbrugh's Mistake (1706); "Ud'slight" in Nathan Field's Amends for Ladies (1618); "Uds my life" in George Farquhar's The Inconstant (1702), and the following:

> DUBOIS: I am your friend and servant: struggle with me, and take my sword. --
> Noble sir, make your way! you have slain an officer. (EXIT)
> MONTAGUE: Some one of them has certainly requited me;
> For I do lose much blood. (EXIT)
> FIRST OFFICER: Udsprecious, we have lost a brother! pursue the gentleman!
> --Francis Beaumont, John Fletcher & Philip Massinger: The Honest Man's Fortune (1613); Act II, Scene 4.

> MATHEO: Go, trot after your dad, do you capitulate; I'll pawn not for you; I'll not steal to be hanged for such an hypocritical, close, common harlot: away, you dog!--Brave i'faith! Udsfoot, give me some meat.
> --Thomas Dekker: The Honest Whore, Part II (1630); Act IV, Scene 1.

> BEAUMELLE: Ah, my sweet Bellapert, thou cabinet
> To all my counsels, thou dost know the cause
> That makes thy Lady wither thus in youth.
> BELLAPERT: Ud's-light, enjoy your wishes: whilst I live,
> One way or other you shall crown your will.
> --Philip Massinger & Nathan Field: The Fatal Dowry (1632); Act II, Scene 2.

> CELADON: I'll fight with you.
> FLORIMEL: Out upon fighting: 'tis grown so common a fashion, that a modish man contemns it: A man of garniture and feather is above the dispensation of a sword.
> OLINDA: Uds my life, here's the Queen's music just going to us; you shall decide your quarrel by a dance.

--John Dryden: Secret Love (1667); Act V.

SAINTLY: Delay no longer, or--
WOODALL: Or! you will not swear, I hope?
SAINTLY: Uds Niggers, but I will; and that so
loud, that Mr. Limberham shall hear me.
WOODALL: Uds Niggers, I confess, is a very
dreadful oath: you cou'd lie naturally before, as
you are a Fanatick: if you can swear such rap-
pers too, there's hope of you; you may be a woman
of the world intime.
--John Dryden: The Kind Keeper (1678); Act IV,
Scene 2.

COURTINE: Sir Jolly is the glory of the age.
SIR JOLLY JUMBLE: Nay, now, sir, you honour
me too far.
BEAUGARD: He's the delight of the young, and
wonder of the old.
SIR JOLLY JUMBLE: I swear, gentlemen, you
make me blush.
COURTINE: He deserves a statue of gold, at the
charge of the kingdom.
SIR JOLLY JUMBLE: Out upon't, fie for shame!
I protest I'll leave your company if you talk so.
But faith they were pure whores, daintily dutiful
strumpets: ha! uddsbud, they'd--have stripped for
t'other bottle.
BEAUGARD: Truly, Sir Jolly, you are a man of
very extraordinary discipline: I never saw whores
under better command in my life.
--Thomas Otway: The Soldier's Fortune (1681);
Act II, Scene 1.

SNAP: By your leave, gentlemen. Mr. Trapland,
if we must do our office, tell us. We have half
a dozen gentlemen to arrest in Pall Mall and Co-
vent Garden; and if we don't make haste the chairmen will be abroad and block up the chocolate-
houses, and then our labour's lost.
TRAPLAND: Udso, that's true. Mr. Valentine,
I love mirth, but business must be done.
--William Congreve: Love For Love (1695); Act I,
Scene 6.

YOUNG FASHION: Pray, sir, let it be done without ceremony; twill save money.

SIR TUNBELLY: Money--save money when Hoyden's to be marry'd? Udswoons, I'll give my wench a wedding dinner, tho' I go to grass with the King of Assyria for't; and such a dinner it shall be, as is not to be cook'd in the poaching of an egg.
--Sir John Vanbrugh: The Relapse (1696); Act III, Scene 4.

SIR TUNBELLY: Gentlemen, you are welcome. Ladies, by your leave. Ha--They bill like turtles. Udsookers, they set my old blood a-fire; I shall cuckold some body before morning.
--Sir John Vanbrugh: The Relapse (1696); Act V, Scene 5.

SIR TUNBELLY CLUMSY: Puppy! puppy!--I might prevent their being beggars, if I chose it; for I could give 'em as good a rent-roll as your lordship.
LORD FOPPINGTON: Ay, old fellow, but you will not do that--for that would be acting like a Christian, and thou art a barbarian, stap my vitals.
SIR TUNBELLY CLUMSY: Udzookers! now six words more, and I'll forgive them directly.
--Richard Brinsley Sheridan: A Trip to Scarborough (1777); Act V, Scene 2.

"Be not wroth with me, good Mike; I did but try whether thou hadst parted with aught of thine old and honourable frankness, which your enviers and backbiters called saucy impudence."
"Let them call it what they will," said Michael Lambourne, 'It is the commodity we must carry through the world with us.--Uds daggers!"
--Sir Walter Scott: Kenilworth (1821); chapter 3.

UNBE: To have no being; to "not be"; to not exist. Found in Richard Francis Burton's Arabian Nights (1885); Thomas Hardy's Wessex Poems (1898), and in the following:

And doun cam his sweet sisters,
    greeting sae sair,
And down cam his bonie wife,
    tearing her hair.
"My house is unbigged,
    my barn's unbeen,

My corn's unshorn,
   my meadow grows green. "
--"Bonnie James Campbell" in Child's English and
   Scottish Popular Ballads; Version A, stanzas 3
   & 4.

     A second meaning of this word, "to cease to be, " is
illustrated in the following:

PETRONIUS:
How oft, with danger of the field beset,
Or with home's mutinies would he unbe
Himself; or, over cruel altars weeping,
Wish that with putting off a vizard he
Might his true inward sorrow lay aside:
The shows of things are better than themselves.
--Anonymous: Nero (ca. 1624); Act III, Scene 3.

UNDERPEEP: To peep under or from under; to look beneath or from beneath. The origin of peep is not certain.

IACHIMO: 'Tis her breathing that
Perfumes the chamber thus: the flame o'the taper
Bows towards her; and would under-peep her lids,
To see the enclosed lights, now canopied
Under these windows, white and azure, laced
With blue of heaven's own tinct.
--William Shakespeare: Cymbeline (1610); Act II,
   Scene 2.

And o'er his steadfast cheek a furrow'd pain
Hath set, and stiffen'd like a storm in ice,
Showing by drooping lines the deadly strain
Of mortal anguish;--yet you might gaze twice
Ere Death it seem'd, and not his cousin, Sleep,
That through those creviced lids did underpeep.
--Thomas Hood: Hero and Leander (1827); stanza
   61.

USQUEBAUGH: A word of many spellings, popular in the
17th century, meaning "whisky. " In fact, our word whisky
is merely a shortening of this word, which comes from the
Irish uisge "water, " and beatha, "life, " similar in construction to aqua vitae, "water of life. " Dr. Johnson tells us:
"It is a compounded distilled spirit, being drawn on aroma-
ticks; and the Irish sort is particularly distinguished for its
pleasant and mild flavour. The Highland sort is somewhat

hotter; and, by corruption, in Scottish they call it whisky. "
Examples of its use can be found in John Derricke's The
Image Irelande (1581); Beaumont & Fletcher's The Scornful
Lady (ca. 1610); Samuel Foote's The Orators (1762); in Haz-
litt (1818); Scott's The Abbot (1820) and The Monastery
(1820); Robert Bremner's Excursions in Denmark, Norway,
and Sweden (1840), and in the following:

> AIMWELL: And have you lived so long upon this
> ale, landlord?
> BONIFACE: Eight-and-fifty years, upon my credit,
> sir--but it killed my wife, poor woman, as the
> saying is.
> AIMWELL: How came that to pass?
> BONIFACE: I don't know how, sir; she would not
> let the ale take its natural course, sir; she was
> for qualifying it every now and then with a dram,
> as the saying is; and an honest gentleman that
> came this way from Ireland made her a present of
> a dozen bottles of usquebaugh--but the poor woman
> was never well after.   But, howe'er, I was obliged
> to the gentleman, you know.
> --George Farquhar: The Beaux' Stratagem (1707);
>   Act I, Scene 1.

-V-

VAIL STAFF: This was the old practice of lowering one's
stick or staff as a respectful salute, coming from vail, "to
lower as a sign of respect. " It comes through the Old
French valer.

> And for the ancient custom of vail staff,
> Claim privilege from me: If any ask a reason why?
>   or how?
> Say, English Edward vaild his staff to you.
> --Robert Greene?: George A Greene (1599); Act
>   V, Scene 1.

VASQUINE: An old Scottish name for a gown or petticoat,
originally worn by Basque and Spanish women.   From the
French vasquine, it is also spelled basquine.

> "I shall endure her presence without any desire to
> damage either her curch or vasquine. "
> --Sir Walter Scott: The Abbot (1820); chapter 31.

VECKE, VEKKE: A very old name for an equally old woman. It comes, probably through the Old French, from the Italian vecchio, "old," and can be found in the works of John Lydgate (1420, 1440), and in Gower:

> This olde wyht him hath awaited
> In place wher as he hire lefte:
> Florent his wofull heved uplefte
> And syh this vecke wher sche sat,
> Which was the lothlieste what
> That evere man caste on his yhe.
> --John Gower: Confessio Amantis (1393); Book I,
>   lines 1672-1677.

VERBY: Full of verbs. Through the Old French verbe from the Latin verbum, "a word." It was used by Hood:

> To Bowring, man of many tongues,
> (All over tongues like rumor)
> This tributary verse belongs
> To paint his learned humor;
> All kinds of gabs he talks, I wis
> From Latin down to Scottish;
> As fluent as a parrot is,
> But far more Polly-glottish!
> No grammar too abstruse he meets,
> However dark and verby, --
> He gossips Greek about the streets,
> And often Russ--in urbe.
> --Thomas Hood: Sir John Bowring (1845); lines 1-
>   12.

VERDUGO: The executioner, hangman; the man who wields the ax; also, a sharp, severe blow, used as a term of contempt. It comes through the Spanish verdugo, and the Italian verduco, a kind of sword. "Pot-verdugo," as in the Beaumont & Fletcher quote, probably means a "stunning blow received from a drink."

> FACE: Sweet Dol,
> You must go tune your virginal, no losing
> O' the least time. And--do you hear? Good action!
> Firk like a flounder; kiss like a scallop, close;
> And tickle him with thy mother tongue. His great
> Verdugoship has not a joy of language.
> --Ben Jonson: The Alchemist (1610); Act III,
>   Scene 3.

WELFORD: Where are my slippers, sir?
SERVANT (DRUNK): Here, sir.
WELFORD: Where, sir? have you got the pot-
verdugo?
Have you seen the horses, sir?
--Francis Beaumont & John Fletcher: The Scorn-
ful Lady (ca. 1610); Act II, Scene 1.

PETRONIUS:
Leave off your tricks, they are hateful,
And mere forerunners of the ancient measures;
Contrive your beard o' the top cut, like Verdugo's,
It shews you would be wise; and burn your night-
cap,
It looks like half a winding-sheet, and urges
From a young wench nothing but cold repentance;
You may eat onions, so you'll not be lavish.
--John Fletcher: The Woman's Prize (ca. 1612);
Act IV, Scene 1.

VIOLER: Chiefly in Scotland, a violinist usually attached to
the household of a nobleman or rich man for the entertainment of family and guests. Through the Old French vielle
from the medieval Latin vitula. Used principally in the 16th
and 17th centuries, it can be found in Sir George Mackenzie's
Discourse upon the Laws and Customs of Scotland in Matters
Criminal (1678); in Sir John Lauder (1722); James' Forest
Days (1843), and in Scott:

The old man struck the earth with his staff in a
violent passion: "The whoreson fisher rabble!
They have brought another violer upon my walk!
They are such smuggling blackguards, that they
must run in their very music. "
--Sir Walter Scott: Redgauntlet (1824); letter 12.

"Here, " said Vidal, "on this hand--this noble hand,
I renounce--"
But, ere he could utter another word, Hugo de
Lacy, who, perhaps, felt the freedom of the action
as an intrusion on his fallen condition, pulled back
his hand, and bid the minstrel, with a stern frown,
arise, and remember that misfortune made not De
Lacy a fit personage for a mummery.
Renault Vidal rose rebuked. "I had forgot, " he
said, "the distance between an Armorican violer
and a high Norman baron. I thought that the same

depth of sorrow, the same burst of joy, levelled,
for a moment at least, those artificial barriers by
which men are divided. "
--Sir Walter Scott: The Betrothed (1825); chapter
30.

VOGIE, VOGEY, VOUGY: A Scottish word meaning "proud,
well-pleased, vain, conceited, puffed-up, " from an unknown
origin. It can be located in Allan Ramsay (1719); in Ross's
Helenore (1789); John Galt's Lawrie Todd, or the Settlers in
the Woods (1830), and in Burns:

> What will I do gin my Hoggie die?
> My joy, my pride, my Hoggie!
> My only beast, I had na mae,
> And vow but I was vogie!
> --Robert Burns: My Hoggie (1788); stanza 1.

Another meaning of the word, "cheerful, joyful, merry, " can be found in the poetry of Robert Fergusson (1774),
and in John Galt's The Provost (1822).

VUSSE: An old word used in oaths of uncertain meaning and
origin; it may be a variation of faith or vows.

> Are you my uncle? sayes Will. I, sir, sayes
> hee. Are you my uncle? sayes hee againe. I,
> sure, and verely too. But are you my uncle, in-
> deed? By my vusse I am, sayes the old man.
> Then, uncle, by my vusse, welcome to court,
> sayes Will Sommers.
> --Robert Armin: Nest of Ninnies (1608).

-W-

WAESUCK, WAESUCKS: An old Scottish exclamation: "Alas!
Woe is me!" It comes from the Scottish wae, "woe, " and
sucks, "sakes, " and can be found in the following poets:

> Waesuck for him wha has nae feck o't!
> For he's a gowk they're sure to geck at,
> A chiel that ne'er will be respekit,
>   While he draws breath,
> Till his four quarters are bedeckit
>   Wi' gude Braid Claith.
> --Robert Fergusson: Braid Claith (1774); stanza 3.

> Waesucks! for him that gets nae lass,
> Or lasses that hae naething!
> Sma' need has he to say a grace,
> Or melvie his braw claithing!
> --Robert Burns: The Holy Fair (1786); stanza 25.

WAGHALTER: Once a common term for a scoundrel, one who is likely to "wag" in a "halter," i. e. be hanged at the gallows. "A wretchless villain," says Cotgrave. It can be found in Thomas Shelton (1620), and in Ford:

> SPADONE: Yes, crimp; 'tis a gallant life to be an old lord's pimp-whiskin: but, beware of the porter's lodge, for carrying tales out of the school.
> NITIDO: What a terrible sight to a libb'd breech is a sow-gelder!
> SPADONE: Not so terrible as a cross-tree that never grows, to a wag-halter page.
> --John Ford: The Fancies, Chaste and Noble (1635); Act I, Scene 2.

WALLYDRAG, WALLYDRAIGLE: An old word of many spellings, referring to a feeble, worthless, or untidy person, especially a woman; the origin is uncertain. It can also refer to a youngster (because he is tiny and feeble), as in John Galt's The Last of the Lairds (1826). Found in Dunbar (1520), and used by Scott in Rob Roy (1817) and in the following:

> "We think mair about the warst wally-draigle in our ain byre, than about the blessing which the angel of the covenant gave to the Patriarch."
> --Sir Walter Scott: The Heart of Midlothian (1818); chapter 19.

WANDLE: An old Scottish adjective: flexible, strong, nimble, agile, supple. It probably comes from the word wand, with reference to its slenderness. Found in James Hogg (1803), and in Scott:

> "But it was a' sowdered up again some gait, and the bairn was sent awa, and bred up near the Highlands, and grew up to be a fine wanle fallow, like mony ane that comes o' the wrang side o' the blanket."
> --Sir Walter Scott: The Antiquary (1816); chapter 24.

WANT-WIT: A person destitute of sense, one who "wants
wit." It can be located in Metham (1449); Bunyan (1684),
and in Shakespeare:

> ANTONIO:
> In sooth, I know not why I am so sad:
> It wearies me; you say it wearies you;
> But how I caught it, found it, or came by it,
> What stuff 'tis made of, whereof it is born,
> I am to learn;
> And such a want-wit sadness makes of me,
> That I have much ado to know myself.
> --William Shakespeare: The Merchant of Venice
>   (1596); Act I, Scene 1.

WAT: A familiar usage of the proper name Walter, referring to a rabbit or hare; similar to "Tom" for a cat, "Rov-
er" for a dog, etc. Found since the late 15th century, it
can be seen in the following writers:

> Quoth the spider, God have mercie on thee!
> Amen (quoth the fly) but why speak you that?
> I speak (and pray) it even of charity.
> Never was there yet any lark or wat,
> Before hawk or dog, flatter dared or squat
> Than by this answer all thy matter is.
> --John Heywood: The Spider and the Fly (1556);
>   Cap. 24, lines 22-27.

> "By this, poor Wat, far off upon a hill,
> Stands on his hinder legs with list'ning ear,
> To hearken if his foes pursue him still:
> Anon their loud alarums he doth hear;
>   And now his grief may be compared well
>   To one sore sick that hears the passing-bell.
> --William Shakespeare: Venus and Adonis (1593);
>   lines 697-702.

> The man whose vacant mind prepares him to the
>   sport,
> The finder sendeth out, to seek out nimble Wat,
> Which crosseth in the field, each furlong, ever
>   flat,
> Till he this pretty beast upon the form hath found,
> Then viewing for the course, which is the fairest
>   ground,
> The greyhounds forth are brought, for coursing

then in case
And choicely in the slip, one leading forth a brace.
--Michael Drayton: Polyolbion (1612); Song 23.

WEANIE: An old Scottish word for a little child, from wean,
a contraction of wee ane, "wee one. " It was used by R. D.
Blackmore (1864), and by Burns:

When skirlin weanies see the light,
Thou maks the gossips clatter bright,
How fumbling cuifs their dearies slight;
            Wae worth the name!
Nae howdie gets a social night,
            Or plack frae them.
--Robert Burns: Scotch Drink (1786); stanza 12.

WELK: To fade or die away; to wilt, wither; to wane, grow
dim (of the sun or moon). It comes through the Middle
English welken, probably from a Germanic origin, and can
be found in Francis Quarles' The Historie of Sampson (1631);
in Milton (1641), and in the following:

The See now ebbeth, now it floweth,
The lond now welketh, now it groweth,
Now be the Trees with leves grene,
Now thei be bare and nothing sene.
--John Gower: Confessio Amantis (1393); Prologus,
        lines 933-936.

As gentle Shepheard in sweete even-tide,
When ruddy Phoebus gins to welke in west,
High on an hill, his flocke to vewen wide,
Markes which do byte their hasty supper best.
--Edmund Spenser: The Faerie Queene, Book I
    (1590); Canto I, stanza 23.

Also, to make fade or wither:

But nowe sadde Winter welked hath the day,
And Phoebus weary of his yerely taske,
Yestabled hath his steedes in lowlye laye,
And taken up his ynne in Fishes haske.
--Edmund Spenser: The Shepheardes Calender
    (1579); November, lines 13-16.

O how hath black night welked up this day!
My wasted hopes, why are they turned to graze

In pastures of despair? ZEPHERIA say,
Wherein have I, on love committed trespass!
--Anonymous: Zepheria (1594); canzon 16.

WHID: 1) an old cant word for "word," and 2) an old Scottish term for a fib or lie, or tall tale. The origin is not
known, but in sense (1) it may come from a perversion of
"word" itself. (1) can be located in Harman's Caveat for
Vagabonds (1567); Head's Canting Academy (1673); Defoe
(1728); Scott's Kenilworth (1821), and in Reade:

> "'Servant,' quo' he, 'I spy a foul fault in thee.
> Thou liest without discretion: now the end of lying
> being to gull, this is no better than fumbling with
> the divell's tail. I pray Heaven thou mayest prove
> to paint better than thou cuttest whids, or I am
> done out of a dinner.'"
> --Charles Reade: The Cloister and the Hearth
>   (1861); chapter 55.

Sense (2) can be found in Samuel Rutherford Crockett's
The Raiders (1894), and in Burns:

> Some books are lies frae end to end,
> And some great lies were never penn'd:
> Ev'n ministers, they hae been kend,
>   In holy rapture,
> A rousing whid at times to vend,
>   And nail't wi'Scripture.
> --Robert Burns: Death and Dr. Hornbook (1785);
>   stanza 1.

WHIPPERGINNIE, WHIP-HER-JENNY: An old term of contempt of unknown origin, used toward a woman. Also, an
old card game.

> NICHOLAS: Master Richard, the good wife would
> not seek her daughter in the oven, unless she had
> been there herself: but, good Lord, you are
> knuckle-deep in dirt!--I warrant, when he was in,
> he swore Walsingham, and chaf'd terrible for the
> time. (ASIDE)--Look, the water drops from you
> as fast as hops.
> COOMES: What need'st thou to care, whip-her-
> jenny, tripe-cheeks? out, you fat ass!
> --Henry Porter: The Two Angry Women of Abing-
>   ton (1599); Act IV, Scene 3.

WINDOLET: A little window. Through the Middle English windoge from the Old Norse vindauga, constructed from vindr, "wind," and auga, "eye." It can be located in Richard Linche (1596), and in the following:

> The heart-sick soul is cur'd by heart-strong
>   health,
> The heart-strong health is the soul's brightest
>   eye,
> The heart-sick body healed by beauty's wealth;
> Two sunny windolets of either's sky,
> Whose beams cannot be clouded by reproach,
> Nor yet dismounted from so bright a coach.
> --Thomas Middleton: The Wisdom of Solomon
>   Paraphrased (1597); chapter 7.

WINK-A-PEEP, WINCOPIPE: A dialect name for the pimpernel plant, Anagallis arvensis, used by Bacon:

> The trefoil, against rain, swelleth in the stalk; and so standeth more upright: for by wet, stalks do erect, and leaves bow down. There is a small red flower in the stubble-fields, which country people call the wincopipe; which if it open in the morning, you may be sure of a fair day to follow.
> --Francis Bacon: Sylva Sylvarum (1626); paragraph 827.

WORRICOW: A scarecrow or scary hobgoblin, or a person resembling these: one of horrifying features. It comes from worry and cow, "hobgoblin" (origin unknown), and can be found in Allan Ramsay (1711); Tobias Smollett (1757); David Davidson's Thoughts on the Seasons (1789); the poetry of Thomas Donaldson (1809); Scott's Heart of Midlothian (1818); Samuel Rutherford Crockett's The Raiders (1894), and in the following:

> "What needs I care for the Mucklestane Moor ony mair than ye do yoursell, Earnscliffe?" said Hobbie, some thing offended; "to be sure, they do say there's a sort o' worriecows and langnebbit things about the land, but what need I care for them? I hae a good conscience, and little to answer for, unless it be about a rant amang the lasses or a splore at a fair, and that's no muckle to speak of."
> --Sir Walter Scott: The Black Dwarf (1816); chapter 2.

WOWF: An old Scottish word of unknown origin: "Crazy, mad, insane, loony." Examples of its use can be found in James Sibbald (1802); Scott's Redgauntlet (1824), and in the following:

> "Allan is right," said his brother; "it is very odd how Allan, who, between ourselves," said he to Musgrave, "is a little wowf, seems at times to have more sense than us all put together. Observe him now."
> --Sir Walter Scott: A Legend of Montrose (1819); chapter 6.

WYLIECOAT: An old Scottish word of many spellings, referring to a flannel undervest or under-waistcoat, originally worn beneath the doublet. The origin is unknown. It can be located in the Aeneis of Gavin Douglas (1513); Allan Ramsay (1737), and in the following:

> I wad na been surpris'd to spy
> You on an auld wife's flainen toy;
> Or aiblins some bit duddie boy,
>   On 's wyliecoat;
> But Miss's fine Lunardi! fye!
>   How daur ye do 't?
> --Robert Burns: To a Louse (1786); stanza 6.

> A hardy little boy, who had taken the lead in the race round the margin of the lake, did not hesitate a moment to strip off his "wylie-coat," plunge into the water, and swim towards the object of their common solicitude.
> --Sir Walter Scott: The Abbot (1820); chapter 1.

Also, the word refers to an under-petticoat: this use can be seen in Allan Ramsay (1715); James Kelly's Scottish Proverbs (1721); John Pinkerton's The History of Scotland from the Accession of the House of Stuart to that of Mary (1797); and in Samuel Rutherford Crockett's The Men of the Moss Hags (1895).

-X-

"X, " says Dr. Johnson, "is a letter, which, though found in Saxon words, begins no word in the English language. "

XERES, ZEREZ: The name of a village in Andalusia, where a famous wine, Xeres sack, was made; hence, sherris or sherry.

> "All the keys are in my keeping; and dear grand-father has the finest wine; not to be matched in the west of England, as I have heard good judges say; though I know not wine from cider. Do you like the wine of Oporto, or the wine of Xeres?"
> --R. D. Blackmore: Lorna Doone (1869); chapter 50.

> There were once, (and could be nothing now, unless they had been) so many skins of Xeres wine--grown and mellowed by pure chalk rock and un-afflicted sunshine. Wine drunk, indeed, long ago--but the drinkers gave the vineyard dressers these tokens which we call pounds, signifying that having had so much good from them they would return them as much, in future time. And, indeed, for my ten pounds, if my lawyer didn't take it, I could still get my Xeres if Xeres wine exists anywhere.
> --John Ruskin: Fors Clavigera (1886); Volume II, letter 16.

-Y-

YAFF: An old Scottish verb meaning "to bark, as a dog"; also, to prate, to nag, to argue with, wrangle with. The origin is echoic; the example cited below is from the related noun:

> By degrees the human tones predominated; but the angry bark of the cur being at the instant changed into a howl, it is probable something more than fair strength of lungs had contributed to the ascendancy.
> "Sorrow be in your thrapple then!" these were the first articulate words, "will ye no let me hear what the man wants, wi' your yaffing?"
> --Sir Walter Scott: Guy Mannering (1815); chapter 1.

YAFFINGALE, YAFFLE: The green woodpecker. Yaffingale is echoic from the laughing cry of the bird, with an ending

similar to nightingale. Yaffle is a simple echoic. These
forms can be found in Charles Butler's Feminine Monarchie;
or The History of Bees (1609); Charlotte Smith's novel Des-
mond (1792); in R. D. Blackmore (1866), and in the following:

> O blessed yaffil, laughing loud!
> O blessed falling glass!
> O blessed fan of cold gray cloud!
> O blessed smelling grass.
> --Charles Kingsley: The South Wind (April 1st,
>   1856); stanza 2.

> "I am woodman of the woods,
> And hear the garnet-headed yaffingale
> Mock them--my soul, we love but while we may;
> And therefore is my love so large for thee,
> Seeing it is not bounded save by love."
> --Alfred, Lord Tennyson: The Last Tournament
>   (1859); lines 694-698.

YARE: An old cry or exclamation: "Quick! Hurry up!"
especially employed by seamen. It comes through the Old
English and Old High German from the Old Norse gerva,
"plainly, completely," and actually means "quickly." It is
found in Beowulf; in John Barbour's The Bruce (1375); Douglas's Aeneis (1513); James Hogg's The Three Perils of Man
(1822), and in the following:

> CLEOPATRA:
> Give me my robe, put on my crown; I have
> Immortal longings in me: now no more
> The juice of Egypt's grape shall moist this lip:--
> Yare, yare, good Iras; quick. --Methinks I hear
> Antony call.
> --William Shakespeare: Antony and Cleopatra
>   (1607); Act V, Scene 2.

> BOATSWAIN: Heigh, my hearts! cheerly, cheerly,
> my hearts! yare, yare! Take in the topsail!
> Tend to the master's whistle!
> --William Shakespeare: The Tempest (1611); Act I,
>   Scene 1.

> "Yare!--for the ebb runs strongly towards the sea,
> The east wind drives the rack to Thessaly,
> And lightly do such kings as this one sleep

If now and then small watch their servants keep. "
--William Morris: The Life and Death of Jason
(1867); Book IX, lines 241-244.

YELLOW-BOY, YELLOW-HAMMER: Any gold coin, but
more specifically, the guinea. Though these words refer to
the same objects, their origins here are different: yellow-
boy comes from the brilliant color of the coin itself; yellow-
hammer is from the bright gold-colored woodpecker of the
same name. These forms can be found in James Shirley's
The Bird in a Cage (1633); John Arbuthnot's The History of
John Bull (1712); James Grant's Sketches in London (1838),
and in the following:

SIMON: Faith, and I thank your bounty, and not
your wisdom; you are not troubled with wit neither
greatly, it seems. Now, by this light, a nest of
yellow-hammers; What will become of me? if I
can keep all these without hanging myself, I am
happier than a hundred of my neighbours.
--Thomas Middleton: The Mayor of Queenborough
(1626); Act II, Scene 3.

BILBOE: But are the pence numbered? Do they
cry chink in thy pocket? How many yellow boys,
rogue? how many yellow boys?
--John Wilson: The Cheats (1662); Act I, Scene 1.

LOVEBY: Now does my heart go pit a pat, for
fear I should not find the money there: I would
fain lift it up to see, and yet I am so fraid of
missing: yet a plague, why should I fear he'll
fail me; the name of friend's a sacred thing; sure
he'll consider that:--methinks this hat looks as if
it should have something under it: if one could
see the yellow boys peeping underneath the brims
now: ha!
--John Dryden: The Wild Gallant (1663); Act III.

"Ah!" cried Isaac List rapturously, "the pleasures
of winning! The delight of picking up the money--
the bright, shining yellow-boys--and sweeping 'em
into one's pocket! The deliciousness of having a
triumph at last, and thinking that one didn't stop
short and turn back, but went half-way to meet
it!"
--Charles Dickens: The Old Curiosity Shop (1840);
chapter 42.

YIRD: The Scottish form of the word "earth. " It can be found in John Spalding (1670), and in Burns:

> When lyart leaves bestrow the yird,
> Or, wavering like the bauckie-bird,
> Bedim cauld Boreas' blast.
> --Robert Burns: The Jolly Beggars (1794); Recita-
> tivo I.

YOUNG: An old use of this word was in a technical sense in optometry, referring to a lens of low magnification; an "old" lens was one of high magnification. It can be seen in John Chamberlaine's The Religious Philosopher (1718), and in Pepys:

> From the Exchange I took a coach, and went to
> Turlington, the great spectacle-maker, for advice,
> who dissuades me from using old spectacles, but
> rather young ones, and do tell me that nothing can
> wrong my eyes more than for me to use reading-
> glasses, which do magnify much.
> --Samuel Pepys' Diary: November 4th, 1667.

YUKE, YEUK, EWK: An old Scottish verb of many spell-ings, meaning "to itch. " Examples of its use can be located in Wyntoun (1425); Dunbar (1508), and in the following:

> ...If sleekit Chatham Will was livin,
> Or glaikit Charlie got his nieve in;
> How daddie Burke the plea was cookin,
> If Warren Hastings' neck was yeukin...
> --Robert Burns: The Following Poem... (1790);
> lines 23-26.

> Poor man, the flie, aft bizzies by,
> As aft as chance he comes thee nigh,
> Thy auld damn'd elbow yeuks wi' joy,
>   And hellish pleasure;
> Already in thy fancy's eye,
>   Thy sicker treasure.
> --Robert Burns: Poem on Life (1796); stanza 6.

"But our folk were at great pains lang syne to big up the passage in some parts, and pu' it down in others, for fear o' some uncanny body getting into it, and finding their way down to the cove: it wad hae been a fashious job that--by my certie, some

o' our necks wad hae been ewking. "
--Sir Walter Scott: The Antiquary (1816); chapter
21.

-Z-

ZAD, ZED: The old name (still used in Britain) for the letter Z; hence, a person or an object of a crooked or bent
shape. Through the French zède and Italian zeta, from the
Greek letter zēta. It may be found in William Holder's
Elements of Speech (1669), in Daniel Defoe, and in the following:

> EARL OF KENT:
> Thou whoreson zed! thou unnecessary letter!
> --William Shakespeare: King Lear (ca. 1606); Act
> II, Scene 2.

> Shall I not think what pains the matron took,
> When first I trembled o'er the gilded book?
> How she, all patient, both at eve and morn,
> Her needle pointed at the guarding horn,
> And how she soothed me, when, with study sad,
> I labour'd on to reach the final zad?
> --George Crabbe: The Borough (1810); Letter 18,
> lines 25-30.

ZECCHIN, ZECCHINE: An old type of gold coin, the "se-
quin, " used in Venice and Turkey. From the Italian zec-
chino, a coin of Venice, from zecca, the mint. Through the
Spanish seca, from the Arabic sikkah, "coin. " Examples of
its use can be located in George Gascoigne, George Sandys,
James Shirley, Mrs. Piozzi, and in the following:

> "There is, " replied Malvoisin, "among those who
> came hither with Bois-Guilbert, two fellows whom
> I well know; servants they were to my brother
> Philip de Malvoisin, and passed from his service
> to that of Front-de-Boeuf. It may be they know
> something of the witcheries of this woman. "
>   "Away, seek them out instantly--and hark thee,
> if a byzant or two will sharpen their memory, let
> them not be wanting. "
>   'They would swear the mother that bore them a
> sorceress for a zecchin, " said the Preceptor.
> --Sir Walter Scott: Ivanhoe (1819); chapter 36.

ZITELLA: An Italian word into English, referring to a young
girl or virgin. Found in Richard Lassels' The Voyage of
Italy (1668), Aphra Behn's The Feign'd Curtizans (1679), and
in the following:

> On our Lady-day, 25th March, we saw the Pope
> and Cardinals ride in pomp to the Minerva, the
> great guns of the Castle of St. Angelo being fired,
> when he gives portions to 500 zitelle (young wom-
> en), who kiss his feet in procession, some destined
> to marry, some to be nuns.
> --John Evelyn's Diary: March 1st, 1645.

ZOOKERS! ZWOOKERS!: An old mild oath, short for Gad-
swookers, Gadzooks, God's sokinges, etc., ultimately from
God's hooks (the nails upon which Christ hung on the Cross).
Very popular in the 17th, 18th, and 19th centuries, and
found in many writers, including Shelton, Ainsworth, Farnol,
and the following:

> COUNTRYMAN:
> Zwain! though I am a zwain, I have a heart yet,
> As ready to do service for my leege,
> As any princox peacock of you all.
> Zookers! had I one of you zingle, with this twig
> I would so veeze you.
> --Philip Massinger: The Emperor of the East
> (1631); Act IV, Scene 2.

APPENDIX A

LIST OF AUTHORS QUOTED IN THE ARCHAICON

Joseph Addison
W. Harrison Ainsworth
Robert Armin
Matthew Arnold

Francis Bacon
John Barbour
R. H. Barham
J. M. Barrie
Francis Beaumont
R. D. Blackmore
James Boswell
Thomas Bridges
Charlotte Bronte
Emily Bronte
Richard Brookes
Robert Browning
Edward George Bulwer-Lytton
Gen. John Burgoyne
Robert Burns
Samuel Butler
George Gordon Byron

"R. C."
Hall Caine
Richard Carew
William Cartwright
James Cawthorn
George Chapman
Geoffrey Chaucer
George Colman
William Congreve
Capt. James Cook

Charles Cotton
William Cowper
George Crabbe
Oliver Cromwell
Richard Cumberland

Charles Darwin
Sir William Davenant
Robert Davenport
Thomas Dekker
Charles Dickens
Benjamin Disraeli
Sir Arthur Conan Doyle
Michael Drayton
John Dryden

George Eliot
Sir George Etherege
John Evelyn

George Farquhar
Robert Fergusson
Nathan Field
Henry Fielding
John Fletcher
Phineas Fletcher
John Ford

John Gay
Oliver Goldsmith
John Gower
Robert Greene
Sir Fulke Greville

Henry Hallam
Thomas Hardy
Bret Harte
Nathaniel Hawthorne
John Heywood
Thomas Heywood
Philemon Holland
Randle Holme
Oliver Wendell Holmes
Thomas Hood
Thomas Hughes

Washington Irving

Richard Jobson
Samuel Johnson
Ben Jonson

John Keats
Charles Kingsley
Thomas Kyd

Charles Lamb
Henry Wadsworth Longfellow
Samuel Longfellow
John Lyly

Rev. S. R. Maitland
Christopher Marlowe
Shackerley Marmion
John Marston
Andrew Marvell
William Mason
Philip Massinger
George Meredith
Thomas Middleton
John Milton
William Morris

Thomas Otway

Margaret Paston
William Paston
Samuel Pegge the Elder
Samuel Pepys
Alexander Pope
Henry Porter

Samuel Purchas

Charles Reade
William Rowley

Michael Scott
Sir Walter Scott
Thomas Shadwell
William Shakespeare
Percy Bysshe Shelley
William Shenstone
Richard Brinsley Sheridan
James Shirley
John Skelton
Tobias Smollett
Robert Southey
Edmund Spenser
Sir Richard Steele
Laurence Sterne
Robert Louis Stevenson
William Stevenson
Gerard van Swieten
Jonathan Swift

Alfred, Lord Tennyson
William Makepeace Thackeray
Bonnel Thornton
Thomas Tickell
Thomas Tomkis
Cyril Tourneur
Anthony Trollope
Mark Twain

Nicholas Udall

Sir John Vanbrugh

George Washington
John Webster
Paul Whitehead
John Wilson
Robert Wilson the Elder
William Wordsworth
William Wycherley
John Wycliffe

William Butler Yeats
Edward Young

APPENDIX B

A SHORT GLOSSARY OF THE CANT, THE SECRET LANGUAGE OF THIEVES, BEGGARS, ROGUES, &C.

abram	naked
abram-cour	a ragged person
autem	a church
autem mort	a married woman
belly-cheat, billy-cheat	an apron
bene	good
bene cofe	good man
beneship	very good
bing	to go
bing a wast	to go away
bleating-cheat	a sheep or calf
blowing	a whore
bord	a shilling
boughar	a cur
boung, bung	a purse
bouse, booze	drink
bousing-ken, boozing-ken	an ale-house
bube	the pox
bufe, buge	a dog
bulk and file	a pickpocket and his mate
buttock	a whore
cackling-cheat	a chicken or cock
calle	a cloak
cant	to speak
cassan	cheese
caster	a cloak
chates, chats	the gallows
clear	very drunk
cloy	to steal
cly the jerk	to be whipped

coale	ready cash
cofe, cove	a man
cokir	a liar
confeck	counterfeit
convenient	a whore
couch	to lie asleep
couch a hogshead	to go to sleep
crackmans	a hedge
crampings	bolts and shackles
crash	to kill
crashing-cheats	teeth
cuffin	a man
cuffin quire	a justice
cut	to speak
cut bene whids	to speak well
cut queer whids	to speak evil
damber	rascal
darkmans	the night
deusea vile, deuce-a-ville	the country
dimber	pretty
dommerer	a madman
drawers	hose, stockings
duds	goods, clothing
dup	to go in, to enter
fencing cully	a fence, one that receives stolen goods
ferme	a hole
fib	to beat
filch	a stick or staff
flag	a groat
fogus	tobacco
fripon	a scoundrel
gage, gauge	a quart-pot
gan	a mouth
gentry cove	a gentleman
gentry more	a gentlewoman
glaziers	eyes
glimmer	a fire
grannam	corn
grunting-cheat	a pig or hog
gun	lip
gybe	a written pass
harman beck	a constable

harmans	the stocks
heartsease	twenty shillings
heave a book	to rob a house
jigger	a door
ken	a house
knapper of knappers	a stealer of sheep
lag	water
lap	butter; milk; pottage; whey
lib	to tumble
libben, libken	a house
libedge	a bed
lightmans	the day
lower	money
lowing-cheat	a cow
lucries	all kinds of clothing
lullabye-cheat	a child
make	a halfpenny
Margery prater	a hen
maund, maunder	to ask, beg
mill	to steal
mint	gold
mish	a shirt
muffling-cheat	a napkin
natural	a whore
niggling	companying with women
nosegent	a nun
pad	a pathway, a way
patrico	a priest
peck	meat
piss upon a nettle	to be anxious or uneasy
poplars	pottage
prancer	a horse
prat	a buttock
prig	a pert fellow
prog	meat
pure, purest pure	a whore
put	a person easily gulled or cheated
quaroms	a body
queer cuffin	a churl
queer ken	a prison

rhino	ready cash
rhinocerical	full of cash
rigging	clothing
Roger or Tib of the buttery	a goose
Rome booze	wine
Rome mort	a queen
Romeville	London
Ruffian	the Devil
ruffmans	woods or bushes
ruff peck	bacon
scout	a watch
sharp	subtle
sharper	a cheater
sheep-biter	a poor, sorry wretch
skew	a cup
skipper	a barn
slate	a sheet
smelling-cheat	an orchard or garden, or the nose
smoky	jealous
Solomon	the Mass
stampers	shoes
stamps	legs
strommel	straw
stuling ken	a house for the reception of stolen property
tackle	a whore
tattler	an alarm
tattmonger	one who cheats at dice
tatts	false dice
tilter	a sword
togeman	a cloak
tower	to see
trining	hanging
vardo	a wagon
win	a penny
yarum	milk

APPENDIX C

A SHORT GLOSSARY OF THE ZINGARO TONGUE, OR THE LANGUAGE OF THE GYPSIES OF BRITAIN

acavat	this
acavo	that
adra	drowned
afta	seven
apra	above
avesi to jallow	to faint
bai	a bough
bar	a rock
bara, baro	a boat or ship
barraw	sand
baulo paramattee	a grape
baurifoki	a nation
bauro	a judge; lightning; the ocean; a sword; a desert
bauro balscoplatti	a tomb
bauro chumbo	a grave
bauro mattahee	a whale
bauro panee	a wave in the sea; the ocean
bebee	an aunt
beng, benga	the Devil
beval	a breath; the wind
bish	twenty
bish u desh	thirty
bittutheim	a country
boot	numbers; much
bootsee	great
boro	a steeple
borwardo	a giant
boshlod	a cock
boshtow	a saddle
bottoo	a dwarf

boyocorat, boyocrot	pitch
bringeree	a waistcoat
briskenoe	rain
burgau	a town
cal	cheese
calabeen	music
callicoe	yesterday
campen	to fight
can	the ear
cappeet	a hen
careoben	copper
cauliban	black
cham	the sun
charrie	a sword
chatto	green
chauk	an uncle
chavo	a son
chericloe	a bird
chinaber	tar
chive	the tongue
chockwan	a coat
chollow	to eat
chucknee	a whip
chumbo	a chin
cockwhur	a nutmeg
colah	a crown
colee	anger
coluri	a desert
commoben	love
congrogre	sulfur
coose	little
corat	oil
corow	a cup
coshtan	old
couloe	soot, filth
covascorook	the laurel
crellis	a king
cumbo, cumbee	hill or mountain
cusht	a bow
dad	father
davies	day
davila	God
deckloo	a flag
delapray	a dream
delvo	a valley

dennam	a tooth
dennoloo	a fool
desh	ten
devus	today
dicken	sight
die, dai	mother
discaloe	to see
doeyave	the ocean
domoe	the back
doriove, doriobb	a river
drom	a road
dromo	a wilderness
drou panee jal	to bathe
due	two
due bisha	forty
dumbo	a mountain
enneah	nine
folivingro	a bridle
foroose	a city
fule	a steeple
gava, geeva	life
gave	a village
georgee	dead body of a woman
georgio	dead body of a man; a dwarf
geronee	an ox
giorgeo	a man
givellan	to sing
givellee, gillee	a song
givengro	harvest
godlie	thunder
godocovan	an ape
gree	a spur; a horse
grove, grovenee	a cow
gur	a house
harrow	a sword
hatcheriban	to burn
havoura	the eye
herree	a leg
hocleben	hatred
hoova	a cap
iasia vallacai	to command
iaw	to walk

ionadass	to wake up
jamoval eo panee	a bath
k'howe	a window
kir	a house
kirchimo podrum	an inn
lasthom	found
lavanah	beer
lesco	the soul
lill	a book
lolo	red
loon	salt
manchouro	harp
mass	meat, food, nourishment
matchee	fish
matchian	a cat
millan	an ass
milo	a mule
miraban	death
modaval	God
moloo	death; a dead body
mormingro	a barber
moughem	to pray
moul	wine
mumallee	a cradle
naphilee phillee	a sick woman
naphilisoli	sickness
naphiloosoli	a sick man
nashedoe	lost
nevo	new
nie	fingernail
nock	the nose
ochano	a lie
ohano	words
oitoo	eight
ovavo devus	tomorrow
paddee	drowned
paiass	good sport
pal	brother
pan, pen	sister
panee	water; the ocean; tears; a drink

pappin	a goose
pappus, paupus	grandfather
pashoo, pawnee	a brook or rill
peng	a crown; five
peola	to drink
per	the belly
peroe	the foot
p'har	silk
phovee, p'hovee	the earth
plastomingree	a couch
poomingro	a peach
porcherie	brass
pordo	full
porgee	a bridge
porno	white
posomiso	a spur
prasthem	to run
pratcheely	a flame
racamansoe	to speak
radchevo	a servant
raiah, riah	sir
raiena, roiena	a lady
rashee	a priest
ratt	blood
rattie	night; dark
ravoo, ravoos	heaven
rogeo, roseo	a flower
romana chil	a gypsy
rome	a man; a husband
romee	a woman
rook	a tree
roop	silver
sallaw	to laugh
sashtaa	iron
sauvee	an eagle
savanow	sleep; to sleep
scholl	a flute
sep, sap	a serpent
shan	he; she
sharrous	the head
sheree	here
shillaloe	winter
shing	a horn
shirn	to hear
sho	six

shocmaloe	smell
shulta	here
sovochollo	to swear
starrie	a star
stor	four
suhakie	gold
tarno	a child
tattabeen	summer
tattoo	heat; warm
tedan	yellow
tedou	oil
thee	the soul
thubh	a needle
tood	lightning; milk
tooph	smoke
tophis	chimney
towamah	to wash
tresh	fear
trin	three
vaccashoe	a lamb
vadon	a wagon
valashtee	a finger
vash	a forest
vasti	the hand
vaunustry	a ring
vongur	a cinder
water jam perall	to fly
wocklee	an image
wooda	a door
woodrous	a bed
yabesh	the year
yaccal	a dog
yaccogaree	an arrow
yack	blue
yacorah	an hour
yarraw	air
yec	one
yec bish	twenty-one
yive	hail
yocne coenue	eyebrows
yog	fire
youee	I (masculine)
youesee	I (feminine)

BIBLIOGRAPHY

Bradley, Henry, The Making of English. New York: Macmillan, 1955.

Brook, G. L., English Dialects. London: Andre Deutsch, 1963.

_____, A History of The English Language. London: Andre Deutsch, 1958.

Clark, John Williams, Early English. London: Andre Deutsch, revised edition, 1967.

Cohen, Marcel, Language: Its Structure and Evolution. Coral Gables: University of Miami Press, 1970.

Earle, John, The Philology of the English Tongue. London: Oxford University Press, 5th edition, 1892.

Fernald, James C., Historic English. New York: Funk & Wagnalls Co., 1921.

Freeman, William, A Concise Dictionary of English Idioms. Boston: The Writer, Inc., 2nd edition, 1963.

Funk, Charles Earle, A Hog on Ice and Other Curious Expressions. New York: Harper & Brothers, 1948.

Granville, Wilfred, Sea Slang of the Twentieth Century. New York: Philosophical Library, 1950.

Hughes, John P., The Science of Language. New York: Random House, 1962.

Hulbert, James Root, Dictionaries British and American. London: Andre Deutsch, 1955.

Lewis, C. S., Studies in Words. London: Cambridge University Press, 1960.

McAdam, E. L., Jr., & Milne, George, Johnson's Dictionary, A Modern Selection. New York: Pantheon, 1963.

McIntosh, Angus, & Halliday, M. A. K., Patterns of Language. Bloomington: Indiana University Press, 1967.

McIntosh, E., The Concise Oxford Dictionary. London: Oxford University Press, 4th edition, 1951.

Morris, William & Mary, Dictionary of Word and Phrase Origins. 2 volumes. New York: Harper & Row, 1967.

Opie, Iona & Peter, The Lore and Language of Schoolchildren.

London: Oxford University Press, 1961.

Partridge, Eric, ed., A Classical Dictionary of the Vulgar Tongue, by Captain Francis Grose. New York: Barnes & Noble, 3rd edition, 1963.

———, A Dictionary of Slang and Unconventional English. New York: Macmillan, 5th edition, 1961.

———, A Dictionary of the Underworld. New York: Macmillan, 1950.

———, Here, There and Everywhere. London: Hamish Hamilton, 2nd edition, 1950.

———, Name into Word: Proper Names that have Become Common Property. London: Secker & Warburg, 1949.

———, Origins: A Short Etymological Dictionary of Modern English. New York: Macmillan, 2nd edition, 1959.

———, Slang To-day and Yesterday. New York: Macmillan, 3rd edition, 1950.

———, & Clark, John W., British and American English Since 1900. New York: Philosophical Library, 1951.

Pei, Mario, The Families of Words. New York: Harper & Brothers, 1962.

———, The Story of the English Language. New York: J. B. Lippincott, revised edition, 1967.

Peters, Robert A., A Linguistic History of English. Boston: Houghton Mifflin, 1968.

Pyles, Thomas, The Origins and Development of the English Language. New York: Harcourt, Brace & World, 1964.

Rodale, J. I., The King's English on Horseback. Emaus, Pa.: Rodale Publications, Inc., 1938.

Shepherd, Henry E., The History of the English Language from the Teutonic Invasion of Britain to the Close of the Georgian Era. New York: E. J. Hale & Son, 1877.

Shipley, Joseph T., Dictionary of Early English. New York: Philosophical Library, 1955.

Skeat, Rev. Walter W., A Concise Etymological Dictionary of the English Language. London: Oxford University Press, 1882.

———, Notes on English Etymology. London: Oxford University Press, 1901.

———, Principles of English Etymology. London: Oxford University Press, 2nd edition, 1892.

———, & Mayhew, A. L., ed., A Glossary of Tudor and Stuart Words. London: Oxford University Press, 1914.

Smith, Rev. H. Percy, Glossary of Terms and Phrases. New York: D. Appleton & Co., 1883.

Starnes, De Witt T., & Noyes, Gertrude E., The English Dictionary from Cawdrey to Johnson 1604-1755. Chapel Hill: University of North Carolina Press, 1946.

Sutherland, James, ed., The Oxford Book of English Talk.
London: Oxford University Press, 1953.
Tilley, Morris Palmer, A Dictionary of the Proverbs in
England in the Sixteenth and Seventeenth Centuries. Ann
Arbor: University of Michigan Press, 1950.
Tucker, Susie I., ed., English Examined. London: Cam-
bridge University Press, 1961.
(°) Warrack, Alexander, A Scots Dialect Dictionary. Edinburgh:
W. & R. Chambers, Ltd., 1911.
Webster, Noah, Dissertations on the English Language.
Gainesville, Florida: Scholars' Facsimiles and Reprints,
1951.
Weekley, Ernest, The English Language. New York: British
Book Centre, 1952.
● Wrenn, C. L., The English Language. London: Methuen,
1958.
Wyld, Henry Cecil, A History of Modern Colloquial English.
London: Oxford University Press, 3rd edition, 1936.
Ziff, Paul, Semantic Analysis. Ithaca, N.Y.: Cornell Uni-
versity Press, 1960.